For permission requests, write to the publisher:
Laprea Education, Inc.
info@StructuredLiteracy.com

www.StructuredLiteracy.com

ISBN: 979-8-88741-959-6

# THE SCIENCE OF READING ACADEMY

**Welcome to the Science of Reading Academy Workbook!**

Welcome to Laprea Education's Science of Reading Academy! We are thrilled to have you join us on this journey to deepen your understanding of the Science of Reading and structured literacy. This workbook is designed to accompany our comprehensive 6-module course, providing you with practical tools and strategies to implement a structured literacy approach in your classroom. To access the course videos, visit ScienceOfReadingAcademy.com, and don't forget to join the Facebook group, The Science of Reading Academy, so you can connect and collaborate with others who are on a similar learning journey.

This workbook is crafted to meet the needs of a diverse audience. Those who will benefit from the course teachings, activities, and bonus content include **teachers** who are looking for a digestible, comprehensive course to enhance their knowledge and practical skills in structured literacy; **administrators and instructional coaches** seeking a training program to support teachers who are making the transition to structured literacy; and **higher education instructors** seeking resources to help educate preservice teachers and graduate-level education students about the Science of Reading and its classroom implications.

To accommodate different schedules and learning preferences, we recommend choosing from three pacing options:

**Deep Dive Option (28 Weeks):** Cover one lesson per week.
*Activities:* Each week, begin by completing the engagement questions in the workbook, then view the video and take notes. Lastly, participate in collaborative learning communities to work through bonus content questions and activities.

**Overview Option (6-12 Weeks):** Cover one module every 1-2 weeks.
*Activities:* For each video in the module, begin by perusing the engagement questions in the workbook, choosing the one that is most applicable to your learning journey, and reflecting on it. Then, watch each video and take notes. Due to the faster pace, learning facilitators should select the most relevant bonus content discussion questions and activities for participants. Learning communities should collaborate to maximize the bonus content.

**Flexible/Self-Paced Option:** Participants decide their own pace.
Choose which modules to complete quickly and which to spend more time on. For example, the theory-based first three modules might be completed quickly, while modules 4-6, which are more practical, might be done at a slower pace of one lesson per week.
*Collaboration:* With this option, it is highly recommended that participants join the Facebook group to engage in discussions and collaborate with others to enhance their learning experience.

**Let's Get Started!**
We are excited for you to embark on this learning journey with the Science of Reading Academy.
As you dive into the course, remember that you are not alone. Whether you are participating as an individual or as part of a group, this workbook and the online community are here to support you every step of the way. Let's work together to bring the Science of Reading into your classroom, empowering your students with the literacy skills they need to succeed. Happy learning!

**Recommended Resources/Extensions** At the end of several video lessons in this course, Dr. Conner makes recommendations for additional resources that allow you to dive more deeply into the topic. A clickable document containing all these resources can be found at https://bit.ly/SOR_Academy_Links.

# Table of Contents

MODULE 1

# Defining the Science of Reading

As educators, you've likely encountered the term "Science of Reading," but its meaning can sometimes be unclear. In Module 1, we will offer a comprehensive overview of what experts define as the "Science of Reading," clarifying common misconceptions along the way. We'll also delve into the tumultuous history of reading instruction, exploring the pedagogical shifts that have shaped our current practices. Finally, we will assess our current reality in reading education and discuss potential next steps for improvement.

As you watch the videos in this module, use the pages that follow to write notes about what you are learning as well as reflect on the new information presented to you.

## Watch

The following videos are part of this learning module. Go to ScienceOfReadingAcademy.com to access each of the videos.

Lesson 1: The Truth about the Science of Reading
Lesson 2: The History of Reading Instruction
Lesson 3: Our Current Reality

## Before you begin

To activate your schema about the module topics, use your current knowledge and experience to reflect on the questions below.

1. What do you think the term "Science of Reading" means? How does it differ from other reading instruction methods you are familiar with?

2. How do you believe reading instruction has evolved over the centuries, and what impact do you think modern technology has had on our understanding of effective reading practices?

3. Why do you think reading scores in the United States have remained stagnant despite various instructional methods being employed over the years? What factors do you think contribute to this trend?

**MODULE 1: Defining the Science of Reading**

# Lesson 1: The Truth about the Science of Reading

*Module 1, Lesson 1 of the Science of Reading Academy clarifies the term "Science of Reading," grounding it in a comprehensive body of research from multiple disciplines, including cognitive psychology, neuroscience, and education. The video emphasizes that the Science of Reading is not a curriculum or a fad but a robust, evidence-based framework that informs effective literacy instruction. The video distinguishes between the Science of Reading and structured literacy, the latter being a practical application of research-based principles in the classroom. Key components of structured literacy include explicit and systematic instruction, cumulative practice, high teacher-student interaction, and the opportunity to apply phonics skills to various texts. Below is the transcript for the Module 1, Lesson 1 video.*

(00:07) Welcome to the Science of Reading Academy. This will be a six-module course that is all focused on learning about the Science of Reading. Each of these modules is designed to take us through learning more about different aspects of current research. So to do this, we're going to follow the E.A.S.E. framework. So the first three modules are focused on exploring the research and the frameworks. Then we'll move to really learning how to apply science-backed strategies to teach decoding. Then, Module 4 will focus on shaping language development. And finally, our last module will really center on executing an SOR approach in your classroom.

(00:57) So we're so excited to get started with you all today, and we're going to be diving right into our first module: Defining the Science of Reading. So this module is all about, really, all about the Science of Reading and anything that is foundational to understanding our next few modules.

(01:22) So today's lesson is titled "The Truth about the Science of Reading," which might seem like an interesting title choice to you. But if you've been in any professional development sessions, if you have looked to purchase a curriculum, if you have been on social media, I am sure you have heard the term *Science of Reading*, and sometimes it can be a little controversial. So we're really wanting to dig down to the basics and figure out what is the truth, what is the science and the research saying is the Science of Reading.

(02:03) So to get started here, we'll just kind of talk about our goals for this Science of Reading Academy. You are in the right place if you want to learn more about the Science of Reading in order to really empower your teaching. The purpose of our academy is to provide research-backed, actionable learning that will elevate your teaching practices. You're also in the right place if the debate and the news and then the teachers' lounge is just daunting or overwhelming to you, and you just want to do what's best for your students. You're in the right place if you believe every student can and should become a proficient reader. And finally, you're in the right place if you are seeking a supportive community where your voice is heard and respected. The SOR Academy is housed in a supportive Facebook group that is really designed to encourage thoughtful questions and discussion between like-minded peers. So these are the objectives of our course, and we are so glad and thankful that you have joined us to go through this journey together.

(03:14) So we're going to start off with just a moment to kind of pause and reflect and just jot down a few ideas in your note guide. What comes to mind when you hear the phrase the Science of Reading? So just jot those down, pause the video, and when you're ready, come back and we'll look at a few phrases that other educators and noneducators have shared.

(03:41) Okay, so take a look here at this Wordle and check your list with the words up on the screen. Did any of these words make your list? Or perhaps you had some words on your list that are not up here. So kind of compare and contrast. Some of the words that really stand out to me: *evidence, foundational, pendulum, logical, essential,* and even the word *books*. So these were words again that were pulled from both educators and noneducators, and we got a variety of responses. And anytime you hear the phrase Science of Reading, it's going to evoke a variety of responses as well as a variety of emotions. But one thing to really keep in mind is the science behind the Science of Reading. And really we could say sciences because there are multiple fields that are contributing to our understanding of how the brain learns to read.

(04:45) So there's cognitive psychology, communication sciences, developmental psychology, education, implementation science, linguistics, neuroscience, and even school psychology. All of these different fields and the research in these fields is coming together to help us know the best way to teach our students to read. So when we say science, we're referencing these many different fields of research, and we're looking critically at the research from all of these different sources in an effort to translate it into our daily classroom practice.

(05:25) Something to really keep in mind that the Science of Reading is *not*, and the first thing is the Science of Reading is not a curriculum, and it's not something you *do*, right? You can't teach the Science of Reading. You're not going to have an SOR block within your day. The Science of Reading is a guiding set of research that informs what our reading block should look like. So for example, small-group reading, you're going to have small-group reading during your day, but you're not going to have an SOR small group. Instead, you're going to have small groups that include research-based practices that have been informed by the body of research that is the Science of Reading.

(06:13) Another thing the Science of Reading is not is only teaching phonics or only teaching any other single aspect of literacy. There are not researchers or advocates of the Science of Reading that are promoting only teaching a single aspect of reading. Rather, they are saying to teach all of the components of the reading rope, one of those reading models that we will discuss in a future video.

(06:46) The Science of Reading is not a pendulum swing or fad, or at least it doesn't have to be, right? The truth is this research, much of it is decades old, and researchers are continuing to add to the body of research as well as refine our understanding. But if, as practitioners, we approach the Science of Reading with the understanding that it truly is a body of research, we will prevent this from becoming another reading war or a pendulum swing, and instead, we're just doing what's best for our kids based on the body of research that we have.

(07:27) This is a quote from Dr. Louisa Motes, and she says, "[The Science of Reading] is the emerging consensus from many related disciplines based on literally thousands of studies supported by hundreds of millions of research dollars conducted across the world and many languages. These studies have revealed a great deal about how we learn to read what goes wrong when students don't learn, and what kind of instruction is most likely to work the best for the most students." What a powerful quote that is, right? What I love about it is how it really paints a picture of the global aspect of the Science of Reading. It is not just a few researchers here and there; it is across the globe, and there are so many different sources that are validating these practices.

(08:21) So with that in mind, take a moment to pause the video and draft your own definition of the Science of Reading based on your current understanding. This could be a definition that you might share with a colleague who perhaps has some misconceptions about what the Science of Reading is.

(08:45) Shifting gears just a little bit, we're going to talk about the term *structured literacy* now. This is another term that you might hear sometimes synonymously with the Science of Reading, but it is something a little bit different. In 2019, the International Dyslexia Association defined structured literacy as "an approach to reading instruction where teachers carefully structure important literacy skills, concepts, and the sequence of instruction to facilitate children's literacy, learning, and progress as much as possible." Louisa Moats said that the term really encompasses both literacy content and instructional methods. So you can think of structured literacy really as putting the Science of Reading in action, and so when we talked earlier, like the Science of Reading is not something that you teach or a block of your day, structured literacy is kind of the answer to that, right? If you're wanting to say that your practices align with these research-backed beliefs, then structured literacy might be a term that you choose to use.

(09:57) There are five key components of structured literacy, according to Spear-Swerling. And the first two kind of go hand in hand. There's explicit instruction, so saying this phoneme is represented by this grapheme. That is explicit instruction. And systematic instruction, so being very intentional with which phoneme-grapheme correspondences you introduce before others and making sure that that is consistent across grade levels, across buildings, and across the district. So explicit and systematic instruction, and that's going to be of phonemes, of phoneme-grapheme correspondences, of syllable patterns, morphemes, as well as text structures, so that goes across the literacy curriculum.

(10:42) Another key component is cumulative practice and reinforcement of, really, any learned skill. So that spiral review that's embedded in what you do.

(10:51) A fourth component is high amounts of interaction between students and their teacher, which is going to give multiple opportunities for that purposeful, meaningful feedback.

(11:03) And last is the application of phonics skills to decodable or controlled text, as well as any text that a child picks up, right, that's always our end goal is that we're creating joyful readers that can engage with any text.

(11:24) In your journal, there is an opportunity to rate yourself on these various areas of structured literacy. So think through which areas your practices are strongly aligned with as well as which areas might need revamping. And just take a moment to rate yourself with that, and that reflection can kind of help guide your learning as you journey through the next few modules to help you know which areas you might want to focus a little bit more on as we go through this learning together.

(11:59) Alright. The last thing I'm going to leave you with are some learning extensions. So to learn more about defining the Science of Reading, check out "The Reading League's SOR Defining Guide." They really sought to find a consensus definition by consulting with a myriad of experts about what the Science of Reading is. Another option is *Melissa and Lori Love Literacy* podcast. They are speaking with Dr. Holly Lane, and she really delves further into knowing how something is truly backed by science and research.

(12:35) We would love to hear from you on the Facebook page, so please find Module 1, Lesson 1, find that thread, and share your working definition of the Science of Reading or share a phrase that came to your mind when you heard the term *Science of Reading*. We would love to hear from you. Thank you so much for joining us today and spending this learning time together. We look forward to seeing you for Module 1, Lesson 2.

What comes to mind when you hear the phrase "the Science of Reading"?

The Science of Reading is NOT

Your turn! Draft your own definition of the Science of Reading based on your current understanding.

Additional Notes

## Structured Literacy

## Structured Literacy Components

## Self-Reflect: Circle to rate yourself on the various areas of structured literacy.

1 = I never do this, 2 = I do this sometimes, 3 = I do this every day

| | | | |
|---|---|---|---|
| Explicit Instruction | 1 | 2 | 3 |
| Systematic Instruction | 1 | 2 | 3 |
| Cumulative Practice and Reinforcement | 1 | 2 | 3 |
| Purposeful Feedback | 1 | 2 | 3 |
| Application and Transfer of Skills | 1 | 2 | 3 |

In which areas are your practices strongly aligned? Which areas might need revamping?

## Additional Notes

# Bonus Content

**Use the questions below to prompt discussion amongst your colleagues.**

1. **Defining the Science of Reading:** How would you define the Science of Reading in your own words? What key elements or principles should be included in this definition?
2. **Multidisciplinary Contributions:** How do the various fields such as cognitive psychology, linguistics, and neuroscience contribute to our understanding of how students learn to read? Can you provide specific examples of insights from these fields?
3. **Structured Literacy:** What is structured literacy, and how does it relate to the Science of Reading? How can structured literacy practices be implemented in the classroom?
4. **Research vs. Curriculum:** Why is it important to distinguish between the Science of Reading as a body of research and reading curriculums or programs? How can this distinction impact classroom practices?
5. **Challenges and Misconceptions:** What are some common misconceptions about the Science of Reading, and how can educators address these misconceptions among colleagues and parents?

**To extend your understanding of this topic, work through the activities below with a small group of peers.**

**Definition Workshop**
In small groups, draft a comprehensive definition of the Science of Reading. Each group can present their definition and discuss the similarities and differences. Aim to create a consensus definition that encompasses the key components discussed.

**Field-Specific Research Exploration**
Assign each group a different field (e.g., cognitive psychology, neuroscience, linguistics) to research how it contributes to the Science of Reading. Groups can present their findings, highlighting key studies or discoveries and their implications for reading instruction.

**Structured Literacy Self-Assessment**
Have teachers individually rate their current practices against the five components of structured literacy (explicit instruction, systematic instruction, cumulative practice, purposeful feedback, application of phonics skills). Then, discuss in small groups which areas are strengths and which need improvement and develop a plan for addressing any gaps.

**Case Study Analysis**
Provide a case study of a classroom implementing structured literacy practices. Groups analyze the case study to identify effective strategies and potential challenges. Discuss how the findings from the case study can be applied to their own classrooms.

**Research and Reflect**
Ask teachers to read "The Reading League's SOR Defining Guide" or listen to the *Melissa and Lori Love Literacy* podcast episode with Dr. Holly Lane. Then, in small groups, discuss how these resources have influenced their understanding of what constitutes evidence-based reading instruction. Share insights and action steps on the Facebook group or during a follow-up meeting.

## Additional Resources

On pages 24-25, you will find a handout that summarizes some of the main ideas in this module. Make copies of this handout to share at a grade-level planning meeting or faculty meeting. Share what you have learned when it comes to defining the Science of Reading and structured literacy.

# Lesson 2: The History of Reading Instruction

*Module 1, Lesson 2 of the Science of Reading Academy covers the evolution of teaching methods from the 1600s to the present. It discusses early phonics-focused primers like the Blue-Backed Speller before transitioning to the whole word approach that was popular in the mid-1800s. The video discusses the look-say method and the subsequent whole language method from the 1970s, which emphasized contextual guessing over phonics. The contentious debate between phonics and whole language approaches led to the development of balanced literacy, which sought to integrate elements of both but often lacked systematic phonics instruction. The video concludes by highlighting the role of technology, specifically fMRI scans, in providing concrete evidence for the effectiveness of structured literacy, which advocates for explicit, systematic instruction to rewire neural networks for reading proficiency. Below is the transcript for the Module 1, Lesson 2 video.*

(00:09) Hello, and welcome back to the Science of Reading Academy. Today we are diving back into Module 1, focused on defining the Science of Reading. Today's lesson is going to be all about the history of reading instruction, which might not sound like a very interesting topic, but honestly, it's fascinating to go all the way back to the 1600s and travel up to present day to learn about how reading has been taught and how even several decades ago those practices continue to impact what we're doing in our classroom today.

(00:47) Now, maybe you've heard the approach to reading referenced as a pendulum swing. Reading can be such a contentious topic in our world today, but as we delve into the history of reading instruction, especially here in the United States, it can be very eye-opening. As we look back at all of these different approaches, it can be really helpful to take a few moments after each approach, pause, and kind of jot down any connections that you have between what was done in the past with what is the same in American classrooms today. And as you do that, I think you'll be able to generate an answer to the question on the screen: Have you ever wondered why reading instruction is a highly contentious topic?

(01:38) So with that, let's get started with the early methods. Early reading instruction in the United States often emphasized phonics. So the New England Primer was published in the Colonies in 1683, and it provided explicit instruction in the alphabet and in phonics. Now, additional primers were later developed. The most famous one is the *American Spelling Book* by Noah Webster, but you've probably heard it called the *Blue-Backed Speller*. That's kind of its common nickname. And this spelling book also taught phonics rules and lessons, and it utilized word lists, syllable practice, patriotic readings, and even biblical passages. So Webster's teaching method continued for around a hundred years or so before methods began to change in the mid-1800s.

(02:26) Horace Mann really denounced that phonics approach that we saw with those early primers. He spoke in 1841 to the American Institute of Instruction, and when he spoke, he really was outlining a case against phonics, and he was advocating for using the whole word approach. So he really did not like letters, and he really did not like phonics. He even described letters in the alphabet as "skeleton-shaped, bloodless, ghostly apparitions," so he had some pretty strong feelings here. His influence persisted all the way into the 20th century when William S. Gray published a book that was titled *On Their Own in Reading*.

(03:26) Now Gray worked to refine Mann's work, and he developed what was known as the *look-say method*. So eventually you'll look at a word, and you just say it, so that whole word memorization, right? So the look-say method taught children to recognize and say whole words by sight rather than using their knowledge of letter sounds to help them decode and sound out words.

(03:54) This look-say method was really influential with the Dick and Jane basal readers, and those were created so that words will repeat on every page enough times for students to just remember them. And even though this method isn't really widely utilized anymore, it still continues to be influential through the three-cueing approach, which is really an integral part of the whole language method.

(04:24) So take a moment and pause and reflect here. In what ways did the whole language approach impact the way that you learned to read and also think, has it impacted any of your teaching methods? After you finish that reflection, go ahead and hop back on the video so that we can move on and talk more about this whole language approach.

(04:50) Okay, so really diving into whole language now. The whole language method evolved from the whole word method, and those are two separate things. The whole language method came about in the 1970s when Ken Goodman's article was published, and his article was titled "Reading: The Psycholinguistic Guessing Game," which is a very interesting title. He hypothesized that readers will use graphic, syntactic, semantic, and phonological clues when they're essentially guessing words as they read. So he claimed that teachers should instruct students in the rules of this guessing game to become more efficient at using contextual clues when reading. This psycholinguistic approach influenced the development of running records and miscue analysis with Marie Clay, which are considered additional components of that whole language approach.

(05:54) Another really important belief of whole language is that learning to read is natural. So if you just give students more exposure to words, more opportunity to read, they're just going to learn to read, right? It's a natural activity, and it's just going to happen.

(06:14) Simultaneously alongside that whole language approach, there's also a push for phonics. In 1955, Rudolph Flesch published his book called *Why Johnny Can't Read*, and this book was very critical of the whole language approach and strongly advocated for a method of reading instruction that taught the alphabetic principle. Now, Flesch tailored his book to mothers and fathers rather than educators. In fact, the introduction of his book even says, "The teaching of reading is too important to be left to the educators." So as you can imagine, that was a very polarizing statement, right? That is not something that's going to make a lot of teachers and educators want to read his book. Now, further research did substantiate Flesch's claims against the whole language method, but because his approach was so polarizing, he just didn't get a lot of people on board.

(07:20) And around this time, the United States really wanted answers. And so that's when the National Conference on Research in English started to assemble, and they're trying to sort out all of this contradictory and really incomplete reading research. So this committee analyzed the research that existed, and they compared all of the different approaches to teaching beginning reading.

(07:48) Jeanne Chall was a prominent researcher in the education field at the time, and she was a member of this assembled committee. She further analyzed the United States' reading issues when she publicized her book, *Learning to Read: The Great Debate*. Now, what was different about her book from Rudolph Flesch's book is that she specifically welcomed and included researchers, educators, preservice teachers, parents, publishers, really everyone that has a stake and is invested in teaching children to read. She included all of them in the introduction of her book. Her book concluded with a call for a code emphasis method for teaching beginning readers that's really going to emphasize that alphabetic code.

(08:40) This code emphasis method was shown to produce a lot better results for kindergarten through third grade students. And she shared that evidence in her book. This was really one of her significant contributions, and the fact that her belief was that reading instruction should be grounded in both research and evidence, right? It doesn't have to be polarizing. We just want to look at what the research says to do.

(09:07) But even after her 1967 publication, phonics instruction continued to be implemented with varying degrees of emphasis throughout the next several years. This period was even referenced as some by the pendulum years. So during this tumultuous time, many educators really desired to find a middle ground between the two philosophies of whole language and phonics. They just wanted to do what's best for their students, just like we do today.

(09:39) The California Department of Education originally coined the term *balanced literacy* to help find this middle ground between the whole language and the phonics approaches. As with other instructional approaches to reading, balanced literacy can really have a variety of definitions. Really though, it's going to include literacy instruction that is designed to maintain equilibrium across various language art domains. So this is going to make sure that teachers are sharing with students foundational skills, comprehension, vocabulary, all of those things through a variety of delivery methods, so including whole-group and small-group instruction and really just working on keeping everything balanced, which sounds like a really good thing. Supporters of balanced literacy really do accept the importance of phonics instruction, but where it kind of comes down to the gray area is what that looks like exactly, right? There's still some debate about the extent and the role of phonics instruction in those early reading classrooms.

(10:58) Now, the findings of the National Reading Panel in 2000 did substantiate those earlier assertions that phonics instruction is a very valuable component of teaching students to read. However, some versions of balanced literacy don't provide a lot of phonics instruction, and when it is provided, it's lacking that systematic approach. It's more just sprinkled in.

(11:25) So in addition to this lack of sequential phonics instruction, balanced literacy often uses the three-cueing or the MSV model to prompt students in guided reading. So that comes from Goodman's psycholinguistic guessing game. As students are reading leveled texts, teachers are taking running records, and they're analyzing the sources of information. So if students are using meanings, syntax, or visual inputs when they encounter difficult words, so that's not a problem, right? Students can use all three systems when they're decoding words. The problem is how we're prompting students. So often balanced literacy educators have been instructed to prompt students to rely on contextual cues at a much higher rate than visual cues. Balanced literacy proponents advise that those contextual cues are more effective than visual cues when determining an unknown word. However, that three-cueing system is really problematic, and it's unsustainable, and eventually it's going to lead to students having word-level decoding difficulties.

(12:40) Blevins cautions us that if students are given texts in which they have to rely on sight words and on context and on picture clues to figure out or guess words, that's what they're going to think reading is, right? But as soon as all of those supports are taken away, the student's ability to read completely falls apart. So balanced literacy really seems to be this plausible solution that was going to end the reading wars, but it's not always as balanced as we want it to be.

(13:12) Moats even refers to balanced literacy as an illusion, suggesting that it's just a repackaging of the whole language approach. She even questions the wisdom of bridging these two methods together of whole language and phonics because they have such polar opposite ideals. Structured literacy advocates say that learning to read is not a natural process. That's where that systematic component comes in.

(13:40) So with all of this background, and you can see how both sides really have valid points, what is different about today, right? What makes today not just another fad, another trend, or another pendulum swing? Well, really, the difference is technology. We now have functional MRIs, so fMRIs, that allow us to know for sure what is happening in the reading brain. So there's no longer a need to debate or to argue. Previously, like Goodman and his psycholinguistic guessing game, that was a hypothesis. That was a scientific method in action, right? He hypothesized this; they tried it out. It was a theory. Well, there was nothing wrong with that. It made sense. But now we have brain scans that say that's not actually what's happening. So we revise our theory. We grow and we learn from what science is saying. That is what good science is.

(14:46) So as neuroscientists have studied these fMRI scans of readers and nonreaders, they have observed key differences in cortical activity as reading improves. So when we teach students to read, we are rewiring those neural networks within their brain. The human brain utilizes something known as synaptic plasticity. So it can grow, and it can change, and it can repurpose areas, but we have to be very intentional with the instructional methods that we're choosing in order for this to happen. Structured literacy proponents really argue that students have to be provided with explicit and systematic literacy instruction in order for all of our students to become proficient readers.

(15:35) Okay. So after all of that history lesson, take a minute to summarize in about two to three sentences why the approach to reading no longer has to be a pendulum swing. After you've done that, come back and join the video for just a few more learning extensions that I'm going to share with you.

(15:58) I'm going to leave you with this quote from Margaret Goldbert: "In order to stop the pendulum, we must commit to staying up to date with reading research and pursuing only evidence-based practices." We as practitioners have the power to stop the pendulum from continuing to swing. It requires ongoing learning and ongoing work, but it really is worth it. And I just want to say thank you for taking the time to learn together with us because it is educators like you that are dedicated to going through this learning process that are going to make the difference. You are going to stop that pendulum from swinging, and you are going to help your students just have what they need to become effective readers.

(16:46) A few learning extensions from our time together today: The first is a blog, "Reading Instruction through the Decades," that's just going to give you a little bit more history if you find that interesting like I do. And there is also a podcast that you can listen to from Iowa Reading Research Center. So thank you again for spending today with us. Please visit the SOR Academy Facebook group and leave a comment on the Module 1, Lesson 2 thread. We can't wait to hear from you.

Have you ever wondered why reading instruction is a highly contentious topic?

Early Methods

The Whole Word Approach

Additional Notes

Pause and Reflect: In what ways did the whole language approach impact the way you learned to read? How has it impacted your teaching methods?

Additional Notes

Whole Language

Phonics

Merging the Two: Balanced Literacy

What is different about today?

Your turn! Explain in 2-3 sentences why the approach to reading no longer has to be a pendulum swing.

Additional Notes

# Bonus Content

**Use the questions below to prompt discussion amongst your colleagues.**

1. **Reflecting on Phonics and Whole Word Approaches:** How do the early phonics methods, such as those used in the New England Primer and the Blue-Backed Speller, compare with the whole word approach advocated by Horace Mann? What are the advantages and disadvantages of each method?
2. **Impact of Historical Methods on Current Practices:** In what ways do the historical methods of reading instruction still influence the way reading is taught in classrooms today? Can you identify any specific strategies or materials that have persisted?
3. **Avoiding Pendulum Swings:** How does emphasizing research in our literacy approach enhance our instruction and help avoid pendulum swings? In what ways does structured literacy incorporate research findings to create a comprehensive literacy instruction model?
4. **Role of Neuroscience in Reading Instruction:** How has the advent of functional MRIs (fMRIs) changed our understanding of reading instruction? What implications does this have for future teaching methods?
5. **Influence of Key Figures:** Discuss the contributions of key figures such as Jeanne Chall, Ken Goodman, and Rudolph Flesch to the field of reading instruction. How did their work shape the conversation on the best methods for teaching reading?

**To extend your understanding of this topic, work through the activities below with a small group of peers.**

**Timeline Creation**

In small groups, create a timeline of the major milestones in the history of reading instruction, including significant publications, influential figures, and key changes in methodology. Present the timeline to the larger group and discuss the impacts of these milestones on current practices.

**Comparative Analysis**

Conduct a comparative analysis of two different reading instruction methods (e.g., phonics vs. whole language). Each group should choose one method, research its principles and effectiveness, and present their findings, highlighting the strengths and weaknesses of each approach.

**Case Study Review**

Find a case study that highlights/corresponds to a specific component of structured literacy. Analyze the outcomes and discuss what factors contributed to the successes or challenges observed in the case.

**Neuroscience and Reading Instruction Workshop**

Host a workshop where teachers can explore the latest neuroscience research related to reading instruction. Activities could include reviewing fMRI studies, discussing how this research supports or challenges current teaching methods, and brainstorming ways to integrate scientific findings into practical classroom strategies.

**Additional Resources**

On pages 24-25, you will find a handout that summarizes some of the main ideas in this module. Make copies of this handout to share at a grade-level planning meeting or faculty meeting. Share what you have learned when it comes to defining the Science of Reading and structured literacy.

**MODULE 1: Defining the Science of Reading**

# Lesson 3: Our Current Reality

*Module 1, Lesson 3 of the Science of Reading Academy examines the reality of reading instruction in the United States through the lens of recent data and research. It highlights the stagnant reading scores reported by the Nation's Report Card (NAEP) over the past few decades, with only slight fluctuations and no significant improvement in reading proficiency. The video contrasts this with meta-analysis data from Nathaniel Hansford, which suggests that 96% of students can reach grade-level reading proficiency with adequate intervention. The video discusses a typical classroom profile, emphasizing that while some students will learn to read without much assistance, the majority require high-quality instruction, and a smaller percentage need additional support. Below is the transcript for the Module 1, Lesson 3 video.*

(00:08) Hello, and thank you so much for joining us for our very last lesson in Module 1, focused on defining the Science of Reading. Today we are going to talk about our current reality. So we talked last episode about the history and the progression of how reading instruction has happened here in the United States and how that has really led to it being such a contentious topic. Because of that, our current reality is not always what we hope it to be, right? We know as educators that we have a lot of students who are not able to read or are not able to read at the level at which we would want. So we're really going to look at some of the data that tells us what's going on and talk about what our own classrooms look like.

(01:04) So as we begin here, I want you to just have a picture in your mind of a typical American classroom. So if you are a teacher, then just think of your students that are in front of you right now, or if you're doing this during the summertime, a group of students that you worked with last year. If you were classroom adjacent, or perhaps you are an administrator or a coach, maybe an interventionist, think about a classroom with students and a teacher that you've worked with and picture those students' faces in your mind, and just come up with an approximate percentage that you would say are grade-level readers, and just jot that down in your note guide somewhere and keep that in the back of your head as we're going through this episode today.

(01:54) So let's look here at the Nation's Report Card. This comes from NAEP, and NAEP is given to a random sampling of fourth, eighth, and twelfth grade students across the nation, and it's typically administered every two years in late January to early March. Because of the pandemic, that didn't happen in 2020, so we went from 2019 to 2022. So there is a bigger gap there, which makes sense, right? And the reason for this is when states are assessing reading, they're using their own state-developed assessment, so it becomes very difficult to compare reading scores across the nation from a really big picture. So we can't compare what students in Florida are doing to students in California because they're using two totally different assessments. So NAEP allows us to get this random sampling and just keep a pulse on how the nation is doing in the area of reading.

(03:02) Now, one thing you'll notice on this chart here is that, unsurprisingly, there was a nationwide drop in scores between 2019 and 2022. We had the pandemic during those years, right? That doesn't surprise anyone who's been in education, but what is surprising, reading scores have not significantly changed since this test was first administered in 1992. When you look at that trend line, it is pretty consistent across the board. Not a lot of improvement, not a lot of really drops either, but no significant change in what our students are doing in the area of reading.

(03:46) When we look at this, this gives us a little bit closer look into what that NAEP performance score meets. So in the year 2022, 37% of students were considered below basic, 29% of students were considered basic, 24% were considered proficient, and 9% were considered advanced. And this is fourth grade students across the nation in the area of reading. Now, one thing to keep in mind is that proficiency on NAEP is not equivalent to grade-level proficiency. Their website states that NAEP basic denotes partial mastery of the knowledge and skills that are fundamental for proficient work at a given grade. NAEP proficient represents solid academic performance for the given grade level and competency over a challenging subject matter, including subject matter knowledge, application of such knowledge to real-world situations, and analytical skills appropriate to the subject matter. So that kind of gives you an idea of what NAEP basic and NAEP proficient means. Obviously, our goal would be for all students to be proficient in advance, but when we look at this report card, that is not our current reality.

(05:07) Now, you might be wondering what is possible, what should we be looking here for? And scientists have wondered that, too. Nathaniel Hansford did a meta-analysis of lots of experimental research that exists to try and figure out what percentage of students can reach grade-level reading expectations. And when he did this meta-analysis, he came up with the average of 96% of students are capable of reaching grade-level reading expectations—with the caveat—as long as there's proper reading intervention support provided within the school. So 96% was the average of these different experimental studies. That is a very different number than what we see as our current reality. So a huge gap between what's happening with reading scores and what could be happening with reading scores.

(06:13) Louisa Moats says: "This we know reading failure can be prevented in all but a small percentage of children with serious learning disorders," and that would really be reflected in that number from Nathaniel Hansford, that 96%, right? 96% of students can learn to read. Some of them may need that intervention, but they can.

(06:36) So with that in mind, pause and reflect: which data set more closely aligns to your reality? Is it the NAEP scores, or is it the Hansford meta-analysis, so that 96% number. As you do this, please give yourself grace as you reflect on your data. This is not a *you* problem. This is a systematic problem that is going to take all of us working together to tackle to get more and more of our students to that reading proficiency.

(07:13) Let's take a look here at a typical classroom profile. So each of these icons represents a student, and there are 20 students up here on the screen. So what research supports is that approximately 30% of students will learn regardless of instruction. Those are the ones that you just give a book to and it seems like they teach themselves to read, right? So those are the students in green there, and they're going to learn pretty much no matter what. 50% of students will learn with high-quality Tier 1 instruction, so those are the students in yellow. Those are the ones that are really going to benefit from teachers that are following that explicit systematic instruction. They're being very intentional to incorporate all aspects of reading, and they're really thinking about what their students need. So those are the yellow students there. So that's 30% green, 50% yellow.

(08:14) So that takes us to 80% with solid Tier 1 instruction, 80% of your students should be able to learn how to read. Now, those silver students over there, those represent 15% of students, and they will learn, but they're going to need more time and more support. So those are your ones that are going to need that Tier 2 and Tier 3 intervention. And finally, there's the red icon. And approximately 5% of students are going to struggle to learn to read just due to cognitive difficulties. So this again is just an average, but it can kind of help you compare your classroom or that classroom that you pictured to this typical classroom profile.

(09:01) The discrepancy between research and practice is caused by several contributing factors, right? It's not just one. And that's everything from inadequate teacher preparation to teacher efficacy to ineffective practices being used in classrooms. But we can close the gap, and one of the best ways to do that is by teacher learning. And that is what you're doing right now. You're doing one of those first major steps, and so thank you so much for your commitment to learning and to doing what's best for our students.

(09:41) As a thank you for completing the first module of lessons, you will have access to some exclusive downloadable content. Module 1's content includes a special handout that summarizes the most important points from our learning. So this can be something that you share with your colleagues, that you use as a reference for yourself. There are some additional resources to explore on there as well. So we just want to say thank you for participating in this learning.

(10:14) One last thing, I do have some learning extensions to share with you on the NAEP topic, so if you're interested in further reading on NAEP, there is a link to the website there, and then there's also a podcast of anything you could ever want to know about that assessment, so some learning extensions there. But we really just appreciate your time and your attention. Please remember to join and visit the SOR Academy Group on Facebook and comment on that Module 1, Lesson thread, Lesson 3 thread. We really look forward to hearing from you. Thank you so much.

Think of a typical American classroom. What percentage would you say are grade-level readers?

Additional Notes

Nation's Report Card: What is so surprising?

A Promising Possibility: What percentage of children can learn to read?

Pause and Reflect: Which data set more closely aligns to your reality?

Additional Notes

Typical Classroom Profile

_____% will learn to read regardless of instruction.

_____% will learn with high-quality Tier 1 instruction.

_____% will learn with a Tier 2 or 3 intervention.

_____% will struggle because of cognitive difficulties.

# Bonus Content

**Use the questions below to prompt discussion amongst your colleagues.**

1. **Current Reality vs. Potential:** How does the current reality of reading proficiency in your classroom compare to the national data presented (e.g., NAEP scores vs. Hansford meta-analysis)? What factors might contribute to any discrepancies?
2. **Teacher Preparation and Efficacy:** How do you perceive the role of teacher preparation and efficacy in the current state of reading instruction? What improvements could be made in teacher training to better address the needs of all students?
3. **Intervention Strategies:** Discuss the effectiveness of Tier 1, Tier 2, and Tier 3 interventions in your experience. How do you identify and support students who require additional help beyond Tier 1 instruction?
4. **Systematic Challenges:** Reflect on the statement that the reading proficiency issue is a systematic problem. What are some of the systematic challenges you face in your school, and what collaborative efforts could help overcome these barriers?

**To extend your understanding of this topic, work through the activities below with a small group of peers.**

**Data Analysis Workshop**
Conduct a workshop where teachers bring their classroom reading data. Compare it with the NAEP and Hansford data. Discuss possible reasons for differences and brainstorm strategies to improve reading proficiency.

**Case Study Review**
Review and analyze case studies of classrooms or schools that have successfully implemented reading interventions. Identify key strategies and discuss how they could be adapted to your own context.

**Peer Observation and Feedback**
Organize sessions where teachers observe each other's reading instruction methods. Provide constructive feedback focusing on the use of explicit, systematic instruction and how it can be enhanced.

**Intervention Planning**
In small groups, develop detailed intervention plans for students who fall into the 15% (Tier 2 and 3) and 5% (severe cognitive difficulties) categories. Share and critique each other's plans to refine approaches.

**Professional Development Series**
Create a series of professional development sessions focusing on the Science of Reading. Include topics such as effective instructional strategies, data-driven decision making, and collaborative approaches to close the gap between current reality and potential reading proficiency.

**Additional Resources**
On pages 24-25, you will find a handout that summarizes some of the main ideas in this module. Make copies of this handout to share at a grade-level planning meeting or faculty meeting. Share what you have learned when it comes to defining the Science of Reading and structured literacy.

LAPREA
EDUCATION
Understanding the
Science of Reading

# Nation's Report Card

**Student reading proficiency (NAEP)**

| | |
|---|---|
| 37% | **Below basic** |
| 24% | **Proficient** |
| 29% | **Basic** |
| 9% | **Advanced** |

*Experimental research supports the idea that 96% of students can reach grade-level reading expectations if there is proper reading intervention support provided within the school.*

# Did you know?

**In a typical classroom ...**

- **30% of students will learn to read regardless of instructional approach**
- **50% of students will learn to read with high-quality tier one instruction**
- **15% of students will learn to read with more time and support (tier 2/tier 3)**
- **5% of students will struggle to read due to cognitive difficulties**

www.structuredliteracy.com

# Defining the Science of Reading

## SOR IS

- Explicit instruction
- Systematic instruction
- Cumulative practice and reinforcement
- Purposeful feedback
- Application and transfer of skills

## SOR IS NOT

- A curriculum or "something to do"
- Only teaching phonics (or any other single aspect of teaching)
- A pendulum swing or fad

# Structured Literacy

"An approach to reading instruction where teachers carefully structure important literacy skills, concepts, and the sequence of instruction"
(The International Dyslexia Association, 2009)

# Resources to Explore

Listed to the right are some of our favorite podcasts, online video trainings, and books about the Science of Reading.

Resources in the first row are great for beginners. Resources in the second row are geared for those ready to move beyond the basics. Resources in the third row are research-dense for those ready for advanced content.

**Sold a Story**

**7 Mighty Moves by Lindsay Kemenay**

**Melissa and Lori Love Literacy**

**Differentiating Phonics Instruction for Maximum Impact by Wiley Blevins**

**Pattan Literacy Symposium**

**Speech to Print by Louisa Moats**

MODULE 2

# Exploring the Reading Models

In Module 2, we will delve into various models of reading, each with practical implications for your teaching. We'll start with Gough and Tunmer's Simple View of Reading, a model that simplifies reading into two key components: decoding and comprehension. Next, we'll explore Scarborough's Reading Rope, a model that weaves together multiple strands of reading skills to illustrate the complexity of proficient reading. We'll then cover the Four-Part Processing Model, which outlines the cognitive processes involved in recognizing words and constructing meaning. Finally, we'll discuss the most recent model, the Active View of Reading, which underscores the dynamic and interactive nature of the reading process. These lessons will equip you with the knowledge to inform your effective reading instruction.

As you watch the videos in this module, use the pages that follow to write notes about what you are learning as well as reflect on the new information presented to you.

## Watch

The following videos are part of this learning module. Go to ScienceOfReadingAcademy.com to access each of the videos.

Lesson 1: The Simple View of Reading
Lesson 2: The Reading Rope
Lesson 3: The Four-Part Processing Model
Lesson 4: The Active View of Reading

## Before you begin

To activate your schema about the module topics, use your current knowledge and experience to reflect on the questions below.

1. How do you think word recognition and language comprehension interact to affect reading comprehension? Can you provide examples of how strengths or weaknesses in these areas might impact a student's reading abilities?

2. What components do you believe are necessary for skilled reading? How might weaknesses in any of these components disrupt reading development?

3. In what ways do you think motivation and self-regulation might influence a student's ability to read proficiently? How could these factors be integrated into reading instruction?

MODULE 2: Exploring Reading Models

# Lesson 1: The Simple View of Reading

*Module 2, Lesson 1 from the Science of Reading Academy introduces the Simple View of Reading (SVR), a model created by Gough and Tunmer in 1986, which asserts that skilled reading is the product of both word recognition and language comprehension. Dr. Conner explains that word recognition encompasses both decoding skills and the ability to recognize words automatically, while language comprehension involves understanding spoken words and deriving meaning from them. The video illustrates how varying levels of these two components affect reading comprehension through examples of different reader profiles. It acknowledges that while the SVR outlines the essential elements for reading comprehension, it doesn't specify the exact methods for teaching these skills. Below is the transcript for the Module 2, Lesson 1 video.*

**(00:06)** Hello, and welcome back to the Science of Reading Academy. Today we are diving into Module 2, which is going to focus on exploring several different reading models. Our reading model of focus today is the simple view of reading. Now, Gough and Tunmer were the creators of the simple view of reading, and they developed this in 1986, really with the intent of showing the role of decoding in the reading process.

**(00:40)** So the simple view of reading can really be summarized with a multiplication equation, so adding in some math to our literacy. Word recognition multiplied by language comprehension is equivalent to reading comprehension. So that is the simple view of reading in a nutshell. And again, really they were trying to address the debate surrounding how decoding affects skilled reading. And they really said that word recognition or that decoding piece is central for skilled reading comprehension. Now they're calling it word recognition and not just decoding because they're also incorporating that instant automatic word recognition piece, right? When you look at a word and you just know what it is without even thinking about it. So they are trying to illustrate that that is essential alongside language comprehension in order for reading comprehension to even be possible.

**(01:47)** Before we dive into each of these individual components, I want you to take a moment, pause the video, jot down in your note guide your own definition of word recognition as well as language comprehension. And this will help you as we go through the next few slides together to kind of focus your learning.

**(02:12)** Okay, so let's dive into word recognition. Word recognition is the ability to look at a word and just automatically know it. So for skilled readers, it appears that we have memorized a wide number of words. We just look at them, we don't think about it, we just know what they are. But in reality, our brains have done something different with words. We have done something called *orthographic mapping*, and we'll cover that in a future video, but our brains treat words a little bit differently, which allows us to be fluid readers and to not have to memorize every single word that we would ever encounter because that would just be an impossible task, right? So to demonstrate this, we're going to do a little activity. I'm going to show you a few different words on the next three slides. And when you look at these next slides, I want you to completely ignore the words and just pay attention to the colors, okay? So those are your instructions. Ignore the words and only pay attention to the colors. Here we go. 3, 2, 1. Okay. Remember, ignore the word. Just look at the color. 3, 2, 1. 3, 2, 1.

**(03:36)** Okay, so what did you notice about that activity? I don't know about you, but even me, and I have done this multiple times, whenever I see the word *blue*, I think blue way before I think green, even though my brain is going color, color, color, color before I can even process that word is written in green letters. I've already read the word *blue*. Like, I just can't help it, right? Our brains are automatically recognizing these words. So we've memorized colors, but we've done something a little bit different with the words, right? We don't even, it's like effortless. And this is because of how our brain has stored these words through orthographic mapping. We haven't just memorized them as whole units, and that is helping with that effortless automatic retrieval. So when Gough and Tunmer are talking about the simple view of reading, and they say word recognition, that's what they're talking about.

**(04:41)** Now the other component is language comprehension, and this is deriving meaning from spoken words, so hearing a spoken word and knowing what it means. So listening to a read aloud and being able to follow the storyline, having a wide range of vocabulary. So this is going to include things like language structure, syntax, background knowledge, all of those things. So language comprehension is a very broad and complex component that has to be combined with that automatic word recognition in order for reading comprehension to occur.

**(05:23)** So let's look at some common reader profiles using the simple view of reading to help us analyze them. So this first reader here is Becca, and she's a typical reader. She's a second grader, and you can see she has great word recognition. So she received a score of 1 for that. She's very strong with her word recognition. This is her third year, so she's a second grader. This is her third year of systematic explicit phonics instruction, and that's really set her up for success. Her language comprehension, also really strong. She's got a 1 in that. She understands, she enjoys read alouds. She has a growing vocabulary. So with those two things, Becca has the prerequisite skills for good reading comprehension. Her reading comprehension is also a 1 because 1 multiplied by 1 is equivalent to 1. So now Becca is going to continue to work to combine and transfer these more isolated skills to the complex process of reading comprehension.

**(06:28)** Our next reader here is Joseph, and Joseph is a third grader, and we would consider Joseph to be a student with a specific word reading deficit. So if you look at his word recognition score, he is below average in this area. So he is scoring 0.25, so he knows about 25% of what he should for a reader of his age. He has a difficult time hearing individual phoneme names within whole words, which is a prerequisite skill to being able to orthographically map those words. Now, when you look at Joseph's language comprehension, it's excellent, 100%. He loves listening to stories, and he has excellent comprehension of text when that decoding piece is not involved. But because Joseph is missing one of the key ingredients to reading comprehension, his overall reading comprehension is going to be harmed. So 0.25 times 1 is still only 0.25. In third grade, he's primarily going to be tested on reading comprehension, but until his missing word recognition skills are remediated, his reading comprehension will not be able to improve. So focusing on comprehension strategies for him is not going to be effective because that is not where his gap is.

**(07:59)** Now this is another reader. This is Daniel, and Daniel is a first grader, and we would consider Daniel to have a specific language comprehension deficit. Now, Daniel is really strong with his word recognition skills. He's right on track for his grade level. He's mastered all of his letter sounds, and he's fluently decoding CVC words. But Daniel recently moved to the United States with his family, and his home language is Spanish. Daniel is rapidly learning English. He's a very bright student, but he still struggles with some of the academic vocabulary and the new language structures. These language comprehension skills are going to impact his reading comprehension skills. So you'll see his 1 for word recognition times 0.75 is leading to a reading comprehension of 0.75. So even though he can decode all of the words, if he's not able to understand all of them, that will impact his comprehension. When Daniel's language comprehension skills are filled in, as long as those word recognition skills continue to develop appropriately, his reading comprehension will also increase. So an intervention for him is going to focus on supporting that background knowledge, supporting his vocabulary development, and all of those things will help his reading comprehension.

**(09:24)** Our last reader that we're going to look at here is Layla, and we would consider Layla to have mixed reading difficulties. Sometimes you'll hear it referenced as a garden variety of reading difficulty. If you look at Layla's word recognition, she struggles with word recognition. About 50% of the skills that she has need some work, especially when it comes to sounding out words with more than three phonemes. Now, Layla also struggles to follow a grade-level read aloud and needs some additional support to keep track of characters and story events. So Layla has some gaps in her language comprehension and her vocabulary skills as well. When you put these two together, so 0.5 times 0.5 only equals 0.25. So because it's a multiplying factor, her reading comprehension is really harmed when she has weaknesses in both of these areas. So that makes the intervention even trickier to really target what that one thing is because it's not just one thing. She needs all pieces of that reading rope to really come together to support her reading comprehension.

**(10:45)** So take a moment, pause, and reflect. Think of those four common reader profiles. So we talked about Becca, who was a typical reader, strong word recognition, strong language comprehension. We talked about Joseph, who had a specific word reading deficit but had strong language comprehension. We also talked about Daniel, who is a student that's still learning English and so he had some language comprehension deficits but is doing great with word recognition. And finally, we talked about Layla, who had some mixed reading difficulties and really struggled with both word recognition and language comprehension. Within those four common reader profiles, jot down the names of any of your students who might fit in each of these areas and as we proceed into Module 3 and we're really focusing on decoding and Modules 4 and 5 and talking about some of those other elements of reading, you can be thinking about what those readers in your classroom or readers that you're working with might need.

**(11:58)** I want to end with this quote from Seidenberg. He states, "The SVR [the simple view of reading] is like a cake recipe that specifies the main ingredients but not the quantities or the procedures for combining them. It's useful to have the ingredients spelled out this way; you just can't bake the cake," right? So the simple view of reading is an incomplete picture. So you might still have some questions about next steps. Don't worry. Our next videos are going to continue to explore some additional reading models that provide more details about skilled reading. This is really just laying the foundation for further learning to come, and it just gives you that bird's eye view of what readers really need. So just like Seidenberg says, this is just the tip of the iceberg. There is a lot more information that you need in order to actually bake the cake or in order to actually produce a skilled reader.

**(12:59)** If you're interested in some learning extensions on the simple view of reading, please check out this infographic. And there's also a video on here that is fantastic from Reading Rockets. So those would be great places to go to learn a little bit more. Thank you so much for joining us today, and please do remember to visit the Facebook group and comment on the Module 2, Lesson 1 thread. We can't wait to hear from you.

How would you define word recognition? Language comprehension?

Additional Notes

Word Recognition: Words we automatically know

Language Comprehension: Deriving meaning from spoken words

Pause and Reflect: Think of the 4 common reader profiles. Jot down the name(s) of any student who fits in each of the 4 areas.

Typical Reader: Good word recognition and language comprehension

SWRD (Specific Word Reading Deficit): Deficit in word recognition but good language comprehension

SLDC (Specific Language Comprehension Deficit): Good word recognition but deficit in language comprehension

MRD (Mixed Reading Difficulties): Deficit in word recognition and language comprehension

Additional Notes

# Bonus Content

**Use the questions below to prompt discussion amongst your colleagues.**

1. **Components of the Simple View of Reading:** How do word recognition and language comprehension each contribute to reading comprehension according to the simple view of reading (SVR)? Can you give examples of activities or exercises that strengthen each component?
2. **Common Reader Profiles:** Reflect on the four reader profiles discussed (Becca, Joseph, Daniel, and Layla). How might you adapt your instructional strategies to meet the needs of students fitting each profile?
3. **Intervention Strategies:** Based on the reader profiles, what targeted interventions would you propose for students with specific word reading deficits versus those with language comprehension deficits? How would your approach differ for students with mixed reading difficulties?
4. **Limitations of the SVR:** Seidenberg's quote likens the SVR to a cake recipe missing specific quantities and procedures. What additional information or models might you need to fully support the development of skilled readers in your classroom?

**To extend your understanding of this topic, work through the activities below with a small group of peers.**

**Reader Profile Analysis**
Create detailed profiles for students in your class who fit into the categories of typical reader, specific word reading deficit, language comprehension deficit, and mixed reading difficulties. Develop and share intervention plans tailored to each profile.

**Simulation Exercises**
Simulate reading challenges by having teachers read text with altered visual or comprehension cues. Reflect on the experience and discuss how it relates to the difficulties faced by students with word recognition or language comprehension deficits.

**Case Study Discussions**
Review case studies of interventions for different types of reading difficulties. Discuss the outcomes and brainstorm how similar strategies could be applied or adapted for students in your own classrooms.

**Resource Exchange**
Organize a resource exchange where teachers share articles, books, and tools related to the simple view of reading and effective reading interventions. Each participant presents a summary and practical application of their resource to the group.

**Additional Resources**
On pages 50-51, you will find four cards, one for each popular reading model. Make copies and hand these out to your colleagues as a quick reference guide for each of the models.

# Lesson 2: The Reading Rope

*Module 2, Lesson 2 from the Science of Reading Academy focuses on Scarborough's Reading Rope, a model developed in 2001 to provide a detailed understanding of the components involved in skilled reading. Scarborough's Reading Rope consists of two main strands: language comprehension and word recognition. The language comprehension strand includes background knowledge, vocabulary, language structures, verbal reasoning, and literacy knowledge, while the word recognition strand encompasses phonological awareness, decoding, and sight recognition. These strands are intertwined to form a strong, skilled reader. The video discusses how weaknesses in any single component can disrupt a student's overall reading development. Below is the transcript for the Module 2, Lesson 2 video.*

**(00:07)** Hello, and welcome back to the Science of Reading Academy. We're in Module 2, and we're exploring all of the different reading models. Now during our last lesson, we talked about this simple view of reading. Today we're going to do the next step and really talk about Scarborough's Reading Rope. So let's jump in and get started.

**(00:31)** To really help you anchor your learning today, I would highly recommend that you pause the video and gather some supplies so that you can follow along and create your own reading rope as we talk about each of the strands. To complete this activity, you're going to need eight pipe cleaners, eight sticky labels, or you could even use a sticky note or computer paper with tape. It does not have to be fancy, just some way to affix a label to your pipe cleaners, as well as a writing utensil. So pause this video and jump back on when you have those things that you need in order to build the rope.

**(01:15)** Alright, so what is Scarborough's Reading Rope? Our last video discussed the simple view of reading, which is really a wonderful model that illustrates the two prerequisite components of reading comprehension. One of the weaknesses of this simple view of reading is its lack of detail. Scarborough, in 2001, provided a more detailed description of the components of skilled reading through the reading rope model. Scarborough created this visual to help parents and teachers understand the many components that are involved in learning how to read, according to the most recent research. The reading rope model has been validated through both meta-analysis and longitudinal research, so we know that it continues to be true to this day. The reading rope model has two strands: an upper strand focusing on language comprehension, so this part up here, the green strands that you see, and a lower strand focusing on word recognition.

**(02:23)** The language comprehension strand includes the subskills of background knowledge, vocabulary knowledge, language structures, verbal reasoning, and literacy knowledge. The word recognition strand includes the subskills of phonological awareness, decoding and encoding, and sight recognition. The two strands language comprehension and word recognition reinforce each other and weave together to produce an increasingly skilled and automatic reader as time progresses. Each of the reading rope components has been well researched and proven to be interconnected. However, students must fully develop both strands of the reading rope to become proficient readers.

**(03:14)** So let's talk through our language comprehension strand. So now is the time for you to pull out those pipe cleaners, and one of them needs to be labeled background knowledge. So when we think about background knowledge, some of our students are going to come to us with a plethora of background knowledge. They're going to have experiences from outside of their home and outside of their classroom, while some of our students are going to need us to be intentional with building that background knowledge through a wide variety of text experiences, songs, poems, videos, photographs. All of those things are going to build background knowledge in your students. So that is the first strand in your language comprehension.

**(04:03)** Your next strand is vocabulary, so making sure that we are building the vocabulary of our students and carefully selecting words that are those high-yield academic words that are going to build a student's performance across the subjects. So your second strand is labeled vocabulary.

**(04:25)** Your third strand is going to be labeled language structure. So this is things like how sentences are formed and the grammar rules and the complex nuanced meanings of words, all of those things make up our language structure. So we need to be intentional with providing students instruction about the language structure. So that's your third piece of the rope.

**(04:53)** Your fourth piece is verbal reasoning. So verbal reasoning is going to be things like making inferences and being able to draw conclusions. This is both with text and being able to explain their thinking to others. So verbal reasoning is the fourth strand of language comprehension.

**(05:15)** And finally, literacy knowledge. So this is everything from print concepts to being familiar with genres. Literacy knowledge is a wide breadth of knowledge that students need.

**(05:31)** So after you've labeled all five strands, I want you to start intertwining them together. So it's kind of hard to braid five different strands. So I would just take your pipe cleaners and twist them together. Now, when we look at the rope, we'll see here that they don't start connecting together at the very tippy top, right? So when students are first learning these things, they're going to learn them in more isolated parts of their day because, cognitively, they're not ready yet to start intertwining them. So that will come later, so leave a little bit of your pipe cleaners at the end that are not raveled yet and then start raveling, twisting them together. All right, and when you're ready, we're going to keep going to word recognition. So pause the video if you need to get caught up and then jump back on.

**(06:33)** Word recognition has less strands. So with your three remaining pipe cleaners, you're going to label the first one phonological awareness. Now, phonological awareness is that big umbrella that's also going to include the subset phonemic awareness, which is being able to hear individual sounds and words and manipulate them. So that's that first piece that students need to be able to hear and understand sounds in our language.

**(07:06)** This second component of this rope is decoding, so being able to look at graphemes or look at written representations of phonemes and sound them out to make a word.

**(07:20)** Finally, the last component is sight recognition. Now, this is not just sight words; this is more automaticity. So being able to look at words and having enough practice orthographically mapping them to be able to see and know the words automatically.

**(07:42)** So these are your three components of word recognition. There's only three of them, so it's a little bit easier to do your braiding process, so you can braid those strands together. Now, one thing that's always really interesting, and you might not want to do it because you've been working so hard on putting your strands together, but if you look at your word recognition braid, if you pull out one of those strands, the whole braid falls apart. So if you have students that don't have decoding or don't have sight recognition or don't have phonological awareness, that whole word recognition strain completely falls apart. Now, language comprehension, if you pull out one of those five strands, it doesn't fall apart. It just gets weaker. So language comprehension is a little bit different than our word recognition. It's not as sequential, but they all work together to make a stronger reading rope.

**(08:40)** Now, after you have your word recognition rope braided together, now you're going to take your language comprehension rope and your word recognition rope and start intertwining them. And the same is true that we talked about earlier. When students are first starting out on their journey to become skilled readers, they need to have an isolated word recognition part of their day and an isolated language comprehension part of their day because it is too much cognitively to do both at once. But as they get older, those skills can become increasingly interwoven until, by the time they are leaving elementary school, you're not going to know if it is a language comprehension or a word recognition lesson because those skills are so closely intertwined. Alright, I hope you had fun making your reading rope.

**(09:43)** Pause and reflect. Jot down in your note guide, think of each strand of the rope. Which strand do you feel is your strength as an educator, and which strand might need more focus? So jot down your thoughts and then jump back on the video for our learning extensions.

**(10:06)** This quote from Hollis Scarborough is one of my very favorites. She states, "Weakness in any strand can disrupt reading, and weakness in SEVERAL strands can disrupt reading more." So I always bring up this quote when I'm talking about reading intervention. When we think about our students, and we're really honing in on that Tier 2, we've got to figure out which area of the rope is their weakness so that we can fill that gap and make their rope strong. But when we think about Tier 1, we've got to make sure that we are providing that explicit instruction in all areas of reading so that our students' ropes don't have any holes so that their reading is not disrupted.

**(10:53)** Our learning extensions for today are both a blog post all about the reading rope—that is a great read—and a reading rope podcast. So if you want to know more, these would be great resources for you to check out. Thank you so much for joining us. Please remember to visit the SOR Academy Facebook group and comment on the Module 2, Lesson 2 thread. We can't wait to hear from you.

## Language Comprehension: 5 Components

Background Knowledge

Vocabulary

Language Structure

Verbal Reasoning

Literacy Knowledge

## Word Recognition: 3 Components

Phonological Awareness

Decoding

Sight Recognition

## Pause and Reflect: Think of each strand of the rope. Which strand do you feel is your strength as an educator? Which strand might need more focus?

Additional Notes

# Bonus Content

**Use the questions below to prompt discussion amongst your colleagues.**

1. **Components of Scarborough's Reading Rope:** What are the two main strands of Scarborough's Reading Rope, and what subskills are included in each strand? How do these subskills contribute to overall reading proficiency?
2. **Building Background Knowledge:** How does background knowledge impact a student's ability to comprehend text? What strategies can teachers use to build background knowledge in students with limited experiences?
3. **Phonological Awareness and Decoding:** Why are phonological awareness and decoding crucial for word recognition? Can you share examples of activities that effectively develop these skills in students?
4. **Interconnectedness of Skills:** Discuss how the subskills within the language comprehension and word recognition strands reinforce each other. What happens when one or more of these subskills are weak?
5. **Application in the Classroom**: How can the concept of Scarborough's Reading Rope be applied to daily reading instruction? Reflect on your teaching practice and identify which strand or subskill you find most challenging to teach and why.

**To extend your understanding of this topic, work through the activities below with a small group of peers.**

**Reading Rope Creation**
Have teachers create their own physical reading ropes using pipe cleaners and labels as described in the video. This hands-on activity will help them visualize and remember the components of Scarborough's Reading Rope.

**Subskill Workshops**
Organize workshops focusing on each subskill within the reading rope. Teachers can rotate through stations where they learn and practice strategies for teaching background knowledge, vocabulary, language structure, verbal reasoning, literacy knowledge, phonological awareness, decoding, and sight recognition.

**Case Study Analysis**
Provide case studies of students with reading difficulties. In small groups, teachers analyze the cases to identify which components of the reading rope are weak and develop targeted intervention plans.

**Lesson Plan Development**
In small groups, teachers develop lesson plans that integrate activities addressing multiple subskills of the reading rope. They then present their plans and receive feedback from their peers.

**Reflection and Goal Setting**
Have teachers reflect on their strengths and areas for improvement in teaching the components of the reading rope. They can set specific goals for enhancing their instruction and share these goals with a peer group for accountability and support.

**Additional Resources**
On pages 50-51, you will find four cards, one for each popular reading model. Make copies and hand these out to your colleagues as a quick reference guide for each of the models.

MODULE 2: Exploring Reading Models

# Lesson 3: The Four-Part Processing Model

*Module 2, Lesson 3 from the Science of Reading Academy focuses on the four-part processing model of reading instruction, developed by Seidenberg and McClelland in 1989. This model, confirmed by later advanced brain imaging studies, illustrates how the brain processes word recognition through four interconnected processors: the orthographic processor (which handles the visual input of written words), the phonological processor (which connects written letters to their corresponding sounds), the meaning processor (which helps understand word meanings and context), and the context processor (which clarifies word meanings based on the surrounding text). The video emphasizes the importance of bottom-up processing, starting with decoding letters and sounds, to develop proficient reading skills and suggests practical applications for supporting struggling readers. Below is the transcript for the Module 2, Lesson 3 video.*

**(00:07)** Hello, and welcome back to the Science of Reading Academy. We are in Module 2, where we are exploring reading models, and today we are going to discuss the four-part processing model.

**(00:23)** The four-part processing model, or the four-part processing system, was developed by Seindenberg and McClellan in 1989. It shows how our brains complete the word recognition process. Scientists figured this out through experiments on reading. They came up with this model back in 1989 to sum up what they found out about how good and not-so-good readers process words. They made this model before they could actually see where and when these brain activities happen during reading. One of the most exciting things, though, is that later, when we had functional MRI and some of the more advanced technology that we have today, those studies confirmed their hypotheses. You can read more about this in a book called *Beginning to Read: Thinking and Learning about Print* by Adams, as well as some articles and magazines such as *Psychological Science* and the *Public Interest* as well as *Scientific American*. This model helps simplify how we understand reading, although scientists have also found smaller parts within each system that do different jobs. So it is a very complex model, but it is really simplifying even more complex research.

**(01:49)** So we're going to start with the orthographic processor. The orthographic processing system is the part of our brain that inputs written words visually. It takes in what we see on a page, so letters, punctuation, spaces, the patterns and words, and it helps us as readers make sense of them. This system lets us do things like copy text, recognize whole words, or even remember how to spell. One of the things that's fascinating about our brain is that when we read, our brain is able to quickly filter and identify the features of the letters and words we're looking at, matching them to what we already know in our memory. If we recognize the letters or words, we link them to their sounds and their meanings. Most people can read various styles of writing or different fonts without much trouble once they know their letters and sounds. So that really tells us that it's not about the shape or the size or the color. It's about connecting letters to sounds. So the size, the style, the font, whether the letters are uppercase or lower case doesn't really matter once we know how to read. We recognize letters by their shapes, whether they have curves or straight lines or angles, and the orthographic system stores information about writing that we need for reading and spelling.

**(03:14)** How fast we recognize and remember letters is really important for letting us read well. Of course, it's also really important that we connect those words that we read with what they mean. So children who struggle with this orthographic processing system might find it hard to learn so-called sight words, or words that they should know by sight; they might not spell as well, and they might read slowly because they're still trying to sound out words long after they should have learned to recognize them quickly.

**(03:46)** The next processor is the phonological processor. The phonological processor is a partner to the orthographic processor in our brains. It helps us connect written letters to their corresponding sounds. Good readers have overlearned this process so that they can almost instantly recognize whole words at a glance. It makes it look like they're only using the visual meaning of words when they read, so they're just looking at a word and knowing what it is—that look-say method that we talked about in the history of reading instruction. However, the phonological processor is always at work, even when we don't realize that. When experienced readers can't silently say the sounds of words to themselves, that's when they're going to read slower and make more mistakes.

**(04:34)** The phonological processor has many important jobs that are all related to how we hear, remember, and speak sounds. One of its jobs is to help us recognize those individual sounds and words. Children who struggle with this might have trouble remembering the sounds that go with letters or blending them together. They might also find it hard to notice the small differences between similar words. They might also struggle to spell words with all of the different sounds within those words.

**(05:07)** The next processor is the meaning processor. So understanding words involves all three parts of our brain: the part that deals with how the word sounds, that phonological processor; the part that handles how the words look, or the orthographic processor; and the part that understands what words mean, the meaning processor. Sometimes you'll also hear this referenced as a *semantic processor*. This meaning processor, or semantic processor, is crucial because it helps us make sense of words in different context. If we're only focusing on how words sound or how words look, and we're not ever involving the meaning processor, we might read words but not really understand them. For example, we might read unfamiliar words or random words without meaning or even we might read our own language without grasping what it's saying. The processor stores all of the words that we know, arranges them in our mental dictionary, and helps us understand the meanings of new words as we come across them in reading. The context of what we're reading helps us figure out what these new words mean. Each word in our mental dictionary has various aspects, like how it sounds or how it's spelled, what it means, how it's usually used, and any other meanings it might have. There are so many multiple meaning words in our language, so it stores all of those.

**(06:34)** The meaning processor is organized in different ways to help us understand words better. For example, it's going to connect words that mean similar things. It's going to break words down into their roots and into their smaller parts and link words with common meanings or association. So that's where that morphology instruction really becomes important. As we learn new words, this part of our brain is going to expand and build new neural pathways. Words in our mental dictionary aren't just learned in isolation. Instead, they're connected to other words, into things that we already know. This connection really helps us learn words more easily, especially when we're linking them to how they sound, how they're spelled, and the context where they're used. When children struggle with vocabulary, have limited English knowledge, or find it hard to reason with words, that's when we know their meaning processor is being impacted, and they might have difficulty with learning to read. In some cases, they might be able to figure out how to see words, but they're going to really struggle to understand what they mean.

**(07:48)** The final processor is the context processor, and the main role of the context processor is to work together with and assist the meaning processor. When we're talking about context, we're referencing the surrounding sentences and the overall topic or ideas discussed in the text. This context helps us understand the meaning of a word. Many words that sound the same can have different meanings, but the correct meaning is determined by this instance that they're used in. For instance, the word *passed* can mean, oh, she passed by the store, or even I saw him in the past. So just listening, they sound the same, but they have different meanings based on the context of the sentence. Context is going to help us understand the intended meaning of a word, especially if we're not familiar with it. It also enhances our understanding of how each word is typically used in our language context, helps clear up any confusion caused by multiple meanings of words, and it can help us spot mistakes in reading and prompt us to go back and read again for clarification.

**(09:00)** One thing that's really important to remember is that context cannot be a substitute for decoding. The context processor comes into play after the orthographic and phonological processors have done their work. It can provide clarity and an opportunity to check what you just read against meaning, but it is not the input method of word recognition. So when we think about the three-cueing system and asking, "Does that make sense?"—that's not a bad prompt. We just really want to be very intentional with when and how we're asking that and always drawing students' attention first to decoding, connecting those letters that are written to sounds that have been sort in their brain, blending them together to read a word, and then thinking through what makes sense in that context to help them self-correct and to help them think of multiple meaning words.

**(09:57)** So take a minute now to pause and think, how does each of the four processors work together and perhaps even challenge yourself: Can you label a blank diagram of that four-part processor? Think about where each piece goes and how they work together. After you've done that, go ahead and come back to wrap up our video together.

**(10:26)** One thing that's really important as we think about this four-part processor is connecting that to our practice. And it's very important that our prompts to support striving readers should promote the bottom-up processing that's demonstrated by the four-part processing model. That means that we're going to start with the letters, right? So always draw students' attention to the word itself, not to the picture, not skipping the word and coming back to it, looking at that word and going through the letters, connecting them to the sounds first, and then moving to the other processors as necessary.

**(11:06)** For further learning, there is a video recorded interview with Dr. Marilyn Adams, and she's the author of the book *Beginning to Read* that was the original source of the four-part processing model, which can also be known as the Adams model. So a great interview if you're interested in learning more about this reading model.

**(11:29)** Thank you so much for joining us, and please remember to visit the SOR Academy Facebook group and comment on the Module 2, Lesson 3 thread.

## The Four-Part Processing Model

## Orthographic Processor (receives visual input [letters])

## Phonological Processor (connects letters to sounds)

Additional Notes

Meaning Processor (makes sense of what words mean)

Additional Notes

Context Processor (provides clarifying information)

Pause and Reflect: Think of how each of the four processors work together. Can you label a blank diagram?

# Bonus Content

**Use the questions below to prompt discussion amongst your colleagues.**

1. **Historical Context:** How did the development of the four-part processing model by Seidenberg and McClellan in 1989 change our understanding of how the brain processes written words? What were the limitations of their original research, and how have modern technologies like fMRI validated their findings?
2. **Orthographic Processor:** Discuss the role of the orthographic processor in reading. How does it help readers recognize and remember letters and words? What challenges might a student face if they struggle with orthographic processing?
3. **Phonological Processor:** Explain the importance of the phonological processor in reading. How does it interact with the orthographic processor, and why is it crucial for reading fluency and accuracy?
4. **Meaning and Context Processors:** How do the meaning and context processors contribute to a reader's understanding of text? Why is it important for these processors to work together, and what might happen if one of these processors is not functioning effectively?
5. **Practical Applications:** How can teachers use the four-part processing model to support struggling readers? What strategies can be implemented in the classroom to enhance each of the four processors?

**To extend your understanding of this topic, work through the activities below with a small group of peers.**

**Diagram Labeling**

Provide a blank diagram of the four-part processing model and have teachers label each part (orthographic, phonological, meaning, context). Then, discuss as a group how each part interacts during the reading process.

**Case Studies**

Review case studies of students with different reading difficulties (e.g., dyslexia, language processing disorders). Identify which processor(s) might be affected and brainstorm intervention strategies to support these students.

**Reading Analysis**

Have teachers bring in examples of a student's reading work. In small groups, analyze the work to identify strengths and weaknesses in the student's use of the four processors. Discuss how instruction could be tailored to support each student's needs.

**Role-Playing**

Create scenarios where one teacher plays the role of a student struggling with a specific processor (e.g., phonological processing) and another teacher acts as the instructor. Role-play different teaching strategies to address the student's needs and discuss the outcomes.

**Book Study**

Assign chapters from *Beginning to Read: Thinking and Learning about Print* by Marilyn Adams for a deeper understanding of the four-part processing model. Have small groups present key takeaways and how they can apply this knowledge to their teaching practices.

**Additional Resources**

On pages 50-51, you will find four cards, one for each popular reading model. Make copies and hand these out to your colleagues as a quick reference guide for each of the models.

**MODULE 2: Exploring Reading Models**

# Lesson 4: The Active View of Reading

*Module 2, Lesson 4 from the Science of Reading Academy focuses on the active view of reading, developed by Duke and Cartwright. This model differs from other reading models by highlighting additional factors beyond word recognition and language comprehension that can cause reading difficulties. It includes the overlap between word recognition and language comprehension, termed bridging processes, which include vocabulary, reading fluency, and morphological awareness. The model also incorporates the concept of active self-regulation, where a reader's motivation, strategies, and executive function skills, such as cognitive flexibility and working memory, play crucial roles in reading proficiency. Below is the transcript for the Module 2, Lesson 4 video.*

**(00:07)** Hello, and welcome back to the Science of Reading Academy. We are in our last lesson of Module 2, which is focused on exploring reading models. Today we're going to discuss the active view of reading. There are three key differences in the active view of reading according to Duke and Cartwright, who are the authors of this model. The first is that the model identifies additional factors that can cause reading difficulties going beyond word recognition or language comprehension. So you'll remember with both the simple view of reading as well as the reading rope, both of those had word recognition, so up here, as well as language comprehension. But in this one, there's a few different areas on this screen.

**(01:00)** So this model aims to acknowledge that different people may struggle with reading for reasons other than word recognition and language comprehension. The second key difference is that the model shows how word recognition and language comprehension overlap and identifies this overlap as something called *bridging processes*. The third difference is that the model includes the role of active self-regulation, referencing that a reader's motivation, use of strategies, and other factors can influence how well they read. Additionally, the model suggests that each aspect of reading can be improved through instruction, which really offers hope for those struggling with reading comprehension and is really empowering for us as educators to know that we can impact how a student learns to read if we can just identify which one of those areas is preventing their reading ability.

**(02:06)** So let's talk a little bit more about active self-regulation. Skilled readers are not just passive recipients of text. They're actively using strategies and their executive function skills to understand what they read. This involves way more than just knowing how to read words and understand language. Readers also need to manage their reading process, they need to use strategies, they need to stay motivated, they need to engage with the text. I don't know about you, but I can picture in my mind several students that, really, it wasn't a decoding issue, it wasn't a comprehension issue. They just could not focus on the text in front of them and the text at hand. They needed support with that self-regulation side of reading in order to be effective readers.

**(03:04)** Executive function skills are those higher-level mental processes that are used for complex, goal-oriented tasks. They include cognitive flexibility, working memory, inhibitory control, attention, and planning. Research on executive functioning skills in relation to reading has really increased significantly in the past few years. Evidence shows that both generalized executive function skills as well as those specific to reading really play important roles in reading ability.

**(03:47)** Reading strategies are deliberate methods that are used to control and adjust reading efforts to better understand text. These strategies are things like breaking down words into morphology parts to decode them and understand them or perhaps using context clues to figure out word meanings. Teaching students these strategies, just like teaching them decoding techniques, can improve their ability to read certain words. So those are the three components that Duke and Cartwright are referencing when they say active self-regulation.

**(04:23)** All right, take a moment to pause and reflect. How can we as educators support the development of active self-regulation with our students? Jot down a few ideas in your note guide and then come back and join us to talk about bridging processes when you're finished.

**(04:40)** Okay, so shifting gears here to talk about those bridging processes. So you'll remember that was where the overlap exists between word recognition and language comprehension. And this overlap is really helpful in predicting reading outcomes, and it's very crucial for educators to consider these processes when they're looking at young readers. It can even suggest that interventions for developing readers need to carefully address factors that bridge both word recognition and language comprehension rather than just focusing on one or the other because it's not just phonics. It's not just language comprehension. It's putting them both together and having them work alongside each other that is going to prevent those or is going to produce those skilled readers.

**(05:33)** So looking first at vocabulary. Vocabulary knowledge is not just about understanding language. It's also going to help with recognizing words. For example, if we know how to pronounce words correctly and understand their meaning, that's going to help our reading comprehension.

**(03:47)** This connection between vocabulary, pronunciation, and meaning is key for creating a mental map of words in our memory. We have a lexicon in our brain that helps us keep track of all of these things, and the better quality lexicon—so the ones that have the meaning and the pronunciation and multiple meanings, synonyms, and antonyms and all of that—the deeper and the higher-quality representation we have, the better our brain is going to remember that work. Executive skills like coordination and connection making are really thought to play a role in this process, and there are brain studies that support that with evidence as well.

**(06:42)** Next, let's look at reading fluency. So reading fluency is commonly linked only to decoding or only to word recognition, but fluency really is influenced by both word recognition and comprehension. Fluency involves accurate word reading, reading with automaticity, and proper expression while maintaining meaning. So it's not just fast reading, right, it's all of those things working together. It's not just about recognizing words but also really understanding their meaning and their structure, and that even includes punctuation because that can really impact syntax and semantics as well. Fluency acts as a bridge between word recognition and comprehension, and that can help us understand why fluency acts as that bridging process. Effective methods for improving fluency will focus on developing both word recognition as well as comprehension skills.

**(07:47)** The final bridging process is morphological awareness, and this is the understanding of how word parts come together to form meaning, and it's crucial for reading. Research shows that morphological awareness will directly impact a child's reading ability, and not having morphological awareness is linked to reading difficulties. Importantly, it's related to both recognizing words and understanding language. So you might've noticed a theme between these three areas. Vocabulary, fluency, morphological awareness are related to both that decoding side and that comprehension side. So that's why Duke and Cartwright identified them as those bridging processes.

**(08:34)** This is a quote from Duke and Cartwright. They say, "Each construct name and the model is instructionally malleable." As educators, we are the difference makers. Each of these components—self-regulation, word recognition, language comprehension, and those bridging processes—can be influenced by us as educators. And that is such a privilege and an honor, but it really takes us being so intentional with our instruction in order for us to be effective at changing those areas.

**(09:11)** So I want you to pause again and choose one of those bridging processes. So remember that was morphological awareness, fluency, and vocabulary. Choose one of those and summarize how it connects word recognition to language comprehension. Jot it down in your note guide and then come back so we can talk about some bonus content and learning extensions.

**(09:34)** Okay, so first up here we have our learning extensions. There are two open access articles that are both from the same journal, *Reading Research Quarterly*. One includes the original publication from Duke and Cartwright about their active view of reading model. And then there's also Gough and Tunmer's response to some assertions in the original article. And Gough and Tunmer were the authors of the simple view of reading, so you can kind of see their response to this.

**(10:12)** Finally, we have some exclusive downloadable content as a thank you for joining us for module 2. So these are some cards that are meant to be printed out back to front that review all four of our reading models that we've discussed. So use these as references for yourself. These would also be great to share with colleagues if you're doing a PD session, these could be used as a cooperative learning activity, all kinds of possibilities. Please download those and use them to share your learning.

**(10:49)** Thank you so much for joining us for Module 2. Please take a moment to comment on the Module 2, Lesson 4 thread within our Facebook group for a chance to win. We so appreciate you joining us today.

## Active View of Reading-The Model

## Active Self-Regulation

Motivation and Engagement

Executive Function Skills

Strategy Use

## Pause and Reflect: How can we support the development of active self-regulation with our students?

Additional Notes

## Bridging Processes

Vocabulary

Reading Fluency

Morphological Awareness

Pause and Reflect: Choose <u>one</u> of the bridging processes. Summarize how it connects word recognition to language comprehension.

## Additional Notes

# Bonus Content

**Use the questions below to prompt discussion amongst your colleagues.**

1. **Key Differences:** How does the active view of reading, as proposed by Duke and Cartwright, differ from the simple view of reading and the reading rope models? What are the implications of these differences for diagnosing reading difficulties?
2. **Active Self-Regulation:** What is active self-regulation in reading, and why is it important for skilled reading? How can educators support the development of active self-regulation in their students?
3. **Bridging Processes:** Discuss the concept of bridging processes in the active view of reading. How do vocabulary, fluency, and morphological awareness act as bridges between word recognition and language comprehension?
4. **Executive Function Skills:** How do executive function skills like cognitive flexibility, working memory, and inhibitory control contribute to the reading process? Provide examples of how these skills can be developed in students.
5. **Instructional Strategies:** Based on the active view of reading, what instructional strategies can teachers use to address both word recognition and language comprehension simultaneously? How can these strategies be implemented in a classroom setting?

**To extend your understanding of this topic, work through the activities below with a small group of peers.**

**Case Study Analysis**
Review case studies of students with reading difficulties that go beyond word recognition and language comprehension. Identify which aspects of active self-regulation or bridging processes are affected and propose targeted interventions.

**Strategy Sharing Session**
In small groups, have teachers share effective strategies they use to develop active self-regulation, such as teaching specific reading strategies or fostering motivation and engagement. Create a shared resource document with these strategies.

**Executive Function Skill Development**
Design and implement activities that target specific executive function skills related to reading. For example, create memory games for working memory or planning tasks that require cognitive flexibility.

**Bridging Process Exploration**
Choose one of the bridging processes (vocabulary, fluency, morphological awareness) and develop a mini-lesson or activity that enhances this skill. Share and discuss the outcomes with peers.

**Model Comparison Exercise**
Create a comparison chart of the simple view of reading, the reading rope model, and the active view of reading. Highlight the strengths and limitations of each model and discuss how they can be integrated into a comprehensive reading instruction approach.

**Additional Resources**
On pages 50-51, you will find four cards, one for each popular reading model. Make copies and hand these out to your colleagues as a quick reference guide for each of the models.

# The Simple View of Reading

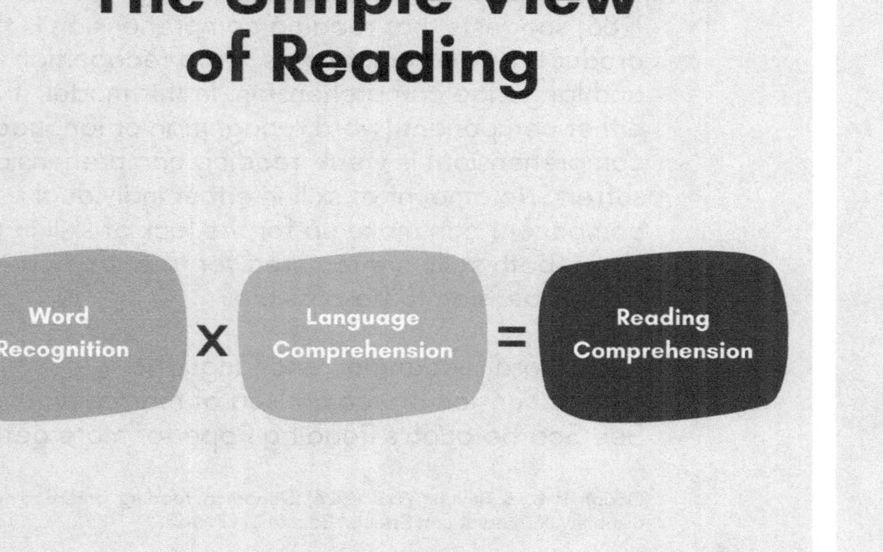


# Scarborough's Reading Rope

Background Knowledge
Vocabulary
Language Structure
Verbal Reasoning
Literacy Knowledge
Phonological Awareness
Decoding
Sight Recognition

# The Four-Part Processing Model

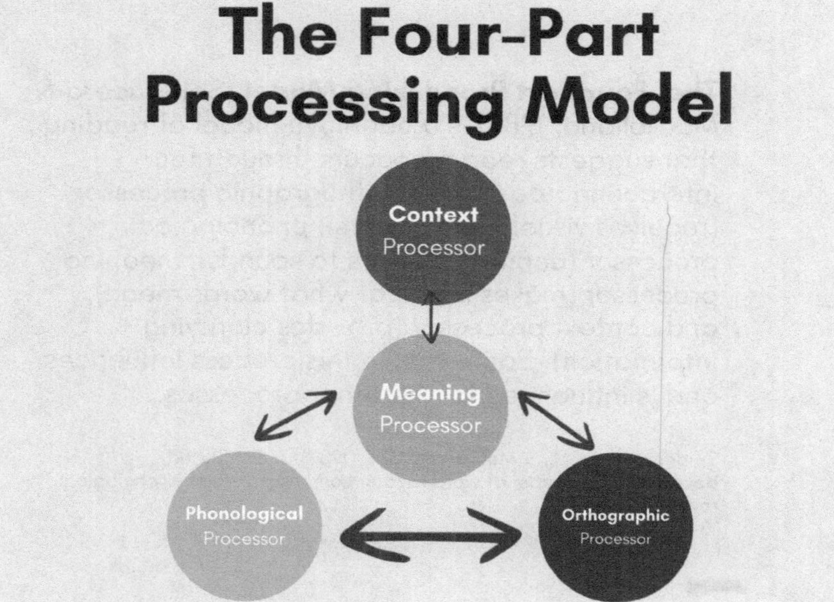


# The Active View of Reading

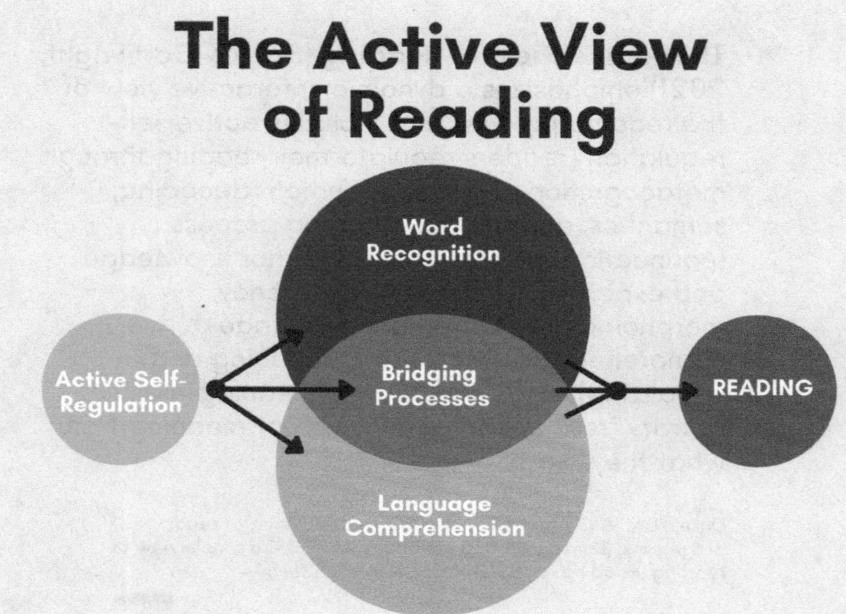

LAPREA

**Scarborough's Reading Rope** (Scarborough, 2001) is a visual model that illustrates all the interconnected components necessary for skilled reading. The rope includes strands related to word recognition (phonological awareness, decoding, sight recognition) and language comprehension (background knowledge, vocabulary, language structures, verbal reasoning, literacy knowledge). In this model, word recognition skills become increasingly automatic over time and language comprehension skills become increasingly strategic over time.

Scarborough, H. S. (2001). Connecting early language and literacy to later reading (dis)abilities: Evidence, theory, and practice. In S. Neuman & D. Dickinson (Eds.), Handbook for research in early literacy. New York: Guilford Press.

LAPREA

**The Simple View of Reading** (Gough & Tunmer, 1986) suggests that reading comprehension is the product of two components, word recognition and language comprehension. In this model, if either component (word recognition or language comprehension) is weak, reading comprehension suffers. No amount of skill in either individual component can make up for the lack of skill in the other; both skills are required for true reading comprehension to be possible.

Note, word recognition and language comprehension are comprised of many elements. See Scarborough's Reading Rope for more detail.

Gough, P. B., & Tunmer, W. E. (1986). Decoding, reading, and reading disability. Remedial and Special Education, 7, 6-10.

LAPREA

**The Active View of Reading** (Duke & Cartwright, 2021) emphasizes a dynamic, interactive view of the reading process that includes active self-regulation (readers regulate their reading through metacognition), word recognition (decoding, semantics, and syntax), bridging process (connecting the text with their prior knowledge and experiences, vocabulary, fluency, morphological awareness), language comprehension (interpreting meaning and visualizing), and reading as a meaning-making activity (readers actively construct meaning from what they read).

Duke, N. K., & Cartwright, K. B. (2021). The science of reading progresses: Communicating advances beyond the simple view of reading. Reading Research Quarterly, 56, S25-S44.

LAPREA

**The Four Part Processing Model** (Seidenberg & McClelland, 1989) is a cognitive model of reading that suggests reading occurs through four interconnected stages: orthographic processor (receives visual input-letters), phonological processor (connects letters to sounds), meaning processor (makes sense of what words mean), and context processor (provides clarifying information). Each level in this process influences and is influenced by the other processes.

Seidenberg, M. S., & McClelland, J. L. (1989). A distributed, developmental model of word recognition and naming. Psychological review, 96(4), 523.

MODULE 3

# Investigating the Reading Brain

In Module 3, we will investigate the fascinating processes of the reading brain. We will start by exploring the brain's reading regions and identify which areas are involved in the reading circuit. Next, we will examine neuroplasticity and how the brain's ability to reorganize itself impacts reading development and instruction. Finally, we will discuss the self-teaching hypothesis, which explains how children can rapidly learn to read independently once they grasp key concepts. These lessons provide a comprehensive understanding of the neurological foundations that underpin effective reading instruction, giving you a deep insight into the brain's role in reading.

As you watch the videos in this module, use the pages that follow to write notes about what you are learning as well as reflect on the new information presented to you.

## Watch

The following videos are part of this learning module. Go to ScienceOfReadingAcademy.com to access each of the videos.

Lesson 1: The Brain's Reading Regions
Lesson 2: Neuroplasticity and the Brain
Lesson 3: The Self-Teaching Hypothesis

## Before you begin

To activate your schema about the module topics, use your current knowledge and experience to reflect on the questions below.

1. What do you know about how different parts of the brain might contribute to the ability to read?

2. In what ways do you think the brain's ability to change and adapt can help in learning new skills, like reading?

3. Why do you think it's important for students to learn how to figure out unfamiliar words on their own?

# Lesson 1: The Brain's Reading Regions

*Module 3, Lesson 1 from the Science of Reading Academy focuses on the brain's reading regions within the left hemisphere, detailing how various lobes and specific areas contribute to reading. The frontal lobe handles complex cognitive tasks, while the parietal lobe integrates sensory information. The occipital lobe processes visual input, and the temporal lobe manages sounds, speech, and emotional responses. The reading circuit involves the visual cortex recognizing letters, the occipital-temporal region processing these letters, and the parietal-temporal region connecting visual input to phonemes. The inferior frontal gyrus is essential for phonological and semantic processing, and the superior temporal gyrus, including Wernicke's area, supports language comprehension. Below is the transcript for the Module 3, Lesson 1 video.*

(00:07) Hello, and welcome back to the Science of Reading Academy. I am so excited to get started with Module 3, which is all about investigating the reading brain. The reading brain is so fascinating to me, and there's so much that we can learn about it. Today's lesson is all about the brain's reading regions, and there's lots of technical terms, but this lesson will really allow you to understand some of the future lessons. When we're talking about the research, this is going to give you that context that you need to understand what those researchers are talking about.

(00:47) So when we think about the brain, there are two hemispheres of the brain. There's the right hemisphere and the left hemisphere. The reading regions that we really want to develop are located in the left hemisphere. So to help us remember the four lobes of the brain, we can use our hands to help us. So you're going to take your hand, and you're going to make kind of an odd fist. So your thumb will go down, and your fingers are going to go on top of it, and your thumb just kind of hangs out here below your fingers. So if you turn it toward the front with your thumb facing toward you, the front fingers here are going to represent your frontal lobe. So these two fingers, and that's right behind your forehead, and this is the part of the brain that's responsible for complex and abstract abilities. This part doesn't develop until you're in your twenties, so it takes a while before that frontal lobe is fully formed.

(01:55) The next part is that parietal lobe. So that is represented by your index and your middle finger here, so it's behind the frontal lobe toward the back, and this is going to integrate the sensory information in your body.

(02:12) Now if you look at the back part of your fist, it kind of looks like an eye. So this can help you remember that your occipital lobe is the area responsible for visual information, and that's located at the very back of your brain. That will come up later when we talk about how words are inputted visually through our brains, but all of the other lobes are also working hard to help us read those words.

(02:41) Now your thumb down here is going to represent that temporal lobe, but it's connected to the parietal and the occipital lobe down here, and it's going to help us with sounds and with speech. The temporal lobe also includes our limbic system, which is responsible for emotions, for learning, and for memory, and that houses the amygdala. So if you've ever heard of the flipping your brain, that's where that temporal lobe comes from. The amygdala is a portion of that temporal lobe.

(03:13) So take a moment now and pause. Use your hand as a model to rehearse those different regions of the brain. So remember, we have the frontal, parietal, occipital, and temporal lobes. So try to remember all four of those using your hand as a guide, and when you're ready, come back and join us. We'll talk about those regions and their role within reading.

(03:40) So the brain's reading regions utilize all four lobes of the brain's left hemisphere. So again, we have that frontal lobe, the parietal, the occipital, and the temporal. All of those are being utilized during the reading process through the neurological reading circuit. When a word is read, the string of written letters is processed through the visual cortex, and then it's analyzed with the left occipital-temporal area on the fusiform gyrus. The gyrus is just like a fold of the brain, and sometimes you'll hear this referred to as the *visual word form area*. So this process, basically, it's inputting words and it's saying, oh, this word is something special. I noticed that those are letters; I'm going to forward it on in the reading circuit. So this process is going to facilitate that circuit for connecting phonemes and graphemes together, which is that essential prerequisite skill for decoding.

(04:50) So even though these connections seem instantaneous to us as skilled readers, it is crucial that we realize that the visual words are being analyzed by their individual graphemes before they're being quickly reassembled and recognized as a whole word. So it appears we're looking at words and we've memorized them, but we haven't. We've done something a little bit different. If you remember from Module 2 when we were practicing word recognition, we were able to recognize strings of letters faster than we were able to recognize colors because our brain hasn't just memorized those words.

(05:30) After the words are processed through that visual word form area down in the occipital-temporal region, they then have to be connected to the parietal-temporal region. So you can see that green area of the brain there. There's an angular gyrus in here, which again is just that fold within the brain. So that's the particular area where that's occurring. This area is responsible for word analysis, and it's helping connect those graphemes that have been processed visually to phonemes or those sounds that are stored in the brain.

(06:09) Words also have to be connected to the frontal lobe, specifically the inferior frontal gyrus, which includes Broca's area, and that's going to help with grammatical and speech processing, and I'm including all of these terms, the angular gyrus, Broca's area, all of that because I think it gets a little confusing when you hear someone talk about the brain's reading regions and they use these terms and then someone else talks about the brain's reading regions, and they use different terms, but really they're all talking about the same thing. Some people are just using more technical terms than others, but if they're talking about the frontal lobe or the frontal gyrus or the inferior frontal gyrus or they're getting specific and talking about Broca's area, all of that is just helping with that grammatical and speech processing.

(07:00) Dehaene summarizes; he says, "When we sound out our words and letters, our temporal and parietal regions light up along with the frontal speech areas, even when we read silently." So it's not just our brain hearing sounds. It's actually producing them as if we were saying them out loud.

(07:25) These neural circuits between each area of the brain that are involved in reading must be well established to develop skilled reading. The connections between these different brain areas do not exist at birth. It's not like our brain is born and these pathways are there and we just have to make them stronger. They're not there at all, so educators must purposefully develop them to teach students how to read.

(07:51) So we're going to zoom into each of these areas a little bit more closely, starting with the occipital-temporal region. So that is in the back of your brain. So remember, occipital is like the eye. So it's where you're inputting words visually, and the temporal is connected to that. So down toward the back there. This is most commonly known as the *visual word form area*; that tells you what's happening there, and it's serving as the brain's filter for visual information that's entering the language system. It selectively analyzes incoming images for the presence of letters and then forwards them onto other brain areas that subsequently transform them into sound and meaning.

(08:36) So I just kind of think of it as this complex filing system where the occipital-temporal region is going letter, not a letter, letter, not a letter. And when there are letters, something special happens.

You'll even hear this region of the brain referred to as the brain's *letterbox*. So it's activated by written words, but it's not activated when words are spoken out loud. This crucial region houses the person's learned dictionary of word patterns and spelling. So all of those things that are really essential for reading and spelling tasks. Within the visual word form area, letter chunks and detailed representations of syllables and words are stored, which enables readers to mentally visualize word spells. But this is where those bigger pieces, the morphology and all of that is going to come into play as well. This is a crucial part of the brain that is believed to really help with the spelling task, not only just the reading task, but also the spelling task. So it's going to help us visualize, visualize a word spelling mentally. If you've ever looked at a word and thought that doesn't look right, that's your visual word form area at work. This area really helps us distinguish between skilled readers and striving readers. So it's really that filter through which visual information must flow in order to enter the language system.

(10:11) Then we have the parietal-temporal region. So that's that area in the green. So we've inputted our words visually. Our brain has said, hey, those are letters. Those are important back in the occipital-temporal region, and now it's moving up to the parietal-temporal region. So the parietal region is also connected to that temporal region, so they're all right there together. This is really a crucial part of the brain for children that are in the beginning stages of learning to read because it's processing both the visual and the auditory information.

(10:48) So it's really making those connections between graphemes and phonemes. When children are just beginning to decode letters into sounds, this area receives input from both letters and from speech, so it's really helping make that solid phoneme-grapheme connection. As learning progresses, this link is going to become automatic so that even a slight mismatch between a letter and its expected sound triggers a signal in the brain. They're like, ooh, that's different than what I knew before. Beginning readers are going to very much rely on this region of the brain until they've had enough exposure to know it with automaticity. So when we look at brain scans of students that are learning to read, we see a lot more activity in this area than we would of a skilled reader.

(11:38) Now moving toward the inferior frontal gyrus, so this is that frontal lobe section. This area is involved in phonological processing, which is also essential for decoding and understanding written words. Even though it's just those phonemes, we have to make those connections to our stored speech sounds. This helps with mapping visual representations of letters and words onto their corresponding sounds, which will help individuals recognize and pronounce words accurately. Additionally, the inferior frontal gyrus is implicated in semantic processing, which allows readers to comprehend the meaning of words and sentences within a given context. So that's where Broca's area really comes into play as well. That's going to help our lips and our teeth and our tongue know what to do in order to articulate certain sounds.

(12:39) Finally, we have the superior temporal gyrus, and this plays a crucial role in the reading process by contributing to various aspects of language comprehension and auditory processing. This area includes Wernicke's area, which is considered to be the language comprehension center of the brain. So all of these areas of the brain work together almost instantaneously for skilled readers to look at a word to match it to our stored spoken language then to understand the meaning of that word. This probably reminds you of that four-part processing model that we learned about in Module 2.

(13:25) I want to read this quote to you. It says, "The herculean job of educators is no less than to help the brain develop a skill it could not otherwise, which requires creating an entirely new circuit in the brain." The work that we do as reading teachers is truly rocket science. To quote Louisa Moats, we are forging new circuits in the brains of our young students. We're helping sculpt the neural landscape of future generations. This is no small feat for either our students or for ourselves. Because we can read, it seems like, oh, that was so easy, but for our little readers, they are making new neural pathways in their brain. It is a lot of work and a lot of effort.

(14:18) So take a moment, pause, and practice. Create a quick sketch that will help you remember the four components of the reading circuit. You can use whatever term you want. It's not as important to know those technical terms. It's more important that you know the process. So create a sketch that will help you remember and explain that process because it can be empowering to not only share that with your coworkers but also with your students so they understand what's happening when you're doing your phonics lessons and your small-group reading lessons; that can really help them see the value and the purpose in that.

(14:55) Okay. Finally, I want to share with you two learning extensions. The first is a fantastic podcast about the reading brain, and the second is actually a picture book by Denise Eide, and it is *How Your Brain Learns to Read*. It would be great to share with a classroom of students, but I also think it's great to share with teachers because it's very informative about the different areas of the brain and how they work together to create skilled readers. So that's another great read to add to your collection.

(15:35) Thank you so much for joining us again for Module 3. Please look for the Facebook group thread for Module 3, Lesson 1. We can't wait to hear from you.

## The Brain's Left Hemisphere

Frontal Lobe

Parietal Lobe

Occipital Lobe

Temporal Lobe

Additional Notes

## The Brain's Reading Regions

Occipito-Temporal Region (visual word form area)

Parieto-Temporal Region (connections between graphemes and phonemes)

Inferior Frontal Gyrus (phonological and semantic processing)

Superior Temporal Gyrus (understanding spoken language)

## Pause and Reflect: Create a quick sketch to help you remember the four components of the reading circuit.

## Additional Notes

# Bonus Content

**Use the questions below to prompt discussion amongst your colleagues.**

1. **Understanding Brain Lobes and Reading Regions:** How do the frontal, parietal, occipital, and temporal lobes each contribute to the reading process? Can you explain the role of the occipital-temporal region in reading, and why is it often referred to as the brain's letterbox?
2. **Neural Pathways and Reading Development:** Why is it important for educators to understand that neural circuits for reading are not present at birth and must be developed through instruction? How does the parietal-temporal region assist beginning readers, and what changes occur in this region as reading skills improve?
3. **Phonological and Semantic Processing:** What are the functions of the inferior frontal gyrus and the superior temporal gyrus in the reading process? How do Broca's area and Wernicke's area contribute to reading and language comprehension?
4. **Application in the Classroom:** How can teachers use their understanding of the brain's reading regions to inform their instructional practices? What strategies can be employed to help students develop the neural pathways necessary for skilled reading?
5. **Integrating Knowledge and Practice:** Reflect on how understanding the brain's reading regions can change your approach to teaching reading. What specific changes would you implement in your classroom? Discuss how explaining the reading process to students can empower them and improve their learning. How would you incorporate this into your lessons?

**To extend your understanding of this topic, work through the activities below with a small group of peers.**

**Create a Brain Model**
Using materials like clay or playdough, create a 3D model of the brain highlighting the key reading regions (frontal, parietal, occipital, and temporal lobes). Label each part and discuss its role in reading.

**Brain Region Mapping Exercise**
Provide diagrams of the brain and ask each participant to color and label the different reading regions. Follow this with a group discussion on how each region contributes to reading.

**Simulation of Neural Pathways**
Conduct a role-playing activity where each participant represents a different part of the brain involved in reading. Act out the process of reading a word from visual input to comprehension, demonstrating the flow of information through the different regions.

**Case Study Analysis**
Present a case study of a student with reading difficulties. Work together to hypothesize which brain regions might be underdeveloped or not functioning optimally. Discuss potential instructional strategies to support the student.

**Podcast Discussion**
Listen to a podcast episode about the reading brain as a group. After listening, discuss the key points and how they relate to your current understanding and practices in teaching reading. Share insights and possible applications in the classroom.

**Additional Resources**
On page 72, you will find a handout with a labeled graphic of the brain's reading regions. Make copies of this handout and share it with your colleagues at a grade-level planning meeting or faculty meeting. Share with them what you have learned about brain science and its implication on reading.

# Lesson 2: Neuroplasticity and the Brain

*Module 3, Lesson 2 from the Science of Reading Academy focuses on neuroplasticity and its profound impact on the reading brain. Neuroplasticity refers to the brain's ability to reorganize and adapt in response to experiences, learning, and environmental changes. As educators, understanding neuroplasticity is crucial because it underscores how teaching practices can reshape the brain's neural circuits involved in reading. Effective reading instruction, such as teaching phonemic awareness and decoding skills, primes the brain to create new neural connections essential for proficient reading. The video emphasizes that neuroplasticity allows both children and adults, including those with dyslexia, to develop more efficient reading circuits through targeted intervention and practice. This highlights the importance of early and intensive instruction for optimal learning outcomes. Below is the transcript for the Module 3, Lesson 2 video.*

(00:07) Hello, and welcome to the Science of Reading Academy. We're in Module 3, which is all about investigating the reading brain. Today we are going to dive into neuroplasticity and its role in the reading brain.

(00:23) So to start, let's review the brain's reading regions. We covered these more in depth during our last lesson, Lesson 1 of Module 3, but just as a quick review. All four lobes of the brain's left hemisphere—so the frontal lobe, the parietal lobe, the occipital lobe, and the temporal lobe—are utilized during the reading process through the neurological reading circuit. We know that words are processed visually through the visual word form area. So that's down here in the occipital-temporal region. And then they are processed visually through the parietal-temporal region. So this is where a lot of that sounding out effort happens. And then finally, they're connected to speech sounds here and the inferior frontal gyrus around Broca's area as well as word meaning and the superior temporal gyrus.

(01:24) All of this is done almost instantaneously with skilled readers, which really makes us feel like surely we're relying on memorization of whole words, right? This is just happening so fast. We're not conscious of all of the steps that our brain has to take. This makes it really tricky for us as educators because we have to develop this process that we're not even cognizant of with our beginning readers.

(01:53) One thing that's important to remember is that although specific regions of the brain have been identified for their roles in the reading process, there are various brain areas collaborating continuously during reading. So it's not necessarily a step by step because it happens so fast. All of these areas are working together through this very complex reading circuit.

(2:17) This is a quote from Dr. Maryanne Wolf, and she states, "The reading brain doesn't exist. It's created." And I think that's really important for us to remember as educators and the fact that these instructional decisions that we're making and everything we do in our classrooms has the ability to impact and to create neural networks in the students that are sitting in front of us. All of our instructional decisions really must be purposeful so we can create this intricate circuit within their brains. As children learn to read, their brains must undergo these functional changes in order to be successful. And that is such a privilege and the fact that we get to create neural networks in our students, but it's also quite a burden, right? We have to be so careful and so intentional with our instructional practices.

(03:23) So one thing that's really important for us to know about is neuroplasticity. And neuroplasticity is the brain's remarkable ability to reorganize and to adapt throughout a person's life and response to experiences, to learning, as well as even environmental changes. And as it's doing this, it's forming new connections between existing neurons as well as reorganizing connections that already exist. So essentially, this is the brain's way of rewiring itself based on inputs and experiences.

(04:03) Understanding neuroplasticity is crucial for reading teachers because it sheds light on how the brain learns to read and how teaching practices can impact this process. So it really increases our efficacy, our self-efficacy as teachers and educators to know that what we do can change brains.

(04:26) When students are exposed to purposeful reading instruction, their brains undergo changes in their neural circuitry to accommodate this new stuff. So for example, when we are teaching phonemic awareness, we're priming the brain to be able to hear individual speech sounds within spoken words. That is not something that many brains will pick up on automatically. They need some explicit instruction because there's no, if you're just having conversation, there's no need to hear individual speech sounds in words. The only reason you have to do that is to learn how to read. So when we're teaching them, we're teaching the brain a skill that it wouldn't have had otherwise.

(05:14) So let's take a closer look here at the brain's letterbox. So that is also known as *the visual word form area*. And one thing that teachers of young readers know is that reversals are very common with their young learners. So think about the letter "B." A lot of young writers and authors and spellers and readers will flip the letter "B" to make it look like a "D," both when they're reading and their spelling. Sometimes people will think, oh, that must mean they have dyslexia, but that's not true. This really is a natural process and something that our brain must unlearn due to something known as *mirror generalization*.

(06:08) So before we learn to read, our brains naturally treat mirror images as the same object. So this comes from just what we needed to survive, right? So if you look at your mom, it doesn't matter if you look at her from the left or the right or upside down or right side up, your brain knows that is your mom's face. The same would be true if there was a predator and we were running away from a tiger in the jungle. It doesn't matter if that tiger is coming at us from the left or the right or upside down or behind us, we know that that is a tiger.

(06:55) Our brains have learned to generalize images and know that directionality doesn't matter until we introduce the alphabet, and then all of a sudden, directionality matters. And so during reading acquisition, this ability, this generalization has to be untrained essentially. And so as students learn to read, this visual word form area in the brain adapts, and it loses its mirror invariance but only for words and not for pictures. And so that's one example of that neuroplasticity. So it's reorganizing the neurons to say, hey, we're going to still know that an image is an image, but there are some letters we can't do that with. So we're going to have to develop special circuitry for those letters. So that takes students a little bit of time. This is not a symptom of dyslexia; it's just a normal part of learning to read. And the process of unlearning neurosymmetry is not a loss. It's granting us the ability to distinguish between mirror images effectively. So this literacy learning really enhances our brain's flexibility to perceive shapes as the same or different just depending on context.

(08:14) So these two images up on the screen represent the brains of typical readers versus the brains of striving readers. So one thing we know from fMRI scans is that more experienced readers have a lot more activity in that visual word form area—so this part of the brain down here—whereas beginning readers show more activity in the parietal-temporal region, or the word analysis region up here. And that makes sense, right? Because our beginning readers are the ones that are sounding out. So they look at the word *cat* and they're having to go /k/ /a/ /t/; their brains are really thinking about those phoneme-grapheme correspondences, while experienced readers just look at the word *cat* and they've orthographically mapped it, and they know that is the word *cat*. So proficient readers really exhibit those well-connected neural networks between all those different language areas in the left hemisphere of the brain. So this enables that swift conversion of visual input into meaning without conscious effort. So that's just one example of how the brain does change over time. So again, beginning readers spending a lot of their cognitive effort here, but for more experienced readers, all of this just happens so quickly that there's not that concentrated effort here in that region.

(09:48) Now, one thing that's very interesting is that brain imaging research reveals that striving readers exhibit fewer reading-related brain circuits and typically the circuits that they do have are located in atypical areas. So not where we would expect to see those brain circuits. Because the pathways for language and cognition that these striving readers develop are less efficient, then it makes their reading process slower and more laborious despite the fact that they are trying just as hard and they're putting forth just as much, if not more, effort as a typical reader. Dyslexic students tend to have underactivation in the left hemisphere and overactivation in the right hemisphere. So that's what researchers refer to as an *inefficient reading circuit*. So their brain is having to use a different way to get the visual input off the page and translate it into meaning. So it's taking more effort because it's not following the most desirable circuit process.

(11:05) The good news, though, is that for people with dyslexia, their brains can rewire themselves through reading instruction that focuses on phonological awareness and decoding skills. So our brains have that neuroplasticity throughout our lives, meaning that they can change to learn new things. Two key factors contribute to strengthening neural pathways for successful reading. They're going to need, first, intense instruction and, second, deliberate practice. So this isn't going to just happen. There's going to have to be very purposeful practice and purposeful instruction.

(11:47) Brain imaging studies do reveal that when dyslexic individuals receive targeted reading instruction and practice, their brains develop new circuits that connect language processing areas with visual processing areas very similar to what we see with students that are not dyslexic. Addressing this difficulty and mapping language to print through intervention provides dyslexic students with the key to reading success. These changes in the brain can occur not only in young students but also in adult dyslexic nonreaders, really demonstrating that brain plasticity allows for learning and change throughout life. It's not just limited to our young students. However, the older the student, the more intensive the instruction and practice is required. So early intervention is key for optimal outcomes.

(12:48) Alright. We talked a lot about neuroplasticity, which can be kind of a tricky concept to understand, so take a moment to pause and reflect. Jot down in your note guide, how would you explain neuroplasticity to a colleague, and why is it important? After you've done that, go ahead and hop back on the video.

(13:10) Alright. My learning extension that I would like to share with you all today is a pretty long book, but I actually listened to it as an audio book, so it is available that way if you enjoy that option. And this is *Proust and the Squid* by Maryanne Wolf. She was the researcher that we read her quote earlier about the reading brain not just existing but needing to be created. So this is a fantastic book to really dive in more to the reading brain. And she talks about many different elements of reading, so I highly recommend this book whether you read or listen to it.

(13:53) Thank you so much for joining us. Please remember to visit the SOR Academy Facebook group and comment on that Module 3, Lesson 2 thread for a chance to win. And we look forward to seeing you for our last lesson in Module 3.

## The Brain's Reading Regions (4)

## Neuroplasticity

## Brain's Letterbox

## Additional Notes

Typical Reader's Brain/Striving Reader's Brain

Good News!

Pause and Reflect: How would you explain neuroplasticity to a colleague? Why is it important?

Additional Notes

# Bonus Content

**Use the questions below to prompt discussion amongst your colleagues.**

1. **Neuroplasticity in Reading:** What is neuroplasticity, and why is it important in the context of learning to read? Discuss the brain's ability to reorganize itself and how this impacts learning processes, especially in reading.
2. **Brain Changes and Reading Interventions:** How does the brain change when children learn to read, and what role do targeted reading interventions play in this process? Explore the changes in neural pathways and the effects of structured literacy programs on brain activity.
3. **Research Insights on Neuroplasticity:** What insights did Dr. Sally Shaywitz and Dr. Bennett Shaywitz's research provide about neuroplasticity and reading instruction? Examine the findings from fMRI scans and their implications for reading instruction.
4. **Fostering a Growth Mindset for Neuroplasticity:** How can educators foster a growth mindset in their students to support neuroplastic changes in reading skills? Discuss Carol Dweck's research on growth mindset and strategies for encouraging effort and persistence in students.
5. **Practice and Persistence in Learning:** Reflect on a personal experience of learning something new. How did practice and persistence contribute to your learning, and how can these principles be applied in teaching reading? Share personal anecdotes and discuss the importance of practice and persistence in developing new skills.

**To extend your understanding of this topic, work through the activities below with a small group of peers.**

**Brain Mapping Exercise**
Have teachers create a visual map of the brain's reading regions, labeling areas involved in reading and explaining their functions. This can help teachers better understand the brain's role in reading.

**Case Study Analysis**
Examine case studies of students with reading difficulties who have undergone targeted reading interventions. Discuss the neuroplastic changes observed and the instructional strategies used.

**Growth Mindset Workshop**
Conduct a workshop focused on Carol Dweck's growth mindset research. Teachers can role-play scenarios and develop strategies to foster a growth mindset in their classrooms.

**Neuroplasticity Journals**
Encourage teachers to keep journals documenting their observations of students' reading progress. Reflect on how targeted instruction and motivation impact their students' neuroplasticity.

**Collaborative Research Review**
Form small groups to review and discuss recent research articles on neuroplasticity and reading. Each group can present their findings and discuss how the research can inform their teaching practices.

**Additional Resources**
On page 72, you will find a handout with a labeled graphic of the brain's reading regions. Make copies of this handout and share it with your colleagues at a grade-level planning meeting or faculty meeting. Share with them what you have learned about brain science and its implication on reading.

# Lesson 3: The Self-Teaching Hypothesis

*Module 3, Lesson 3 from the Science of Reading Academy focuses on Share's self-teaching hypothesis, a pivotal concept in reading instruction. This hypothesis states that once readers develop a strong reading circuit through explicit teaching, they can independently decode unfamiliar words by continuously connecting graphemes to phonemes. This process of self-teaching occurs through repeated successful decoding encounters, where each instance builds a lasting orthographic representation of the word in the reader's brain. Key prerequisites include automatic knowledge of phoneme-grapheme correspondences and proficiency in segmenting and blending phonemes. Below is the transcript for the Module 3, Lesson 3 video.*

(00:07) Hello, and welcome back to the Science of Reading Academy. Today we are in our very last lesson of Module 3, which has focused on investigating the reading brain. Today's lesson is going to be all about the self-teaching hypothesis, which is an important concept for us to understand when we're preparing our students to become lifelong readers and lifelong learners.

(00:34) So here's the conundrum: Human memory is typically limited to approximately 2,000 individual symbols. In contrast, the average adult has around 40,000 or more words within their lexicon, so words they know and use and speaking vocabulary. It's possible that well-educated adults know upwards of 200,000 words. So I mean, really, we have a lot of words in our speaking lexicon. So you can see these numbers are very different, right? 2,000 is very different from 40,000 or 200,000. So it begs the question, how are we learning to read all of these words. If we know how to speak 40,000 words, but we can only remember 2,000 symbols, how could a teacher ever possibly teach each of us the words that we need to know individually? And really, it's just not possible.

(01:40) This is a quote from a French neuroscientist, and his name is Dr. Dehaene. He states, "The mastery of reading lies, above all, in our ability to decode new words." We've learned about the brain's reading circuit, and we've talked about neuroplasticity. So once our brains have developed that reading circuit and it's well established, then our brain's neuroplasticity allows us to keep decoding and decoding and decoding.

(02:18) David Share calls this *self-teaching hypothesis*. So essentially, once our reading circuit has been formed through good, explicit teaching, then we can start decoding any word that we come across, and we don't have to memorize each word separately.

(02:37) This is known as the *self-teaching hypothesis*. And according to this hypothesis, every successful decoding encounter with an unfamiliar word provides an opportunity for the brain's reading circuit to build a representation of that word in our brains. It doesn't take a lot, just a relatively small number of successful exposures appear to be sufficient for acquiring this orthographic representation or just looking at a word and knowing what it is. This is true for both adult skilled readers as well as young children. So we call this self-teaching. So this girl in our slide here, she is reading *birthday*, and she's going /b/ /ir/ /th/ /d/ /ay/. She's connecting those individual graphemes to their sounds. Then she's able to decode the word *birthday*. So a teacher didn't have to stand right next to her. She was able to do this by herself. And now, after only a few more times of practicing decoding this word, she is going to know it, and she has essentially taught it to herself.

(03:51) There are some prerequisites for self-teaching to occur, and the first one is phoneme-grapheme correspondences. And these really have to be known automatically. So not just being familiar with them but knowing them automatically. If you think back to that parietal-temporal region of our brain where it's connecting sounds to written representations, we have to be very automatic and very quick with that process. If a child does not have a connection to retrieve, then a word can't be decoded. So this is an absolute prerequisite.

(04:33) Second, students need to be able to segment and blend phonemes. They have to be able to break a word apart into its individual sounds and then put it back together. So if you think back to the picture with *birthday*, she is taking that whole word and breaking it apart into sounds so that she can make those connections between individual graphemes and individual sounds. This is necessary for that reading circuit to be complete. So this is why we have times of our day where we're instructing phonemic awareness and where we're providing instruction for phonics and phoneme-grapheme correspondences. We're giving students those prerequisite skills to be able to self-teach or to go through that reading circuitry in their brain.

(05:22) So take a moment just to pause and reflect. What implications does Share's self-teaching hypothesis have on teaching children to read? Jot down your thoughts in your note guide and then come back and join us for some special downloadable content for the end of Module 3, as well as some learning extensions.

(05:44) So starting with some learning extensions here. This is an article that was published in 2022, and it has a meta-analysis on the self-teaching hypothesis. Within the article, there's a quote that states, "Our findings advance the original self-teaching hypothesis, reveal the gaps in the self-teaching research, and point out new directions for future work." So this is a great article to read through if you're interested in knowing more about the current research on this topic.

(06:17) Finally, I would like to share our Module 3 downloadable content for you that is exclusive to those of you that have finished Module 3. So this is a wonderful handout about the brain's reading regions and will be a great resource to both you and your colleagues when you're talking about how this reading circuit is formed in our students.

(06:39) Please remember to visit the SOR Academy Facebook group. Find that Module 3, Lesson 3 thread and comment for a chance to win. Thank you so much for joining us again today, and we can't wait to see you for Module 4.

## The Conundrum

## Self-Teaching Hypothesis

## Additional Notes

## Prerequisites

Phoneme-Grapheme Correspondences

Able to Segment and Blend Phonemes

## Pause and Reflect: What implications does Share's hypothesis have on teaching children to read?

## Additional Notes

# Bonus Content

**Use the questions below to prompt discussion amongst your colleagues.**

1. **Self-Teaching Hypothesis:** What is the self-teaching hypothesis, and how does it explain the acquisition of a large vocabulary despite the brain's limited memory for individual symbols? Discuss the implications of this hypothesis for reading instruction and student independence in learning new words.
2. **Phoneme-Grapheme Correspondences and Phonemic Awareness:** Why are phoneme-grapheme correspondences and phonemic awareness critical prerequisites for the self-teaching hypothesis to work? Explore how these skills facilitate the automatic decoding process necessary for self-teaching.
3. **Decoding Unfamiliar Words:** How does the process of decoding unfamiliar words contribute to the formation of orthographic representations in the brain? Discuss the role of repeated successful decoding encounters in building a mental lexicon.
4. **Instructional Strategies for the Self-Teaching Hypothesis:** What are the potential instructional strategies that teachers can use to foster the development of the reading circuit and support the self-teaching hypothesis? Consider specific teaching practices that align with the principles of phonics and phonemic awareness instruction.
5. **Impact of the Self-Teaching Hypothesis:** How can understanding the self-teaching hypothesis influence the way teachers assess and support struggling readers? Reflect on the importance of targeted interventions and the role of neuroplasticity in helping students who face reading challenges.

**To extend your understanding of this topic, work through the activities below with a small group of peers.**

**Decoding Practice Sessions**

Organize sessions where teachers practice decoding unfamiliar words using phoneme-grapheme correspondences. This hands-on activity can help teachers understand the process their students go through and identify effective strategies for instruction.

**Phoneme-Grapheme Correspondence Drills**

Create a series of drills focusing on quick and automatic recognition of phoneme-grapheme correspondences. Teachers can practice these drills in small groups, discussing the challenges and benefits they observe.

**Orthographic Mapping Workshop**

Conduct a workshop where teachers learn to identify and map out orthographic representations of words. This activity helps teachers visualize how repeated decoding encounters build a mental lexicon in students' brains.

**Case Study Discussions**

Provide teachers with case studies of students at different stages of reading proficiency. Discuss how the self-teaching hypothesis applies to each case and brainstorm targeted interventions that could support each student's reading development.

**Article Review and Reflection**

Assign teachers to read and discuss the 2022 meta-analysis article on the self-teaching hypothesis. Encourage them to reflect on the findings, identify gaps in the research, and propose new directions for future studies in the context of their own teaching experiences.

**Additional Resources**

On page 72, you will find a handout with a labeled graphic of the brain's reading regions. Make copies of this handout and share it with your colleagues at a grade-level planning meeting or faculty meeting. Share with them what you have learned about brain science and its implication on reading.

This page is intentionally blank.

# The Brain's Reading Regions

"The herculean job of educators is no less than to help the brain develop a skill it could not otherwise, which requires creating an entirely new circuit in the brain." -Gottlieb et al., 2022

**ɪe Left Hemisphere of the Brain**

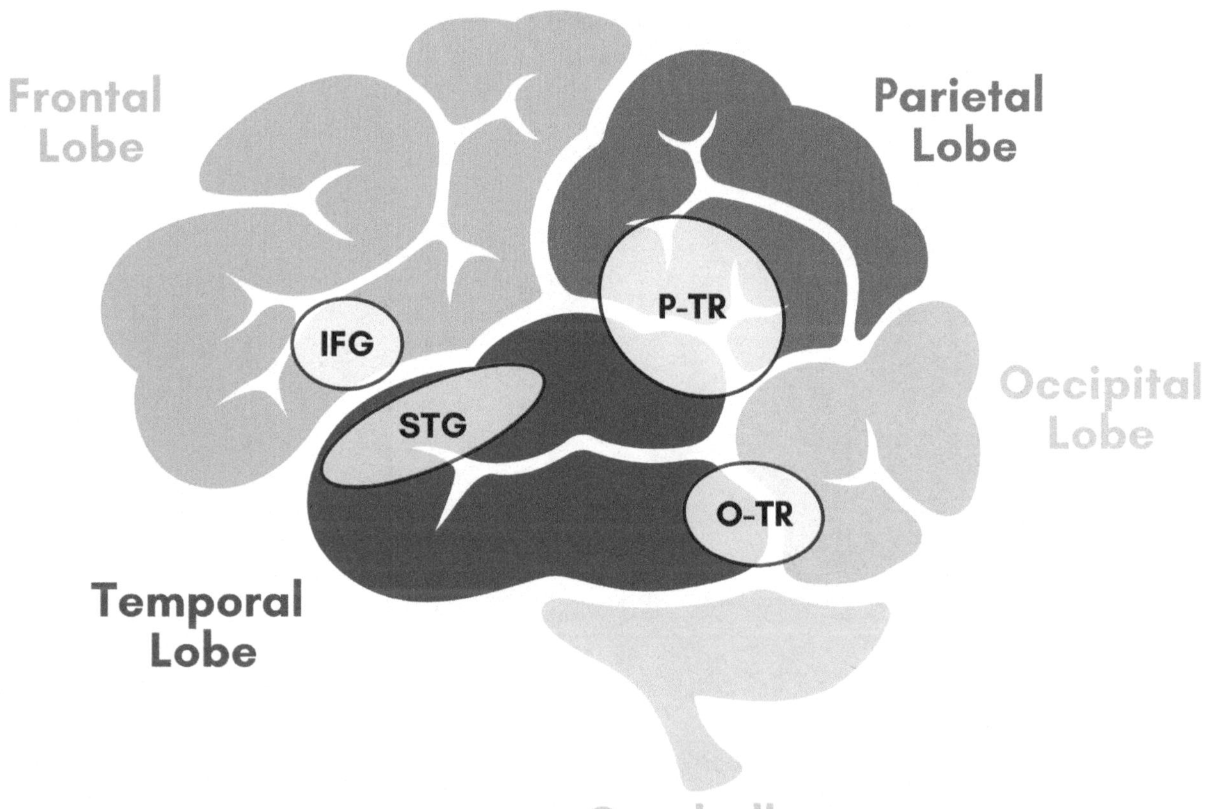


### Occipito-Temporal Region (O-TR)

Visual word form area

Orthographic knowledge

### Parieto-Temporal Region (P-TR)

Links graphemes to phonemes

The conversaion center of our reading brain

### Inferior Frontal Gyrus (IFG)

Includes Broca's area

Phonological and semantic processing

### Superior Temporal Gyrus (STG)

Includes Wernicke's area

Essential for understanding spoken language

This page is intentionally blank.

MODULE 4

# The Road to Decoding

In Module 4, we will explore the integral components that combine to produce skilled decoders. We will begin with the importance of word recognition and its foundational role in reading. Ehri's phases will help us understand where students are developmentally on their journey to becoming skilled readers. We will discuss the important foundational understandings we must facilitate for our early readers, including phonemic awareness and the alphabetic principle. We will then explore orthographic mapping, the process our brain uses to store words in long-term memory. We will discuss how orthographic mapping can apply to any word students read, including high-frequency words. Finally, we will look at decodable texts and their importance in providing accountable practice with phonics skills. These lessons will equip educators with a comprehensive understanding of the decoding process in reading instruction.

As you watch the videos in this module, use the pages that follow to write notes about what you are learning as well as reflect on the new information presented to you.

## Watch

The following videos are part of this learning module. Go to ScienceOfReadingAcademy.com to access each of the videos.

Lesson 1: The Importance of Word Recognition
Lesson 2: Ehri's Phases
Lesson 3: The Alphabetic Principle
Lesson 4: Phonemic Awareness
Lesson 5: Orthographic Mapping
Lesson 6: High-Frequency Words
Lesson 7: Syllabication
Lesson 8: Decodable Texts

## Before you begin

To activate your schema about the module topics, use your current knowledge and experience to reflect on the questions below.

1. Why do you think it's important for students to recognize words quickly and easily when they read?

2. What stages do you think children go through as they learn to read?

3. How do you think understanding the sounds in words (phonemic awareness) helps with reading and spelling?

MODULE 4: The Road to Decoding

# Lesson 1: The Importance of Word Recognition

*Module 4, Lesson 1 of the Science of Reading Academy focuses on the critical importance of word recognition in the process of reading development. Word recognition enables readers to identify words automatically without needing to sound them out letter by letter. This automaticity frees cognitive resources, allowing readers to focus more on understanding the meaning of the text rather than struggling with individual words. The lesson emphasizes that while word recognition is foundational, it is just one strand of Scarborough's Reading Rope, which also includes language comprehension. Effective reading instruction must therefore integrate systematic phonics instruction alongside broader literacy skills to ensure that students develop both fluent word recognition and comprehensive reading abilities. Below is the transcript for the Module 4, Lesson 1 video.*

**(00:07)** Hello, and welcome back to the Science of Reading Academy. Today we are beginning Module 4, which focuses on the road to decoding. So how do we get our students to be able to sound out the words that are on the page and make them meaningful?

**(00:26)** Today's lesson is going to focus on why word recognition is important. So word recognition is sometimes used synonymously with decoding, but really word recognition is that automatic decoding process so that when students are looking at a word, they know what it is without having to laboriously sound it out. So word recognition is kind of the end goal of decoding.

**(00:55)** When we look at Scarborough's Reading Rope, we can see that word recognition is that bottom strand, so it's comprised of phonological awareness, decoding, and sight recognition, so that automatic knowing what a word is. However, word recognition is not the only component that is needed to produce skilled readers. We also have all of these very important language comprehension strands as well. So although Module 4 is going to focus only on word recognition, the truth is that skilled readers have to have all of these components in order to be successful with reading. So that's one of the controversies with Science of Reading is the misunderstanding that Science of Reading is just phonics. That's not true, right, we talked about how the Science of Reading is just a body of research, and phonics is one of the components that our readers need in order to achieve those bottom strands of the reading rope. By mastering word recognition skills, our readers are going to become more efficient at decoding text, which allows them to focus more on understanding the meaning of the text rather than just struggling with individual words. So that's going to help them with their overall reading comprehension and literacy development.

**(02:25)** If you can think about this process like hiking up a mountain, if you are a hiker and you're going up a mountain and you are stumbling over every other step while you're trying to climb this mountain, that is really going to slow you down and make your journey really tough. You're not going to be able to enjoy the process; you're not going to be able to take in the scenery. You're just going to be focused on putting one foot in front of the other, and you're going to be really frustrated because when you do that, you keep falling down. But if are going up this mountain trail and you're not falling, you're able to actually focus on taking in the scenery, you're enjoying the process of the hike without tripping over every other rock, then you're going to have a completely different experience with that hike, and you're really going to get a better feel for all of the things that are around you.

**(03:26)** The same thing is true for our readers. If they are struggling to decode, if they are stumbling over every other word, they're not going to be able to focus on the big picture of the text that they're reading. They're going to have a very narrow view. They're not going to enjoy the process, and they're going to be frustrated. And that in turn is going to really impact their reading comprehension because they're not going to have extra cognitive space for focusing on things like inferencing and making connections because they're so bogged down with that decoding process. So smoothing out our reader's word recognition skills helps them have more cognitive space to really focus on all of the strands of Scarborough's Reading Rope.

**(04:17)** So let's talk about why it can be kind of tricky for readers to be able to decode, and that really is because of the English language. Our language is a little bit complicated, right? It has a deep orthography, which means that it is not just a one-to-one correspondence between a letter and a sound. So if you look at the top row here, we have 44 phonemes in our English language, and some researchers will say 46, some will say 44, the exact number doesn't really matter. There are multiple phonemes, and we can all agree that there's only 26 letters. So there's a big discrepancy between those two. If we have 44 speech sounds but only 26 letters, we have to do something to be able to represent those other sounds. We have multiletter graphemes. So these are things like vowel teams, "ai" working together to represent the /ā/ sound. So that is one of the ways that our English language works to use only 26 letters to represent 44 phonemes.

**(05:44)** Another way is through spelling rules. So if you think about hard and soft "c," if "c" is followed by "e," "i," or "y," it's going to make this soft sound instead of the hard sound. So if students are able to master the 26 letters, the 49 multiletter graphemes, and those spelling rules, they've really unlocked all of the pieces they need in order to be successful decoders. That's not an easy process, like it's not going to just happen in one year of kindergarten if they're just focused on those single-letter graphemes, but it is possible to do with a very particular and explicit systematic scope and sequence, which we'll talk about a little bit later.

**(06:33)** So my challenge for you right now is to pause the video and think through how many different spellings of the /ā/ sound can you list. Jot down all of them. See if you can come up with as many as I'm going to show you. Pause the video and then jump back on when you're ready to compare your list to mine.

**(06:55)** Okay, so these are my eight ways to spell the /ā/ sound. The first grapheme is just a single-letter grapheme, the letter "a" by itself, like in the word *table*; it's working as an open syllable there. There's also "a-consonant-e," that would also be part of a spelling rule, right? When there's a consonant in between a vowel and an "e" at the end, then it's going to make its long sound, so *cake*. "ai" is a multi-letter grapheme, *rain*; "ay," a multiletter grapheme like in *tray*. "ey," another multiletter grapheme like in *they*. "eigh," that is a four-letter grapheme all representing one sound, /ā/, like in *eight*. "ei" like in *rein*, and "ea" like in *steak*. So as you can see, our language is complex, but it does follow rules, so we can help unlock these rules for our students.

**(08:03)** Now, there have been some studies that really compare different methods of teaching reading to our students. The first is the whole word method. So when researchers looked at really it was adults that were learning a false language and they were using the whole word method to teach this false or fake language, what they noticed was that those students were able to learn the words a lot faster than students that were taught using the phonics method. So they were just memorizing the words, but what happened was after a certain point, they kind of hit a wall. So they weren't able to continue to accelerate in their process of learning to read because it didn't extend to unfamiliar words, whereas those that were utilizing the phonics method, they had a much slower start because they had to learn all of those individual connections between sounds and graphemes. But in the end, they achieved better results because their decoding skills were able to transfer to new words. So they ultimately surpassed those sight word learners. The sight word learners had to rely on only the words that were taught to them by the researchers.

**(09:39)** It also looked at the brain. So when students were taught using the whole word method, their brains did not develop those efficient reading pathways that we talked about in Module 3. But when students were taught using the phonics method, their brain pathways were activated that we want to see for efficient reading skills.

**(10:06)** So this can show you the downfall of that whole word method but can also help you see why it has been so persistent because early educators—kindergarten teachers, first grade teachers—see success with that method, right? Their students do just fine. They're able to memorize, they're able to read those pattern books, they know their sight words, and they do fine until they get to the point where their vocabulary that they need in order to read is way surpassing their ability to memorize words. And unless they've been taught those connections that they need to be able to sound out the words, they're not able to find success and able to continue their pathway to becoming skilled readers.

**(11:03)** 84%, that is the number that cognitive researchers tell us that if students know all of the phoneme connections to single-letter graphemes, multiletter graphemes, and the spelling rules, that students will be able to decode 84% of words. That is a lot of words, and the rest of the words often are going to come with some of those morphology pieces that students will get in higher grades. So this really represents a significant and valuable skill set that we need to be very intentional about providing to our kindergarten, first, and second grade students.

**(11:53)** So my challenge to you, my second challenge for you today, would be to go through your scope and sequence that you're utilizing both in your grade level but also if you're in a position to think about your school system as a whole. Go through the K-2 scope and sequence and see, are you introducing the key concepts that students need to unlock the code? Will students have enough exposure and purposeful practice with not only the 26 letters of the alphabet but also the 49 phonograms and 31 spelling rules? So that is a really important piece that sometimes is left out. So take some time to go through your scope and sequence, identify any holes that you have, and work on filling those so that you are providing students with a very explicit and systematic exposure to the English language.

**(12:54)** My recommendation to you for a learning extension would be Denise Eide's book, *Uncovering the Logic of English*. This is an excellent read that really helps give information on important patterns in our language and helps us make sense of our English language. So there really is a logic to a lot of the ways that words are spelled and used.

**(13:21)** Thank you so much for your time today. Please remember to visit our SOR Academy Facebook group and comment on the Module 4, Lesson 1 thread. We can't wait to hear from you.

Scarborough's Reading Rope: What can happen to a reader who is missing word recognition skills?

Additional Notes

The English Language

Challenge! How many different spellings of the "long a" sound can you list?

## Whole Word Method vs. Phonics Method

## 84% of Readers

## Take a look at your scope and sequence. What do you notice?

Additional Notes

# Bonus Content

**Use the questions below to prompt discussion amongst your colleagues.**

1. **Word Recognition in Reading Proficiency:** Why is automatic word recognition considered the end goal of decoding, and how does it contribute to overall reading proficiency? Discuss the process and benefits of automatic word recognition compared to laborious decoding.
2. **Scarborough's Reading Rope:** How does Scarborough's Reading Rope illustrate the relationship between word recognition and language comprehension? Review the different components of the rope and their importance in developing skilled readers.
3. **Word Recognition in English's Deep Orthography:** What are the challenges associated with teaching word recognition in the context of the English language's deep orthography? Discuss the complexity of English phonemes and graphemes and the implications for teaching decoding skills.
4. **Effectiveness of Phonics:** What evidence supports the effectiveness of phonics instruction in teaching reading? Reflect on the research findings regarding brain development and long-term reading success.
5. **Designing Effective Word Recognition Instruction;** How can educators ensure their scope and sequence covers the essential components for effective word recognition instruction? Discuss strategies for evaluating and improving the curriculum to include all necessary phoneme-grapheme correspondences and spelling rules.

**To extend your understanding of this topic, work through the activities below with a small group of peers.**

**Phoneme-Grapheme Mapping Exercise**
Teachers can work in small groups to map out the phoneme-grapheme correspondences for various words, discussing strategies to teach these connections effectively.

**Scope and Sequence Review**
Conduct a collaborative review of the existing K–2 scope and sequence, identifying any gaps in phonics and decoding instruction and brainstorming ways to fill these gaps.

**Decoding and Spelling Rules Workshop**
Facilitate a workshop where teachers practice applying various spelling rules and decoding multi letter graphemes, discussing the challenges and strategies for teaching these rules to students.

**Book Study on Uncovering the Logic of English**
Organize a book study where teachers read and discuss Denise Eide's *Uncovering the Logic of English*, sharing insights and practical applications for teaching word recognition in the classroom.

**Additional Resources**
Scan to access an editable lesson plan template that walks you through developing a well-rounded word recognition lesson plan. You will be prompted to force a copy of the template into your own drive. The template has directions in each box to help guide you in your lesson planning; delete the directions to type in your actual lesson plans.

# Lesson 2: Ehri's Phases

*Module 4, Lesson 2 of the Science of Reading Academy focuses on Ehri's phases of reading development, providing a structured framework for understanding how children progress in learning to read. Ehri outlines four key phases: the pre-alphabetic stage, where children recognize words visually and contextually without understanding grapheme-phoneme correspondences; the partial alphabetic stage, characterized by beginning phoneme awareness and reliance on initial and final sounds; the full alphabetic stage, where decoding becomes more systematic as children connect graphemes to phonemes throughout words; and finally, the consolidated alphabetic stage, where readers proficiently decode complex letter patterns and morphemes. Below is the transcript for the Module 4, Lesson 2 video.*

**(00:07)** Hello, and welcome back to the Science of Reading Academy. We're in Module 4, which focuses on the road to decoding. Today's lesson is going to zoom in to Ehri's phases of reading development.

**(00:22)** We've talked about how reading instruction can rewire a student's brain, so it can be really helpful for us to view students through a developmental lens when we're making instructional decisions. We want to know where they are on the path of becoming skilled readers. Ehri's phase theory can be a really valuable framework to help us understand this. She proposes there are four phases that students progress through when they're learning how to read: the pre-alphabetic stage, the partial alphabetic stage, the full alphabetic stage, and the consolidated alphabetic stage. So we're going to talk about each one of these phases or stages in more depth.

**(01:07)** Starting with the pre-alphabetic phase, in this phase, children are going to use visual and contextual cues to "read" words, and I'm putting read in air quotes because they're not decoding the words, but they are beginning to recognize them. This phase typically occurs in preschool-aged children up through around the age of five. In this phase, students will have limited knowledge of letters, including their names, their shapes, and their sounds. So that makes sense because it's called pre-alphabetic, so this is before alphabet knowledge. Children may begin to recognize their names or words that have environmental print. So for example, they might see the jar of Nutella and say, I love Nutella. They might see the McDonald's sign when they're driving down the road and say, oh, that's McDonald's. So they're beginning to attend to print meaning correspondences, so recognizing that the print in our world carries meaning, but they are not yet attending to grapheme-phoneme correspondences, so they're not making the connections between speech sounds and written letters. To move students to the next learning phase, educators should provide instruction about the alphabet, providing explicit instruction on phoneme-grapheme correspondences and give students lots of practice with phonological and phonemic awareness.

**(02:44)** The next stage is the partial alphabetic stage. So in this stage or this phase, students are going to have some knowledge of phoneme-grapheme correspondence. They tend to notice the word's first sound and the word's last sound but ignore the middle ones when they're reading words. Often this is going to be because they haven't yet been taught all of the graphemes that they know, that they need in order to decode anywhere that they encounter. There's some decoding that occurs at this stage but not a lot. Students are mainly relying on context and memory to understand new words. A student in the partial alphabetic phase may look at the picture of the Nutella logo and say, Nutella starts with /n/. So they're recognizing that that's Nutella, but they're utilizing that letter to help them start to make those connections, but they didn't decode the whole word. Students typically enter this stage early in their kindergarten year, and to move students from the partial alphabetic phase to the full alphabetic phase, instruction should focus on phonemic awareness, decoding skills, and exposure to print. We want to move students to being able to decode throughout a whole word.

**(04:12)** That will take us to the full alphabetic phase. So in this phase, students can decode unfamiliar words. They're beginning to attend to individual graphemes and connecting each grapheme to its phonological correspondent. As students decode more and more words, they're developing their orthographic knowledge, so the connection between those sounds and those written spellings. Students in the full alphabetic phase still dedicate a large amount of their cognitive attention to sounding out words as they map speech sounds to print sounds. So when we talked about the different areas of the brain, we talked about how our beginning readers have more concentrated effort in that part of the brain that's connecting those sounds to those graphemes, whereas skilled readers use less cognitive effort there. So for example, if they see the word Nutella, they might not be able to read all of it, but they are going to say, Ooh, I know that first word, /n/ /u/ /t/, nut. They're beginning to use those decoding skills. A typically developing reader will enter this phase towards the beginning of first grade, and they're going to need more instruction in decoding to help them become automatic with their reading.

**(05:35)** The next phase is the consolidated alphabetic phase. When readers progress to the consolidated alphabetic phase, they transition to decoding chunks of letters rather than just individual phonemes. This means that they start recognizing multiletter patterns like consonant blends, digraphs, and vowel teams more readily. Common word families, affixes, and other letter patterns are also stored in their memory and recognized instantly. So these students have started to go through the orthographic mapping process, which we'll talk about later on in Module 4. Additionally, readers are beginning to identify syllables and morphemes as cohesive units. And just as a reminder, although all of these units and pieces of words are stored in the brain, they have not just been stored through memorization. Students have to go through the process of becoming aware of individual phonemes, connecting those to graphemes so that their brain can store them in the memory, but it's not just rote memorization.

**(06:39)** This phase is considered the most advanced stage of reading development, and typically it will begin in second grade and progress as readers refine their word reading skills. Instruction during this phase should emphasize with identifying and understanding the various word parts within words, so looking at morphology, as well as some of those more complex phoneme-grapheme correspondences. To enhance orthographic mapping, students should pronounce each new word while they're reading and really think about those sounds and those letters to reinforce the spelling sound connections and strengthen their phonological memory for the word.

**(07:21)** So pause the video here and reflect. Think about a student that you might know or that you've worked with. Which phase of word recognition is the child in, and how do you know? So jot down that student, and I would also encourage you to jot down some instructional moves that you might make based on where the child is in Ehri's phases.

**(07:47)** The learning extensions for today's lesson are an article on the "Phases of Development in Learning to Read and Spell Words" by Linnea Ehri herself, so a great place to go for more information, as well as a podcast that interviews Linnea Ehri.

**(08:04)** Thank you so much for joining us today. Please visit our SOR Academy Facebook group and comment on the Module 4, Lesson 2 thread. We can't wait to hear from you.

## Ehri's Phases of Word Recognition

Pre-Alphabetic

Partial Alphabetic

Full Alphabetic

Consolidated Alphabetic

## Pause and Reflect: Think of a student you know. Which phase of word recognition is the child in? How do you know?

Additional Notes

# Bonus Content

**Use the questions below to prompt discussion amongst your colleagues.**

1. **Understanding Phases:** How can recognizing a student's phase of reading development (pre-alphabetic, partial alphabetic, full alphabetic, consolidated alphabetic) impact instructional strategies and interventions?
2. **Transitioning Phases:** What are the key indicators that a student is moving from one phase to another in Ehri's phases of reading development? How might teachers facilitate this transition effectively?
3. **Instructional Approaches:** What specific instructional methods or activities can be used to support students in the partial alphabetic stage as they begin to connect initial and final sounds to letters?
4. **Orthographic Mapping:** Why is orthographic mapping considered crucial in the consolidated alphabetic phase? How can teachers help students strengthen their ability to recognize multi letter patterns and word families?
5. **Assessment and Feedback:** How can teachers use knowledge of Ehri's phases to inform assessment practices and provide targeted feedback to students at different stages of reading development?

**To extend your understanding of this topic, work through the activities below with a small group of peers.**

**Case Studies**
Analyze case studies of students at different reading phases. Discuss observations, assessments, and interventions that would be appropriate for each phase.

**Phonemic Awareness Tasks**
Design and practice phonemic awareness tasks tailored to each phase (e.g., segmenting and blending tasks for pre-alphabetic, initial and final sound identification for partial alphabetic).

**Reading Samples**
Bring in reading samples from students representing each phase. Analyze how each student approaches decoding and comprehension tasks differently.

**Instructional Strategy Role Play**
Role-play scenarios where teachers implement instructional strategies specific to each phase. Discuss the effectiveness of different approaches.

**Reflective Journaling**
Reflect on past experiences with students in different phases. Write about successes, challenges, and insights gained from applying Ehri's phases in real-world teaching contexts.

**Additional Resources**
See the Module 4, Lessons 1 bonus content page for access to an editable word recognition lesson plan template.

# Lesson 3: The Alphabetic Principle

*Module 4, Lesson 3 of the Science of Reading Academy focuses on understanding the alphabetic principle, a foundational concept in literacy development. The alphabetic principle is the fundamental realization for students that letters represent sounds in spoken words and vice versa, forming the basis for both reading and writing skills. This principle enables children to both decode and encode words by connecting phonemes (individual sounds) to graphemes (written letters or combinations of letters). Mastery of the alphabetic principle is critical as it supports students in navigating the complexities of English spelling and enhances their ability to read and write fluently. Below is the transcript for the Module 4, Lesson 3 video.*

**(00:07)** Hello, and welcome back to the Science of Reading Academy. We are in Module 4, which is focusing on the road to decoding. How do we get our students to understand the important components of word recognition? Today's lesson is going to focus on the alphabetic principle, what it is, and why it's important.

**(00:32)** In our last video, we did a deep dive on Ehri's phases of word recognition. Her phases really help us understand the path that students follow as they build those neural pathways in their brain and become skilled readers. This progress that students make really hinges on their grasp of the alphabetic principle. Ehri's phases illustrate the developmental journey towards this mastery, which might cause you to wonder, what exactly is the alphabetic principle?

**(01:10)** Really, the alphabetic principle is the a-ha moment that students have when they realize that sounds and spoken words are represented by letters and written words, and letters and written words also represent the sounds and spoken words, and they make connections between the two. So this seems so easy and straightforward to us, right, because we're skilled readers; we do this all the time. But for our beginning readers, this is pivotal, and this is huge. First of all, for students to recognize that spoken words can be broken down into individual sounds, that is not something that they just develop naturally through casual conversation. When we're just talking, we hear words in large units of sound, but when we're reading, we have to be able to break those words down into individual sounds that we call *phonemes*. You'll also recognize with some of your very beginning writers that they will just write strings of letters or even just symbols on their paper, and they use those symbols to tell a story, but those are not connected to sounds and spoken words. So when students start to recognize that what they write down should match the sounds and their spoken words, that's another huge a-ha that they have toward grasping this alphabetic principle. This collective understanding of the connection between sounds and letters is known as the *alphabetic principle*, and it's crucial for developing both reading and writing skills.

**(03:01)** So really, knowing that letters represent sounds and sounds can be represented by letters is the basic principle. But in order to apply this understanding, children really need to know the specifics of our language. So students need to know the phonemes within words so that they can connect those phonemes to specific graphemes or the written representations of those phonemes. They really need to know the opposite; they need to know how to form and how to identify the written representations of sounds or letters. So for basic mastery of the alphabetic principle, you're just going to start with letters and their most common sounds.

**(03:54)** So take a moment here to pause and reflect. Have you ever worked with a student who did not understand the alphabetic principle? How did this correlate with his or her reading performance? And you might also talk about how this correlated with this student's writing performance because the alphabetic principle really impacts both reading and writing. So take a moment, pause, jot down your thoughts in your note guide, and then come back and join us in the video.

**(04:24)** Okay, so after we've learned about the alphabetic principle, you might be wondering how this impacts your instruction. And one instructional shift that we can make to help foster the development of the alphabetic principle is by using really intentional teacher language that I'm going to call *phoneme first language*. So instead of saying, the letter "p" says /p/, we're instead going to use this sound first, so we can spell /p/ with the letter "p." So it seems like a really small shift because it is, but it can be helpful to remember the phrase that letters don't talk. Letters are just representations. And so this is going to help students, especially your striving students, think about letters in a way that will facilitate the building of those neural networks in their reading brain.

**(05:22)** This is an example on the screen from the Structured Literacy with E.A.S.E. program, where they're introducing the most common spelling of the sound /k/. So you can kind of hear what this phoneme first language would sound like. "A common sound the letter 'c' represents is /k/. It can be heard at the beginning of words like *cat* and *clam*. Words that begin with /k/ are spelled 'c' when they're followed by the letter 'a,' the letter 'o,' or the letter 'u,' like in *cat*, *cob*, or *cup*. We'll complete activities to help us identify the /k/ sound in words."

**(06:09)** So you can hear how that's very different from just showing students the letter "c" and saying "c" says /k/. You're really getting students to start thinking about some of those very important spelling rules, even though you're certainly not expecting them to master it; you're exposing them to it, and you're also getting them to think about the complex nature of the English language where phonemes can be represented by multiple graphemes.

**(06:39)** The learning extension today is a brief on the alphabetic principle from the National Center on Improving Literacy. They have several wonderful briefs on different literacy practices, but this one is specific to the alphabetic principles, so I would highly recommend that you check that out if you would like to learn more.

**(07:00)** Thank you so much for joining us again today for Module 4, Lesson 3. Don't forget to visit our SOR Academy Facebook group and comment on today's module's thread so that you can have a chance to win. Talk to you soon.

## Ehri's Phases

## Additional Notes

## The Alphabetic Principle

## Prerequisites

Pause and Reflect: Have you ever worked with a student who did not understand the alphabetic principle? How did this correlate with his or her reading performance? What about his or her writing performance?

Additional Notes

Instructional Shift—"Phonemic First" Language

# Bonus Content

**Use the questions below to prompt discussion amongst your colleagues.**

1. **Definition and Importance:** How would you explain the alphabetic principle to someone unfamiliar with it? Why is understanding this principle crucial for early literacy development?
2. **Developmental Milestones:** What are some observable milestones that indicate a student is beginning to grasp the alphabetic principle? How can teachers support students who struggle with this concept?
3. **Integration into Instruction:** How can teachers integrate phoneme-first language into their daily instruction to reinforce the alphabetic principle effectively? What are the benefits of this approach compared to traditional letter-sound instruction?
4. **Challenges and Strategies:** Reflecting on your teaching experience, what challenges have you encountered when teaching the alphabetic principle? What instructional strategies have proven effective in overcoming these challenges?
5. **Connections to Reading and Writing:** Discuss instances where understanding (or lack thereof) of the alphabetic principle has impacted both reading and writing performance in your students. How did you address these challenges?

**To extend your understanding of this topic, work through the activities below with a small group of peers.**

**Word Mapping**
Create and share examples of phoneme-first language statements for common phonemes (e.g., /k/ as in cat, cob, cup). Discuss how this approach helps students connect sounds to their corresponding letters.

**Interactive Case Studies**
Analyze case studies of students at different stages of understanding the alphabetic principle. Discuss effective instructional strategies tailored to each student's needs.

**Letter-Sound Correspondence Activities**
Design and participate in activities where each participant takes turns presenting a letter and discussing its most common sound, followed by examples in words.

**Lesson Plan Critique**
Bring in lesson plans or activities focused on teaching the alphabetic principle. Discuss strengths, areas for improvement, and modifications for different learner profiles.

**Reflective Journaling**
Reflect individually on your journey in teaching the alphabetic principle. Write about personal successes, challenges, and future goals in improving instructional practices related to this fundamental concept.

**Additional Resources**
See the Module 4, Lessons 1 bonus content page for access to an editable word recognition lesson plan template.

**MODULE 4: The Road to Decoding**

# Lesson 4: Phonemic Awareness

*Module 4, Lesson 4 of the Science of Reading Academy focuses on phonemic awareness, which involves understanding that words are made up of individual sounds, or phonemes, and is an essential prerequisite for decoding and spelling. In contrast to spoken language, where sounds merge seamlessly to form whole words, phonemic awareness requires consciously identifying and manipulating the individual sounds within words. This foundational skill progresses through levels from word boundaries to phonemes, building upon understanding syllables and onset-rime patterns along the way. Effective instruction integrates phonemic awareness with phonics, aligning the auditory skills of phonemic awareness with the visual representations of letters to enhance reading proficiency. Below is the transcript for the Module 4, Lesson 4 video.*

**(00:07)** Hello, and welcome back to the Science of Reading Academy. We're in Module 4 and focused on everything decoding. Today's topic is phonemic awareness, a really crucial step to help students become proficient readers.

**(00:23)** During our last video, we discussed the alphabetic principle, which is that very critical understanding readers must develop that sounds and spoken words can be represented by letters and written words, and those letters and written words represent sounds and spoken words, so that reciprocity between sounds and letters. One of the necessary skills that students need in order to foster the alphabetic principle is phonemic awareness, which is the focus of our learning today.

**(00:59)** Phonemic awareness is the understanding that individual words are made of individual sounds. I touched on this briefly in our last lesson, but it's really important to know that phonemic awareness is not a natural understanding. This is something that our brains have to learn in order to use our invented system of the alphabet. Spoken language, so when we're having conversations and we're listening to other people speak, those words and phrases and sentences, that language is continuous. So it can be really difficult to understand all of the individual sounds that we're saying because of how we articulate our words. And there's even something called *co-articulation* where letters that are right up next to each other when we're pronouncing words can slightly change how they sound just based on the letter that they precede. So our language gets really complicated; our sounds get tangled and blended together when we see them, and that's normal. That's what our language is supposed to be like, but we want to develop phonemic awareness with our students. So in order to do that, we have to rewire our brains to listen inside of words for little bits of sound. We call those *phonemes*. We pull words apart, we rearrange them, we reassemble them with all of those individual sounds, and that whole process would really be pointless if reading didn't exist. But reading does exist, and it's a wonderful thing. So if we want our students to become readers, this work is really essential.

**(02:54)** On this screen, you can see the linguistic hierarchy, and it's not called the phonemic awareness hierarchy because many of the layers, starting down at the bottom all the way up here to the green, these levels or layers are phonological awareness. So phonemic awareness is a subset of phonological awareness. Phonological awareness is recognizing sounds all the way from words to phonemes in spoken language. Phonemic awareness is a subcomponent of that phonological awareness that's focused on individual phoneme sounds.

**(03:38)** So when we think about the typical progression that students are going to have as they are becoming familiar with the phonemic awareness process, they're going to start with the word boundaries level, so being able to hear phrases and sentences and know that within sentences there are individual words. That is the foundation to this linguistic hierarchy. That often is going to happen at the preschool level.

**(04:07)** After students become familiar with word boundaries, then you're going to move them to the syllable level. That's still larger units of sound, some that might even be words on their own, but getting students to start that process of breaking words apart into parts.

**(04:25)** After syllable level, the onset-rime level is really that bridge between the syllable level and the phoneme level, so getting students to hear that initial first sound or first phoneme of a word and then everything after it. So everything after that vowel is going to be the rime. So your onset can also be a beginning blend or a beginning digraph. Then you're moving to the phoneme level, so the individual sound level. And that's the goal that we want students to get to.

**(05:01)** Now, at each level in this hierarchy, you can also have multiple levels of challenge with what you're doing at that level. So for example, at the syllable level, you can do blending and segmenting. Those are a little bit easier, but you can also do substituting and other manipulation tasks, and those are going to be a little bit more challenging.

**(05:27)** Okay, so we're going to play a true or false game here. So take out either your note guide or a piece of paper or a sticky note, something where you can jot down your answer as we go through each slide of if you think this statement is true or false, and then we'll go over the answer after each one.

**(05:48)** So first, phonological and phonemic awareness skills can develop in tandem. So for example, thinking about: Do students have to master syllable blending before moving to onset-rime blending, or can both skills be taught together? So true or false? Alright. The answer to this is true; although children are most often able to master larger linguistic units before moving to smaller units such as phonemes, these skills do not develop in discrete steps or in isolation of each other. Students may find more success with words of greater familiarity, so they might be able to do the phoneme level for a word they've heard but maybe only the onset-rime level for an unfamiliar word. Students can also simultaneously develop two skills at once, so for example, they can be working at both syllable segmentation and beginning sound isolation.

**(06:54)** Next, true or false: Phonemic awareness should be taught separately from phonics. This is false. Phonics and phonemic awareness are not the same thing, but they should be connected. Blevins tells us, from his 2024 book, that we achieve the maximum benefit when phonemic awareness and phonics are tightly connected. So phonics is going to be more powerful and phonemic awareness is going to be more powerful if they both align. Phonemic awareness is training one section of our reading circuit, but to complete that circuit, we need all of the parts. So we need to include visual inputs. Phonemic awareness can be done as a warmup to kind of prime our brain and ease future cognitive burden.

**(07:53)** So on the screen here, you can see an example from the Structured Literacy with E.A.S.E. program. They have phonemic awareness activities for the phoneme that they're going to really focus on throughout the lesson. So the phoneme focus is the /sh/ sound. Before the lesson introduces the grapheme or the letters to represent that sound, they have a phonemic awareness warmup that is going to really include that sound in each exercise to kind of warm up students' brains.

**(08:33)** Alright, next. True or false: Phonemic awareness should be taught with letters. This one's kind of tricky. So it's true and a little bit false. So oral-only phonemic awareness has its place, but don't be afraid of adding in letters quickly. So always remember, phonemic awareness instruction is a means to an end. We don't want students who are proficient at phonemic awareness in isolation but can't transfer those skills to reading.

**(09:15)** Phonemic awareness is just one piece of many in that complex reading circuit. For our beginning readers, simply breaking a word into individual sounds isn't a natural process, right? And so for many students, that doesn't come easily. For those young readers in kindergarten or first grade, or even for our striving readers in older grades, it is really important that we do include some oral-only phonemic awareness work where their brains can just focus on that one task, isolating individual sounds within words. That helps prevent cognitive overload. However, our goal is always to include print as soon as possible. So after doing that phonemic awareness-only activity, do the same activity again, but pull in letters. Remember that closely integrating phonics and phonemic awareness is where the magic happens. Activities such as sound boxes or dictation routines can help us integrate phonemic awareness with phonics in really meaningful ways.

**(10:25)** On this screen here, you can see a picture of the Map-It routine from that Structured Literacy with E.A.S.E. program, and we'll cover this more in depth during our orthographic mapping video, but this is a really great example of how you're going to start with these sounds and then connect those sounds to written letters.

**(10:47)** Alright. So that was a lot of information about phonemic awareness. So take a moment, pause and reflect: Where and how do you incorporate phonemic awareness instruction into your practice? Are there any components that you want to add or adjust? So think about some of those things that we talked about with the ultimate goal of phonemic awareness being that it's just a component on the path to producing skilled readers. So jot down your thoughts and then come back and join us for the rest of the video.

**(11:20)** Alright, so our two learning extensions for today, the first is a quick blog about "Which Is Better, Phonemic Awareness with or without Print," and that will go into a deeper dive of that last true or false statement that we talked about. And there's also a podcast for you all about phonemic awareness. So great places to go if you're looking to learn some more.

**(11:45)** There is also some downloadable content for you. This will be available at the end of Module 4 with several other bonus downloadable contents that we have. But the one that is correlated to today's learning is the phonological awareness assessment, so this will be a great resource for you to figure out where your students are at in that linguistic hierarchy.

**(12:10)** So thank you for joining us again for our Module 4, Lesson 4. We really appreciate your time and can't wait to see you for our next lesson.

Alphabetic Principle

Additional Notes

Phonemic Awareness

## Linguistic Hierarchy

Word Boundaries

Syllables

Onset-Rime

Phoneme

## True or False: Phonological and phonemic awareness can develop in tandem.

## Additional Notes

True or False: Phonemic awareness should be taught separately from phonics.

True or False: Phonemic awareness should be taught with letters.

Pause and Reflect: Where and how do you incorporate phonemic awareness into your practice? Are there an components you want to add or adjust?

Additional Notes

# Bonus Content

**Use the questions below to prompt discussion amongst your colleagues.**

1. **Definition and Importance:** How would you explain phonemic awareness to someone who is new to the concept? Why is it considered a foundational skill for reading development?
2. **Developmental Progression:** What are the different levels within the phonological awareness hierarchy, and how does phonemic awareness fit into this framework? Discuss the progression from word boundaries to phonemes.
3. **Integration with Instruction:** How can teachers effectively integrate phonemic awareness activities with phonics instruction? Why is this integration crucial for supporting early readers?
4. **Challenges and Strategies:** Reflecting on your teaching experience, what challenges have you encountered when teaching phonemic awareness? What instructional strategies have you found effective in addressing these challenges?
5. **Assessment and Differentiation:** How do you assess students' phonemic awareness skills? What are some strategies for differentiating instruction based on students' varying levels of phonemic awareness proficiency?

**To extend your understanding of this topic, work through the activities below with a small group of peers.**

**Phonemic Awareness Progression**
Create a timeline or visual representation of the phonological awareness hierarchy, highlighting the stages from word boundaries to phonemes. Discuss how each stage builds upon the previous one.

**Interactive Case Studies**
Analyze case studies or student profiles to identify specific phonemic awareness challenges and corresponding instructional strategies. Role-play scenarios to practice implementing these strategies.

**Phonemic Awareness Games**
Design and participate in phonemic awareness games such as segmenting, blending, deleting, and substituting phonemes. Discuss how these games can be adapted for different age groups and skill levels.

**Phonemic Awareness Assessments**
Review and discuss various phonemic awareness assessments. Practice administering sample assessments and interpreting results to inform instructional planning.

**Integration with Phonics Activities**
Plan and execute a phonemic awareness activity followed by a related phonics lesson. Reflect on how integrating these activities enhances students' understanding of the alphabetic principle and decoding skills.

**Additional Resources**
See the following pages for a phonological and phonemic awareness assessment that can be administered to students to evaluate proficiency with specific skills.

# Phonological Awareness Assessment

## Assessment Details and Administration

The Phonological Awareness Assessment can be used to evaluate auditory knowledge of the sounds in words. Phonological awareness should be assessed before students begin a phonics program and continuously revisited when breakdowns in mastering phonics skills arise; challenges with phonological skills can provide insight into these breakdowns.

**To Assess Phonological Awareness**: This is an auditory/oral assessment. Students do not need any booklets or papers. Students may use small discs to isolate, segment, or blend phonemes and/or words into syllables. When allowing the use of manipulatives, model one example for each skill set before asking students to do the activity.

**How to Administer the Phonological Awareness Assessment:** This assessment is comprised of seventeen subtests that assess phonological awareness skills. It should be administered to each student individually three times per year (beginning, middle, and end of the year) in kindergarten and as needed in first grade and second grade.

Place check marks in the boxes for correct answers. A student must correctly answer 5/6 of the items in a subtest to show proficiency; when this happens, the student does not need to be reassessed on the skill. If a student misses three answers consecutively, discontinue that subtest. If this happens with two subtests consecutively, discontinue administration of the entire assessment until the next testing date.

The following is a list of subtest skills as well as directions and language to administer them.

**Sentence Segmentation** – Students identify the number of words in a sentence.
Teacher: *How many words are in the sentence?* (Teacher reads a sentence.)
Student: (responds with the number of words.)

**Syllable Blending** – Students blend separate syllables to create a word.
Teacher: Put the two parts together to create a word: /ig/ (pause) /lū/.
Student: igloo

**Syllable Detecting and Segmentation** – Students identify the syllables in a word.
Teacher: How many syllables do you hear in the word seahorse? What are the syllables?
Student: two syllables, sea/horse

**Syllable Addition** – Students identify what word is created when a syllable is added.
Teacher: Say /bak/. Add /pak/ to the end.
Student: backpack

**Syllable Deletion** – Students identify what word is created when a syllable is deleted.
Teacher: Say monkey without /mən/.
Student: key

**Syllable Substitution** – Students identify what word is created when a syllable is changed.
Teacher: Say comfort. Change /fort/ to /plān/.
Student: complain

**Rhyme Recognition** – Students determine if words have the same ending sounds (rimes).
Teacher: Do the words pad and sad rhyme?
Student: Yes.

**Rhyme Production** – Students list words that rhyme with a given word.
Teacher: What rhymes with pin?
Student: (produces rhyming words)

**Alliteration** – Students identify words with the same initial sound as another word.
Teacher: What words begin with the same beginning sound as log?
Student: (produces words that begin with the /l/ sound)

**Onset and Rime** – Students blend the beginning consonant, blend, or digraph (onset) and the vowel and sounds that come after it (rime).
Teacher: Say /p/. Say /ot/. What's the word?
Student: pot

**Initial Phoneme Isolation** – Students identify the initial sound they hear in a word.
Teacher: What sound do you hear at the beginning of tap?
Student: /t/

**Initial Phoneme Deletion** – Students identify what sounds remain when the initial sound is deleted.
Teacher: Say bat. Now say it without the /b/.
Student: at

**Phoneme Segmentation** – Students identify the individual sounds in a word.
Teacher: Say the sounds you hear in cab.
Student: /k/ /a/ /b/

**Phoneme Blending** – Students blend individual sounds together to create a word.
Teacher: Say /sh/ /i/ /p/. What's the word?
Student: ship

**Phoneme Substitution** – Students substitute one sound for another in a word.
Teacher: Say map. Change the /m/ to /t/. What's the word?
Student: tap

**Final Phoneme Isolation** – Students identify the final sound they hear in a word.
Teacher: What sound do you hear at the end of cake?
Student: /k/

**Final Phoneme Deletion** – Students identify what sounds remain when the final sound is deleted.
Teacher: What is the word raft without the /t/?
Student: raf

**Student Data Sheets**

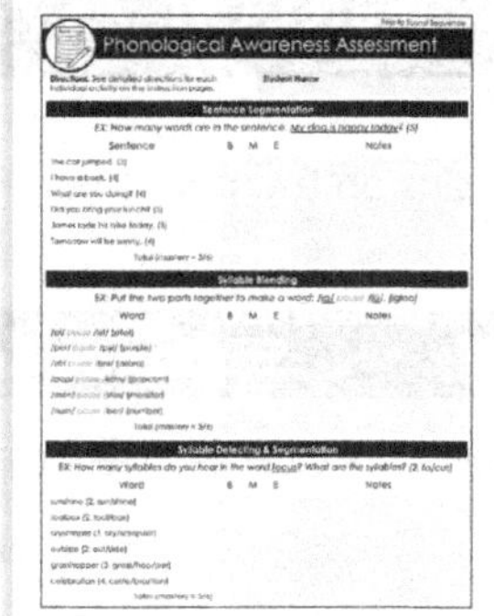
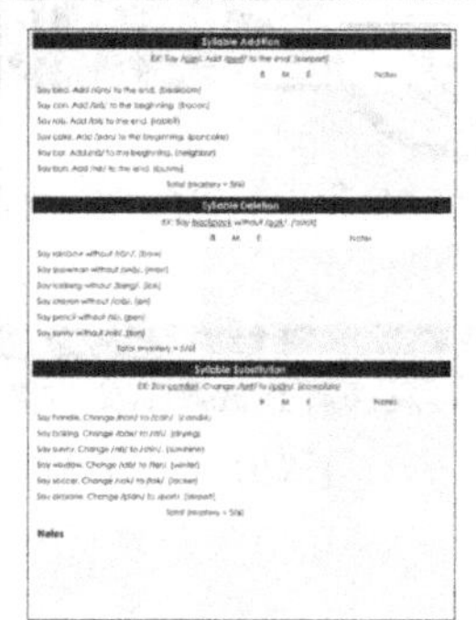
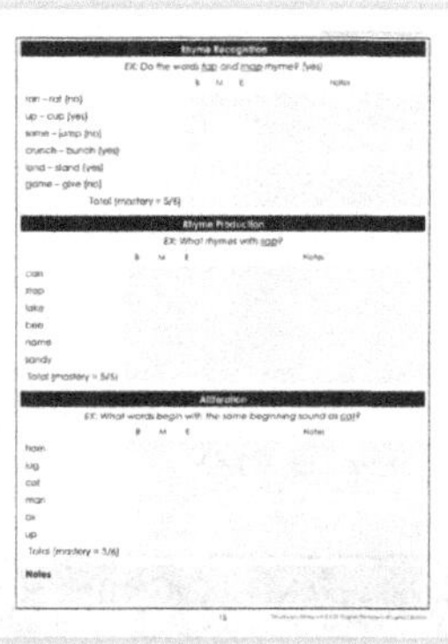
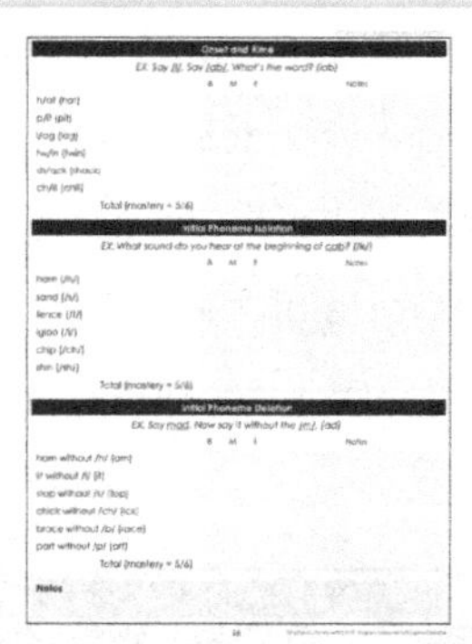
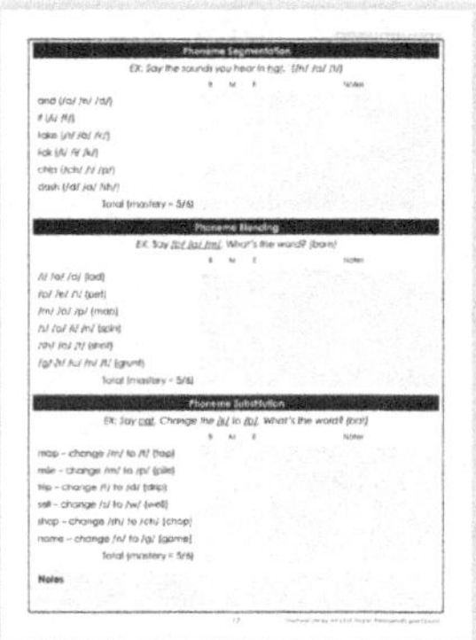
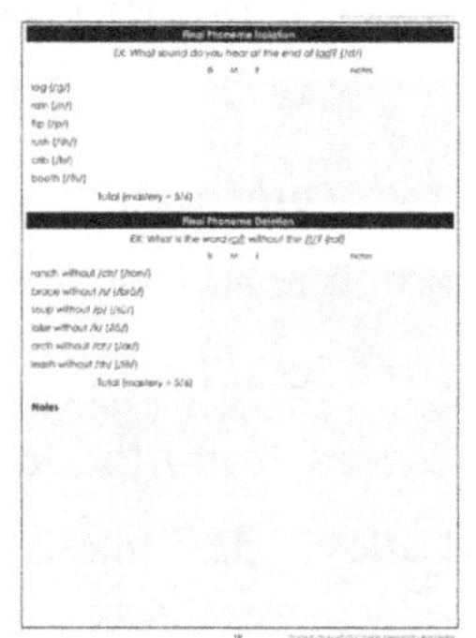

# Phonological Awareness Assessment

**Directions:** See detailed directions on the prior two pages.

**Student Name**

## Sentence Segmentation

*EX: How many words are in the sentence: My dog is happy today? (5)*

| | B | M | E | Notes |
|---|---|---|---|---|
| The cat jumped. (3) | | | | |
| I have a book. (4) | | | | |
| What are you doing? (4) | | | | |
| Did you bring your lunch? (5) | | | | |
| James rode his bike today. (5) | | | | |
| Tomorrow will be sunny. (4) | | | | |
| Total (mastery = 5/6) | | | | |

## Syllable Blending

*EX: Put the two parts together to create a word: /ig/ pause /lū/. (igloo)*

| | B | M | E | Notes |
|---|---|---|---|---|
| /pī/ pause /lət/ (pilot) | | | | |
| /per/ pause /pəl/ (purple) | | | | |
| /zē/ pause /brə/ (zebra) | | | | |
| /pop/ pause /korn/ (popcorn) | | | | |
| /mon/ pause /ster/ (monster) | | | | |
| /num/ pause /ber/ (number) | | | | |
| Total (mastery = 5/6) | | | | |

## Syllable Detecting and Segmentation

*EX: How many syllables do you hear in the word focus? What are the syllables? (2, fo/cus)*

| | B | M | E | Notes |
|---|---|---|---|---|
| sunshine (2, sun/shine) | | | | |
| toolbox (2, tool/box) | | | | |
| skyscraper (3, sky/scrap/er) | | | | |
| outside (2; out/side) | | | | |
| grasshopper (3; grass/hop/per) | | | | |
| celebration (4; cel/e/bra/tion) | | | | |
| Total (mastery = 5/6) | | | | |

## Syllable Addition

*EX: Say /car/. Add /port/ to the end. (carport)*

| | B | M | E | Notes |
|---|---|---|---|---|
| Say bed. Add /rūm/ to the end. (bedroom) | | | | |
| Say con. Add /bā/ to the beginning. (bacon) | | | | |
| Say rab. Add /bit/ to the end. (rabbit) | | | | |
| Say cake. Add /pan/ to the beginning. (pancake) | | | | |
| Say bor. Add /nā/ to the beginning. (neighbor) | | | | |
| Say bun. Add /nē/ to the end. (bunny) | | | | |
| Total (mastery = 5/6) | | | | |

## Syllable Deletion

*EX: Say backpack without /pak/. (back)*

| | B | M | E | Notes |
|---|---|---|---|---|
| Say rainbow without /rān/. (bow) | | | | |
| Say snowman without /snō/. (man) | | | | |
| Say iceberg without /berg/. (ice) | | | | |
| Say crayon without /crā/. (on) | | | | |
| Say pencil without /sil/. (pen) | | | | |
| Say sunny without /nē/. (sun) | | | | |
| Total (mastery = 5/6) | | | | |

## Syllable Substitution

*EX: Say comfort. Change /fort/ to /plān/. (complain)*

| | B | M | E | Notes |
|---|---|---|---|---|
| Say handle. Change /han/ to /can/. (candle) | | | | |
| Say baking. Change /bāk/ to /drī/. (drying) | | | | |
| Say sunny. Change /nē/ to /shīn/. (sunshine) | | | | |
| Say window. Change /dō/ to /ter/. (winter) | | | | |
| Say soccer. Change /sok/ to /lok/. (locker) | | | | |
| Say airplane. Change /plān/ to /port/. (airport) | | | | |
| Total (mastery = 5/6) | | | | |

**Notes**

## Rhyme Recognition

*EX: Do the words tap and map rhyme? (yes)*

| | B | M | E | Notes |
|---|---|---|---|---|
| ran – rat (no) | | | | |
| up – cup (yes) | | | | |
| some – jump (no) | | | | |
| crunch – bunch (yes) | | | | |
| land – stand (yes) | | | | |
| game – give (no) | | | | |
| Total (mastery = 5/6) | | | | |

## Rhyme Production

*EX: What rhymes with sap?*

| | B | M | E | Notes |
|---|---|---|---|---|
| can | | | | |
| stop | | | | |
| lake | | | | |
| bee | | | | |
| name | | | | |
| sandy | | | | |
| Total (mastery = 5/6) | | | | |

## Alliteration

*EX: What words begin with the same beginning sound as cat?*

| | B | M | E | Notes |
|---|---|---|---|---|
| ham | | | | |
| lug | | | | |
| cot | | | | |
| man | | | | |
| ox | | | | |
| up | | | | |
| Total (mastery = 5/6) | | | | |

**Notes**

## Onset and Rime

*EX: Say /l/. Say /ab/. What's the word? (lab)*

| | B | M | E | Notes |
|---|---|---|---|---|
| h/at (hat) | | | | |
| p/it (pit) | | | | |
| l/ag (lag) | | | | |
| tw/in (twin) | | | | |
| sh/ack (shack) | | | | |
| ch/ill (chill) | | | | |
| Total (mastery = 5/6) | | | | |

## Initial Phoneme Isolation

*EX: What sound do you hear at the beginning of cab? (/k/)*

| | B | M | E | Notes |
|---|---|---|---|---|
| ham (/h/) | | | | |
| sand (/s/) | | | | |
| fence (/f/) | | | | |
| igloo (/i/) | | | | |
| chip (/ch/) | | | | |
| shin (/sh/) | | | | |
| Total (mastery = 5/6) | | | | |

## Initial Phoneme Deletion

*EX: Say mad. Now say it without the /m/. (ad)*

| | B | M | E | Notes |
|---|---|---|---|---|
| ham without /h/ (am) | | | | |
| lit without /l/ (it) | | | | |
| stop without /s/ (top) | | | | |
| chick without /ch/ (ick) | | | | |
| brace without /b/ (race) | | | | |
| part without /p/ (art) | | | | |
| Total (mastery = 5/6) | | | | |

**Notes**

## Phoneme Segmentation

*EX: Say the sounds you hear in hat. (/h/ /a/ /t/)*

| | B | M | E | Notes |
|---|---|---|---|---|
| and (/a/ /n/ /d/) | | | | |
| if (/i/ /f/) | | | | |
| take (/t/ /ā/ /k/) | | | | |
| lick (/l/ /i/ /k/) | | | | |
| chip (/ch/ /i/ /p/) | | | | |
| dash (/d/ /a/ /sh/) | | | | |
| Total (mastery = 5/6) | | | | |

## Phoneme Blending

*EX: Say /b/ /a/ /m/. What's the word? (bam)*

| | B | M | E | Notes |
|---|---|---|---|---|
| /l/ /a/ /d/ (lad) | | | | |
| /p/ /e/ /t/ (pet) | | | | |
| /m/ /a/ /p/ (map) | | | | |
| /s/ /p/ /i/ /n/ (spin) | | | | |
| /sh/ /o/ /t/ (shot) | | | | |
| /g/ /r/ /u/ /n/ /t/ (grunt) | | | | |
| Total (mastery = 5/6) | | | | |

## Phoneme Substitution

*EX: Say cat. Change the /k/ to /b/. What's the word? (bat)*

| | B | M | E | Notes |
|---|---|---|---|---|
| map – change /m/ to /t/ (tap) | | | | |
| mile – change /m/ to /p/ (pile) | | | | |
| trip – change /t/ to /d/ (drip) | | | | |
| sell – change /s/ to /w/ (well) | | | | |
| shop – change /sh/ to /ch/ (chop) | | | | |
| name – change /n/ to /g/ (game) | | | | |
| Total (mastery = 5/6) | | | | |

**Notes**

## Final Phoneme Isolation

*EX: What sound do you hear at the end of lad? (/d/)*

| | B | M | E | Notes |
|---|---|---|---|---|
| lag (/g/) | | | | |
| rain (/n/) | | | | |
| flip (/p/) | | | | |
| rush (/sh/) | | | | |
| crib (/b/) | | | | |
| booth (/th/) | | | | |
| Total (mastery = 5/6) | | | | |

## Final Phoneme Deletion

*EX: What is the word raft without the /t/? (raf)*

| | B | M | E | Notes |
|---|---|---|---|---|
| ranch without /ch/ (/ran/) | | | | |
| brace without /s/ (/brā/) | | | | |
| soup without /p/ (/sū/) | | | | |
| lake without /k/ (/lā/) | | | | |
| arch without /ch/ (/ar/) | | | | |
| leash without /sh/ (/lē/) | | | | |
| Total (mastery = 5/6) | | | | |

**Notes**

# Lesson 5: Orthographic Mapping

*Module 4, Lesson 5 of the Science of Reading Academy explores orthographic mapping as a crucial process in reading development. Orthographic mapping involves linking the sounds of spoken language to written letters or patterns, facilitating rapid and accurate word recognition. This process occurs in specific brain regions involved in visual processing, phonemic awareness, and language comprehension. Effective instruction integrates phonemic awareness and phonics to strengthen these connections, emphasizing the importance of repeated exposure and practice for all learners, especially those with dyslexia. Below is the transcript for the Module 4, Lesson 5 video.*

**(00:07)** Hello, and welcome back to the Science of Reading Academy. We are jumping back into Module 4, focused on the road to decoding. Today we are going to focus on the concept of orthographic mapping, and I'm really looking forward to discussing this with you because it's a crucial aspect of the reading process.

**(00:29)** Much of what we'll talk about today will connect back to previous principles covered, especially from Module 2 where we discuss the reading brain. So let's take some time to review the reading circuit in our brain. We input words visually, and then they are processed in the occipital-temporal region. So this is our occipital region and our brain, our occipital lobe. This is the temporal lobe in our brain. This is the occipital-temporal region. Some researchers will reference this as the *brain's letterbox*. Some will call it the *visual word form area*, but what's most important to know is that this part of the brain recognizes that strings of letters are something special, and they are words that carry meaning.

**(01:21)** The parietal-temporal region will be activated next, and this region is helping connect those written representations of words, or the graphemes, to stored phonemes, so stored speech sounds, and bridging the two together. So that's where phonemic awareness is really important to help us make those connections.

**(01:44)** The inferior frontal gyrus is going to come into play next. So you might hear this called *Broca's area*. The gyrus is a fold in the cerebellum of our brain. So this is just a fold in the frontal lobe of our brain that's going to help with articulation, so help us know what to do with our mouth and our tongue and our teeth when we're seeing those stored speech sounds.

**(02:10)** And then finally, the superior temporal gyrus, also known as *Wernicke's area*, is going to help with language comprehension, so accessing those stored meanings of words.

**(02:23)** When our brain is completing this circuit, it is facilitating *orthographic mapping*, which is a term coined by Linnea Ehri. She was also the researcher that we looked at when we talked about Ehri's phases of word development. And this orthographic mapping process references how our brain stores words in our long-term memory for that instant retrieval. The word orthographic, so *ortho* meaning straight and *graph* meaning spelling or written, if we have *orthographic*, we're making a straight or correct connection between what is written and how it's spelled. So orthographic mapping is the process of connecting the sounds of spoken language to the written letters or letter patterns that represent those sounds. It involves learning the relationships between sounds and their corresponding letters, so phonemes and graphemes. This process allows individuals to recognize words quickly and accurately while reading, and it's essential for developing strong reading skills. So if you think about this with the word *crab*, so if you see the written representation of the word *crab*, your brain is having to connect that to speech sounds that are stored from your oral lexicon. Then those speech sounds, you're having to think about how to articulate those sounds to make meaning. And then you're thinking, oh, /k/ /r/ /a/ /b, *crab*, I know what a crab is. That's an animal on the beach. And then you're making that connection back to the written word. That is all happening so quickly, and Ehri references that as *orthographic mapping*.

**(04:23)** All three distinct regions of the brain must be activated for us to learn and automatically retrieve a word. So we need the visual, we need the auditory, and we need the meaning, all of those components working together.

**(04:38)** Now, orthographic mapping can't be taught, and it's not something we really do. We don't have an orthographic mapping lesson, but it is something that we can promote. Readers need three essential components in order for orthographic mapping to be able to occur. None of these elements are going to surprise you because they are three elements that have already come up in a lot of our video series.

**(05:05)** The first is phonemic awareness. Students must be able to pull apart individual sounds from a spoken word. If they don't have this down, then the whole circuit breaks apart, and they're left to memorizing words. That is why phonemic awareness is so essential for our youngest learners.

**(05:29)** The next component is phoneme-grapheme correspondences. For our youngest readers, that's just alphabet knowledge, but it doesn't stop there. Sometimes, that's where we go wrong. Remember, we have 44 sounds and over 75 graphemes. So for typical readers, it will take around three years to master all of these phoneme-grapheme correspondences, and students need to have them down automatically so the orthographic process doesn't get bogged down in that parietal-temporal region where the phonemes and graphemes were being connected. We want students to have them automatically linked so that that process is facilitated automatically.

**(06:12)** Finally, students need to be able to decode words. They need to know what to do when they come to an unfamiliar word that their brain hasn't mapped yet. That is one of the reasons why it is so important that we don't draw students' attention away from print when they come to an unfamiliar word by asking them to look at the pictures or just skip it and come back later and fill it in based on meaning. When we do that, they're losing the opportunity to go through that orthographic mapping process and store those parts in their brain for future retrieval. So the next time they see the word, they're still not going to know it because they've just had to resort to inefficient strategies to figure it out, whereas if they go through that more laborious process of sounding it out and making those connections, then they're starting that orthographic mapping process, and the next time they see it, they're going to have some strategies and skills to be able to make those important connections.

**(07:22)** So orthographic mapping is kind of complex. So take a moment to pause, reflect, and challenge yourself to summarize orthographic mapping in 50 words or less. So you might even just do a brain dump of everything you know about orthographic mapping and then try to condense it into 50 words or less, and that's really going to help you remember those key components that are essential.

**(07:49)** Okay, so one thing that we need to remember is that we want high-quality lexical representations of words in our brains. So we don't just want to have memorized what words look like. We want to have that lexical quality of what the word looks like, sounds like, and means. For most students, this will take multiple exposures and multiple times of orthographic mapping. For our striving readers and students with dyslexia, it can take literally hundreds of times. The brain of a student with dyslexia is really reluctant to rewire. They rely on their frontal lobe and an inefficient reading circuit and the right hemisphere of the brain instead of the left hemisphere. Creating those neural circuits just requires a lot more repetition. It is possible, and all of the components that those students need are the same components. They don't need a completely different lesson; they just need repetition of those high-yield instructional activities.

**(09:02)** One activity that provides meaningful repetition while building the brain's lexical quality of a word is Map-It. And on the screen here, you can see the Map-It activity and Map-It boards that come from Structured Literacy with E.A.S.E. Orthographic mapping isn't something that we can do with students, but this activity helps teach those essential components. You can do this Map-It activity with both regular and irregular words. So you can use it for your sight words, but you can also just use it for words that have that focus phoneme of the day. So when you're thinking about these steps for the Map-It, the first is Echo-It. So you're saying the word, and you're having students repeat it orally to get them thinking about those individual sounds. Then they're going to tap it. So over here you can see these green counters. You can use anything to tap it. You can even just have them tap in the boxes or highlight the boxes if it's a printed sound box on a piece of paper. So they're going to tap the sounds. So if this word is *pull*, they're going /p/ /u/ /ll/. Then they're going to push it. So that's going to help them know that there are three sounds, so they need to have three boxes with graphemes. Finally, they're going to write it. So that's where they're making those connections between the phonemes and the graphemes. And then the last step is reading it.

**(10:37)** If you think back to our last lesson where we talked about how phonemic awareness and phonics are really that powerful duo that go together, this is a great example of that. These first three steps, Echo-It, Tap-It, Push-It, that is all phonemic awareness. It's drawing students' attention to the individual phonemes, but letters have not been introduced yet. Now, once you add letters, then that becomes phonics, but the phonemic awareness piece is foundational to that connection. So this is a great activity to facilitate all of those good pieces of reading.

**(11:17)** So my challenge to you right now would be to practice the Map-It routine with the word *orthographic*. So if you are with a group of teachers or educators, you can take turns being the teacher and the student with the word. If you are by yourself, I would just challenge you to put the word *orthographic* into sound boxes, so go through the steps of tapping out the sounds, drawing the sound boxes for that many sounds, and then writing the graphemes that represent that phoneme that you hear. After you have completed that, then go ahead and join us so that we can talk about our learning extensions and downloadable bonus content.

**(12:02)** Today's learning extensions are from Dr. Linnea Ehri. She provided information for a blog post about instructional guidelines. She recommends to really enhance orthographic mapping and word learning. This is a really fast read that has some great practical applications for all educators. I would highly recommend that you check it out.

**(12:26)** Your downloadable bonus content is some Map-It mats from Laprea's Structured Literacy with E.A.S.E. program. So you have both a teacher display chart here to help you remember the steps, and also to help your students know the steps, and then a student version as well. And when you get to the end of Module 4, you'll be able to download this with your other bonus content from the rest of our lessons.

**(12:59)** Thank you so much for joining us today. Don't forget to comment on the Module 4, Lesson 5 thread for a chance to win.

## The Brain's Reading Regions

## Orthographic Mapping

## Essential Components: Phonemic Awareness

## Additional Notes

## Essential Components: Phoneme-Grapheme Correspondences

## Additional Notes

## Essential Components: Decoding

## Pause and Reflect: Summarize orthographic mapping in 50 words or less.

## Repetition is Key!

## How to Map-It

## Try it Out!: Practice the Map-It routine with the word "orthographic."

## Additional Notes

# Bonus Content

**Use the questions below to prompt discussion amongst your colleagues.**

1. **Brain Processes and Orthographic Mapping:** How do different regions of the brain contribute to the process of orthographic mapping? Why is this understanding important for designing effective reading instruction?
2. **Integration of Skills:** How can phonemic awareness, phoneme-grapheme correspondences, and decoding skills work together to support orthographic mapping? Discuss examples of activities that integrate these components effectively.
3. **Challenges and Strategies:** What challenges might students face during the orthographic mapping process? How can educators address these challenges through targeted instructional strategies?
4. **Role of Repetition:** Why is repetition crucial for developing strong lexical representations through orthographic mapping? How can educators ensure that students receive adequate practice without overwhelming them?
5. **Application in Instruction:** Reflecting on your teaching practice, how can the Map-It routine or similar activities help students build orthographic mapping skills? Share experiences or ideas for implementing such activities in the classroom.

**To extend your understanding of this topic, work through the activities below with a small group of peers.**

**Case Study Analysis**
Analyze case studies or student profiles to identify how different students approach orthographic mapping. Discuss strategies to support students with varying levels of proficiency.

**Brain Model Discussion**
Use diagrams or models to simulate how different brain regions are involved in orthographic mapping. Discuss implications for instructional practices based on these insights.

**Map-It Activity Workshop**
Conduct a workshop where participants practice the Map-It routine with unfamiliar words or specific phoneme-grapheme correspondences. Discuss variations and adaptations for different grade levels.

**Cross-Grade Collaboration**
Pair educators from different grade levels to discuss how orthographic mapping skills progress over time. Create a timeline or developmental chart based on shared insights.

**Instructional Strategy Design**
Design new instructional strategies or modify existing ones to enhance orthographic mapping skills in struggling readers or students with dyslexia. Share and receive feedback on these strategies.

**Additional Resources**
See the following pages for word mapping mats (one with five sounds and one with seven sounds). Additionally, detailed procedures for word mapping are provided.

# Word Mapping Information and Procedures

## Word Mapping

Phonemic skills are essential "for fluent, word-level reading in alphabetic writing systems" (Kilpatrick, 2020, p. 15). According to researchers, "Taking the spoken word and the written word apart and then matching up the two—phonemes and graphemes—is how the spelling of a word gets locked in long-term memory" (Burkins & Yates, 2021, p. 95). This is orthographic mapping, and it is a central concept in the science of reading. When students are engaging in word mapping, they are linking the sounds letters make to the symbols (or letters) that make them. This is foundational for developing both reading and writing skills.

**References**

Burkins, J., & Yates, K. (2021). Shifting the balance: 6 ways to bring the Science of Reading into the Balanced Literacy classroom. Stenhouse Publishers. 480 Congress Street, Portland, ME 04101.

Kilpatrick, D. A. (2020). How the phonology of speech is foundational for instant word recognition. Perspectives on Language and Literacy, 46(3), 11-15.

## Map-It Procedure

**Word Mapping Procedure**

1. **Echo-It**: Read the word aloud. Students repeat the word.
2. **Tap-It:** Students tap each sound they hear in the word with their fingers. Using their free hand, students count the phonemes by putting up a finger for each sound they hear. Students place that number of chips/counters in the Tap-It squares. Next, write the word where students can see it and say it aloud as you underline the graphemes that represent the individual sounds you are saying. Conceal the word before students move to the next step.
3. **Push-It:** Students look at the chips they placed inside the boxes and say the sound that corresponds with each chip as they push the chip out of the box and into the circle above it.
4. **Write-It:** In each empty box, students spell each sound they hear. Once the entire word is written in the boxes, students write the word on the handwriting lines.
5. **Read-It:** Students read the word three times as they drag a finger under the written word.

This page is intentionally blank.

# MAP-IT

1 Echo-It

2 Tap-It

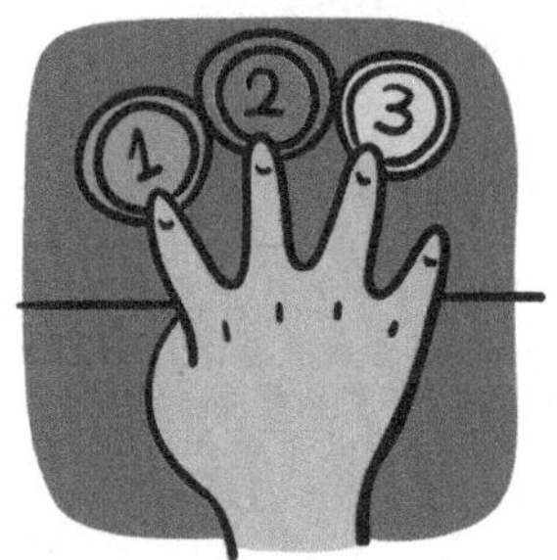


3 Push-It

4 Write-It

5 Read-It

This page is intentionally blank.

# MAP-IT

| Echo-It | Tap-It | Push-It | Write-It | Read-It |
| --- | --- | --- | --- | --- |
|  | 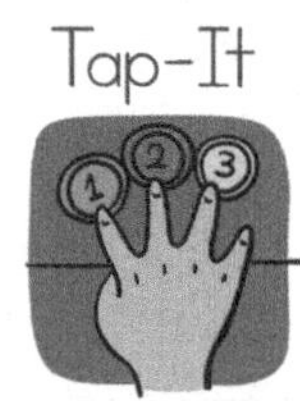 |  |  |  |

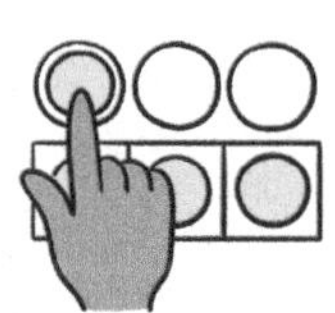

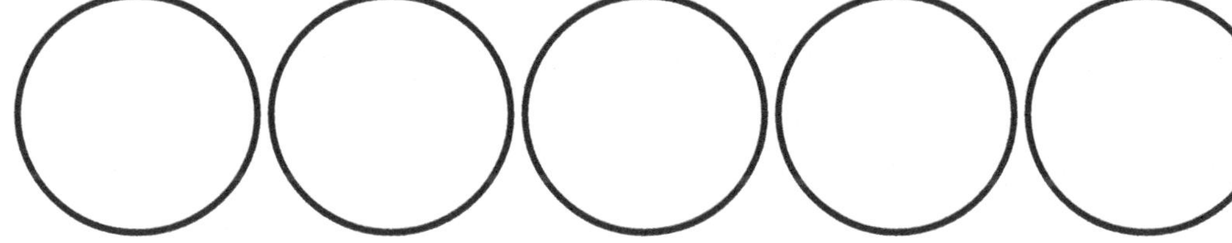

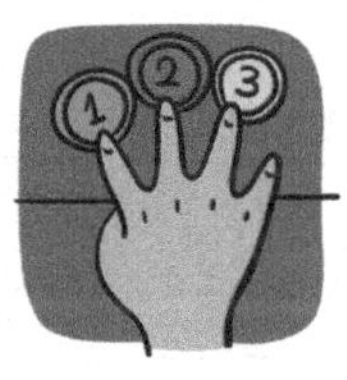

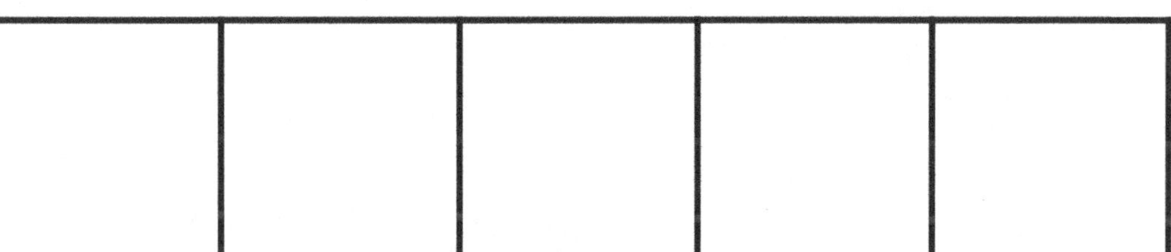

abcdefghijklmnopqrstuvwxyz

This page is intentionally blank.

# MAP-IT

| Echo-It | Tap-It | Push-It | Write-It | Read-It |
|---|---|---|---|---|
| 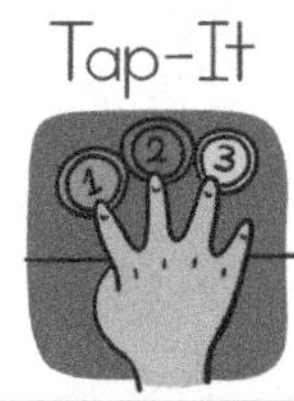 | 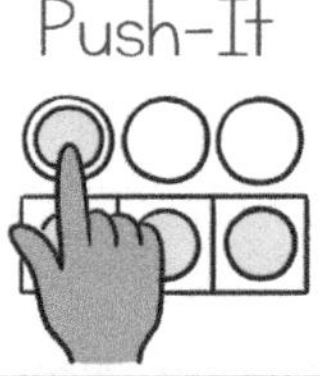 |  |  | |

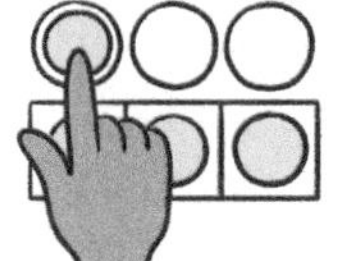

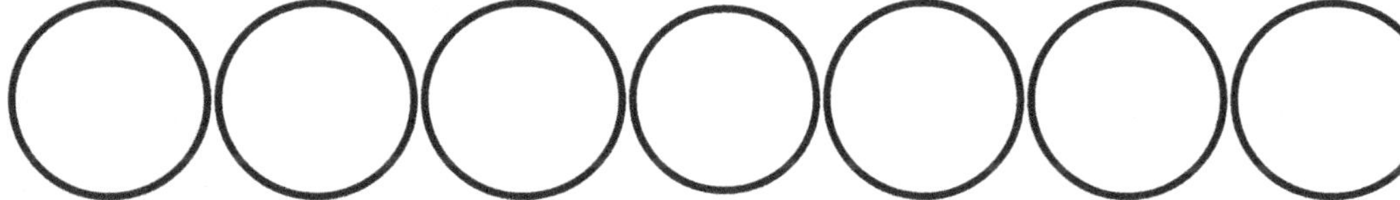

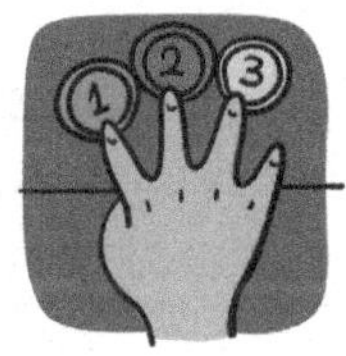

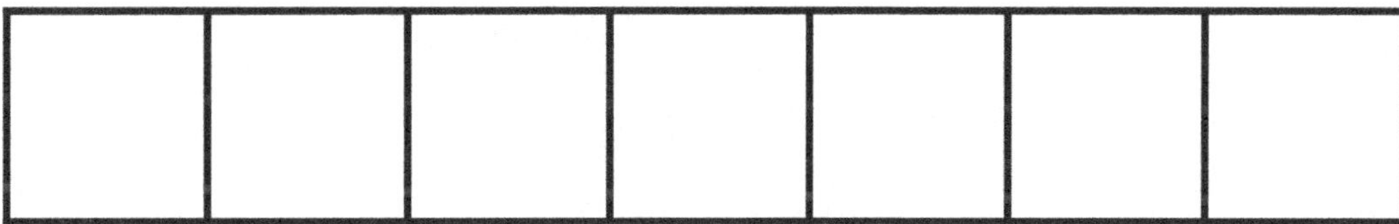

abcdefghijklmnopqrstuvwxyz

This page is intentionally blank.

# Lesson 6: High-Frequency Words

*Module 4, Lesson 6 of the Science of Reading Academy focuses on high-frequency words and their role in reading instruction. High-frequency words are those frequently encountered in text and are crucial for developing reading fluency and comprehension. These words, whether regular or irregular, are processed through orthographic mapping, linking visual cues, phonemes, and word meaning in the brain. Effective instructional strategies like the Read-Spell-Write-Extend routine help students master these words by integrating reading, spelling, writing, and meaningful usage, ensuring robust word recognition skills essential for proficient reading. Below is the transcript for the Module 4, Lesson 6 video.*

**(00:07)** Hello, and welcome back to the Science of Reading Academy. We are on Lesson 6 of Module 4, focused on the road to decoding. Today's lesson will focus on high-frequency words.

**(00:21)** Our last video discussed orthographic mapping, which is the brain's process for storing words into long-term memory. In order for our brains to orthographically map a word, we must connect a word's visual properties to its phonemes and to its meaning. The wonderful thing of all orthographic mapping is that this is the process our brain uses for all words, including irregular words and high-frequency words. So all of those components and steps and procedures that we've talked about in the past several videos still apply regardless of what kind of word a student is learning to read.

**(01:05)** So let's talk about some definitions. There are a lot of different phrases that might come to mind when you hear the term *high-frequency words*. So you might think of them as sight words or heart words or popcorn words. Really the language that you use with your students is not as important, but when we have this conversation as educators, we want to be really precise.

**(01:34)** A sight word is any word that a reader knows automatically. So we've talked some about the difference between decoding and automatic sight recognition. So if a student is having to sound out each of the graphemes in a word and connect those to phonemes, and it's kind of a slower, laborious process, they don't have that word as an automatic sight word, but that's our eventual goal.

**(02:02)** A high-frequency word is a word that appears often in text. So these are often going to be words that you would find on sight word lists for K-2 students, just because of how often they come up in text. High-frequency words that do not follow the rules can still become sight words. They just might need more practice, and so we need to be more intentional with exposing students to these words.

**(02:35)** So you can think about it this way: "All words want to be sight words when they grow up!" This is a saying from Jan Wasowicz, and I love it because it helps me picture the difference between a sight word, a high-frequency word, a heart word. We want all of our words to be sight words, and they might just be classified differently as we're learning them. Essentially, we want our students to orthographically map each and every word they encounter. That's our end goal of all reading instruction. Automatic word recognition, which is fostered through orthographic mapping, leads to reading fluency, which allows for strong reading comprehension. It really doesn't matter if the word is decodable or irregular; we want it to be a sight word.

**(03:26)** So take a moment to pause and reflect. In your own words, sum up our learning by explaining the difference between a sight word and a high-frequency word. After you've jotted that down in your note guide, go ahead and jump back onto the video for some high-frequency word routines.

**(03:46)** Okay, so we've talked about the difference between a high-frequency word and a sight word. So we're now going to be focusing on high-frequency words. So those words that we know students are going to encounter, and it is going to benefit them if they become automatic with those words earlier in the reading process.

**(04:09)** The best instructional practices for high-frequency words are those that accelerate learning and focus on mastery. Research shows that we store irregular words in the same way that we store regular words. It's not a separate reading circuit in our brain, and thank goodness, right, that we only have to learn one reading circuit. We just might need to practice more with words that don't follow the rules because we're having to learn a new phoneme-grapheme connection that's different from the others. So that's another piece of learning that has to occur. So we've talked about that automaticity that really helps students when they're going through that reading circuit; if they know this grapheme represents this phoneme and they know it automatically, that's going to be very helpful. Well, here we're introducing a grapheme that doesn't connect to the phoneme that they're expecting, so they're going to need a little bit more practice with that.

**(05:07)** An easy to remember routine for this process comes from Wiley Blevins. This is the Read-Spell-Write-Extend routine. So we're going to talk through this routine with the word *want*. So the first step is reading. You're going to write the word on a notecard or on a whiteboard and put it in a sentence to give students some context to its meaning.

**(05:35)** So this is an example from the Simply or from the Structured Literacy with E.A.S.E. program, where they have the word *want* and they have a sentence here that puts it in context for you: They want to come with us. So that is a great resource that is already going to have this done for you, but you can also just write it on an index card and come up with your sentence with your students. After reading the word and pointing to the target word, reading it aloud to students, guide your students to tap or see the sounds in the word, so drawing their attention to those individual phonemes like we've talked about before. Our phonics practices are a lot more powerful when we combine them with phonemic awareness. So even though students can see the letters, it can be really helpful to also get them to think about those sounds. That's going to set them up for success for the subsequent steps here.

**(06:34)** Step 2 is focused on spelling. So this is your opportunity to help students connect the sounds in the word to the spelling. On the cards from the Structured Literacy with E.A. S. E. program, you can see an example of what each word would look like when it's mapped. So that's, again, just a great resource. Sometimes words are not as straightforward when we're mapping them as you might think that they would be, so it can be great to have a place to look, but the power of this is really going to come from doing the process with your students. So just showing them a word that's already mapped is not going to be helpful, but talking them through, okay, we hear this sound /w/; I'm going to write that at the beginning. I hear this sound /a/; I'm going to write that next. And talking them through that process, doing it as a class or doing it as a small group, is going to be very powerful.

**(07:32)** During this step, you're also going to discuss any irregular parts, and those parts might be temporarily irregular or permanently irregular. And what I mean by that is a part would be temporarily irregular if the student hasn't learned it yet but they're going to, so for example, the word they has two parts that would be considered irregular if a student hasn't been introduced to digraphs yet. So a beginning kindergartner might encounter that word in text, but they're not going to know the /th/ sound is represented by "th." Once the student learns that particular grapheme, then that part is no longer irregular, so it was just temporarily irregular, while "ey" representing the /ā/ sound is very rare and most likely will not be covered by your phonics curriculum explicitly, and if it is, it will be much later, so most likely that would be a permanently irregular part for your students.

**(08:41)** The third step is writing. So you're going to ask your students to write the word multiple times as they spell it out loud. So you'll remember some students can orthographically map a word in just a few exposures, but many of our students will need several exposures before mastery, especially for words that have irregular parts. Students should have the opportunity to physically write the word.

Handwriting is an important component to facilitating that reading circuit in our brain. They might do this on a whiteboard. They might do this in sand; they might do it with paper pencil, but that physical activity of putting a writing utensil on a writing surface is very helpful. You can also bring in some multisensory components here with skywriting and arm spelling as well.

**(09:33)** The fourth step is extension, so we're going to complete that reading circuit by pulling in meaning. This is where you can ask students to use the word in a sentence and connect the new word to previously learned words at this time. So you can talk about synonyms, antonyms, morphology. You can go as deep as you want here with this extension step because remember, we want good quality representations of words in our long-term memory. So we want to have that deep orthography of words taught to students.

**(10:13)** Okay, so take a moment now to try it out. Pause the video and practice the Read, Spell, Write, Extend routine with the word *pull*. If you're with a group of educators, you can do it together, but if you're by yourself, just think through those steps and what that would look like with your students.

**(10:33)** Okay. Our learning extension for today is a book, but it's a really good book. It's by Wiley Blevins, and I've quoted him several times in our series together. This is his most recent book called *Differentiating Phonics Instruction for Maximum Impact*, and he has a section in here that is specific to high-frequency words, but he also has several other wonderful word study routines, so I would highly recommend you check this out.

**(11:02)** Our bonus downloadable content is wonderful for this lesson. The 109 most frequent high-frequency words are all in a packet with these practice sheets for you, where students can practice some of the steps of the Read, Write, Spell, Extend routine. So this is a great resource that you will receive at the end of Module 4.

**(11:31)** Alright, thank you so much for visiting our SOR Academy Facebook group and continuing to comment on those threads. We can't wait to hear from you this go around as well. Thank you.

## Orthographic Mapping

## Sight Words

## High-Frequency Words

## Additional Notes

Pause and Reflect: What is the difference between a sight word and a high-frequency word?

Additional Notes

High-Frequency Words Routine

1.Read

2. Spell

3. Write

4. Extend

Try It Out!: Practice the Read, Spell, Write, Extend routine with the word "pull."

# Bonus Content

**Use the questions below to prompt discussion amongst your colleagues.**

1. **Understanding Automaticity:** Why is it important for students to achieve automatic recognition of high-frequency words? How does automaticity contribute to overall reading fluency and comprehension?
2. **Differentiating Instruction:** How can educators differentiate instruction to support students in mastering high-frequency words, especially those with irregular spelling patterns? Discuss specific strategies and examples.
3. **Integration with Phonics:** In what ways does the Read-Spell-Write-Extend routine integrate phonics principles with high-frequency word instruction? How does this approach enhance students' understanding and retention of these words?
4. **Addressing Challenges:** What are some common challenges students face when learning high-frequency words, and how can educators address these challenges effectively? Share practical tips and experiences.
5. **Long-Term Memory and Orthographic Mapping:** How does orthographic mapping relate to the process of learning high-frequency words? Discuss strategies for promoting deep orthographic representations of these words in students' long-term memory.

**To extend your understanding of this topic, work through the activities below with a small group of peers.**

**Word Study Analysis**
Analyze a set of high-frequency words and categorize them based on regular and irregular spelling patterns. Discuss implications for instructional strategies tailored to each category.

**Interactive Word Mapping**
Use interactive tools or software to visually map the phonemes and graphemes of high-frequency words. Discuss how this visual representation enhances students' understanding and retention.

**Case Study Review**
Review case studies or student profiles to identify effective interventions for mastering high-frequency words. Discuss and share insights on personalized learning approaches.

**Peer Teaching Workshop**
Conduct a workshop where educators take turns teaching the Read-Spell-Write-Extend routine with different high-frequency words. Provide feedback and discuss variations in implementation.

**Resource Evaluation**
Evaluate and discuss resources like the Structured Literacy with Ease program or books by Wiley Blevins focused on high-frequency words. Share insights on integrating these resources into daily instruction.

**Additional Resources**
Scan to access a high-frequency word workbook with activities that can be used to review the 109 words that are the most critical high-frequency words students need to master.

# Lesson 7: Syllabication

*Module 4, Lesson 7 of the Science of Reading Academy focuses on syllabication and its importance in advancing students' decoding skills from single-syllable to multisyllabic words. Syllables are defined as speech units containing a vowel sound, critical for both decoding and meaning in reading. Understanding the six types of syllables—closed, open, silent "e," vowel team, R-controlled, and consonant -le—equips educators to provide explicit instruction on syllable division and pronunciation rules. This foundational knowledge supports students in transitioning from basic word recognition to more complex text comprehension, crucial for overall reading proficiency. Below is the transcript for the Module 4, Lesson 7 video.*

**(00:07)** Hello, and welcome back to the Science of Reading Academy. We are in Module 4, focused on all things decoding. Today's lesson is going to talk about syllabication, so how we transition our students from decoding one-syllable words to two-syllable words and why this is important.

**(00:28)** A few lessons ago we talked about Ehri's phases of word recognition. As students are on this road to decode, we want them to get to the consolidated alphabetic phase where they're beginning to recognize larger chunks of words. Introducing multisyllabic words is going to help students transition to this new phase of word learning, so from the full alphabetic to the consolidated alphabetic, and that is going to help them have more effective access to words for both decoding and meaning. So when you have students in that full alphabetic stage, this is a great thing for your instruction to focus on to get them to that next stage.

**(01:11)** So the first thing we need to talk about is: What is a syllable? Syllables are speech units of language that contain one vowel sound and can be represented in written language as words, like *cat, mop, or sad*, or parts of words, *mu* in *music*. Syllables do not have to carry meaning. I teach students that a syllable is a beat in a word because that is usually something they can kind of connect to, whereas just saying that they're units of language is not necessarily something that helps the student think, oh, I know what a syllable is. I also make sure to teach that every syllable has a vowel sound. Those are two key pieces of information that are going to help your students transition to this multisyllabic phase of decoding.

**(02:09)** There are six different types of syllables represented in written English. Having awareness of syllable types allows readers to determine how to pronounce a vowel sound in a syllable. Vowels are what make our language so very tricky, so giving students a way to categorize these vowel sounds can be very helpful.

**(02:31)** So the first syllable type is closed syllable. A closed syllable ends in at least one consonant after one vowel. The vowel sound is short. An open syllable ends in one vowel, and the vowel in an open accented syllable is long, like in *hi*. A silent "e" syllable ends in one vowel, one consonant, and a final "e." The "e" is silent; the vowel is long, like in *tape*.

**(03:10)** This next syllable type is the vowel pair syllable, or vowel team. This syllable type has two vowels right next to each other, and each vowel has a different letter combination and sound. This syllable type can also include diphthongs. The next type is R-controlled syllables. So R-controlled syllables have a vowel followed by an "r," and the vowel makes an unexpected sound in these syllables because it's neither short nor long. The last type is consonant -le syllables, and these are one type of final stable syllables. A consonant -le syllable ends in a consonant followed by an "l" and a final "e." The "e" is silent, and you will hear a schwa sound with these syllable types.

**(04:04)** Alright, so take a moment, pause the video, try this out. Label each of these words by syllable type, and then when you're ready, jump back on the video so we can talk about some next steps.

**(04:20)** Okay, so this is a quote from Dr. Suzanne Carreker, and she says, "Even students who read monosyllabic words accurately and automatically may struggle to read multisyllabic words and require explicit instruction." And I know I would definitely agree with this from my time as a first and second grade teacher. Our students don't have the attached strategies when they come to multisyllabic words, even if they've been very successful with one-syllable words. Skilled readers can typically sense where to divide longer words because they have an innate awareness of syllables and they've internalized the orthographic patterns of our language very well, but some of our striving readers or those borderline students, they're going to need that explicit instruction.

**(05:14)** So these are some instructional activities that can help you provide that explicit instruction to your students. These activities can heighten students' visual awareness of syllables as well as syllable division patterns. The first activity is Separated Syllables. So in this, students will identify syllable types of separated syllables, join them into words, and then read the words out loud. So you might have this syllable "cac" written on an index card and this syllable "tus" written on an index card, the syllable "mas" written on an index card and "cot" written on an index card and just put all four of them into a pocket chart. Read the syllables with students and ask them what kind of syllable it is and how they know, and then ask students to match them to create real words.

**(06:08)** The next activity is Syllable Puzzles. So you're going to write syllables on index cards or sentence strips and ask students to arrange them into words and then read the words out loud. So similar, but with the Separated Syllables, you're going to have them closer together, so there's less of that cognitive burden on the matching part, but you're just separating the words a little bit, whereas with the Syllable Puzzles, you're mixing it all up.

**(06:37)** The last part is Spot and Dot. So this activity draws students' attention to the syllable in the words by dotting the vowels to help them divide each word. So these kind of get harder in difficulty here, like this would be the easiest one. This one's a little bit harder, and then this one would be the hardest because students are looking at the word as a whole and then breaking it apart into syllables by themselves.

**(07:05)** Alright, so you're going to try it out again. Try out the Spot and Dot routine with the words *cat, tiger, ostrich, mice,* and *flamingo*. So for this activity, you're going to spot the vowels, dot the vowels—so just put a dot above or below them—and then think about how many vowel sounds you hear in each of the words. After you've done that, jump back on the video for our learning extension and our bonus content.

**(07:38)** Alright. Today's learning extension is a video from the Reading League all about reading longer words. So it's going to cover syllable types and irregular sounds in much greater depth than we did during our time today. So if you're looking for more information, this is a great resource.

**(07:55)** Our bonus downloadable content that will be available at the end of Module 4 are some syllable posters, as well as that Spot and Dot poster that we covered earlier, so that will be a great resource.

**(08:09)** Thank you again for joining us today. Please remember to visit that Facebook group and comment on the Module 4, Lesson 7 thread. We can't wait to hear from you.

## Ehri's Phases

## What is a syllable?

## Additional Notes

| Types of Syllables |
| --- |
| Closed |
| Open |
| Silent "e" |
| Vowel Pair |
| R-controlled |
| Consonant -le |

Additional Notes

**Try It Out!: Label each of these words by syllable type.**

boil

me

bark

test

cake

table

**Instructional Activities**

Separated Syllables

Syllable Puzzles

Spot and Dot

**Try It Out!: Try the Spot and Dot routine with these words.**

cat

tiger

ostrich

mice

flamingo

Additional Notes

# Bonus Content

**Use the questions below to prompt discussion amongst your colleagues.**

1. **Understanding Syllables:** How do syllables contribute to the process of decoding multisyllabic words? Discuss why teaching syllabication is crucial for students' reading development, particularly as they transition from one-syllable to multisyllabic words.
2. **Types of Syllables:** What are the six types of syllables discussed in the video? How can awareness of these syllable types help students improve their pronunciation and understanding of words in written English?
3. **Challenges in Multisyllabic Words:** According to Dr. Suzanne Carreker, why do some students struggle with multisyllabic words even if they read one-syllable words accurately? How can explicit instruction in syllabication address these challenges?
4. **Instructional Strategies:** Discuss the effectiveness of activities like Separated Syllables, Syllable Puzzles, and Spot and Dot in teaching syllabication. How do these activities promote visual awareness and understanding of syllable division patterns?
5. **Application in Instruction:** How can educators integrate syllabication instruction into their daily teaching practices across different grade levels? Share specific examples and experiences.

**To extend your understanding of this topic, work through the activities below with a small group of peers.**

<u>**Syllable Sorting Game**</u>
Prepare a set of cards with words of varying syllable types (closed, open, silent "e," etc.). In small groups, sort these words into their respective syllable categories and discuss why each word belongs to its category.

<u>**Syllable Type Analysis**</u>
Analyze a passage from a grade-level text and identify different types of syllables present. Discuss how recognizing these syllable types can aid in pronunciation and comprehension of the text.

<u>**Multisensory Syllable Breakdown**</u>
Use tactile materials (like sand or manipulative letters) to physically break down multisyllabic words into their component syllables. Discuss how multisensory approaches can support students' understanding of syllabication.

<u>**Syllable Scavenger Hunt**</u>
Create a scavenger hunt activity where educators search for examples of different syllable types in educational materials or children's books. Discuss findings and strategies for incorporating these examples into classroom instruction.

<u>**Peer Coaching on Syllabication**</u>
Pair up educators to observe each other's syllabication teaching techniques. Provide constructive feedback on clarity, engagement, and effectiveness in facilitating students' understanding of syllables.

**Additional Resources**
See the following pages for three posters that define syllables, show a strategy for counting syllables, and show an example for how to identify syllable types in multisyllabic words.

# Syllable Posters

## Understanding Syllables

Syllable analysis (identifying and dividing syllables) is an important part of learning how to read through a structured literacy approach (Jiban, 2022). Long words can seem intimidating for young readers. But with some basic knowledge of syllable patterns, students can break longer words into manageable parts. This is where knowledge of syllable types and division becomes crucial. When a child learns and practices syllable division strategies in isolation, they can transfer those skills when reading text (Schukraft, 2020).

In order for students to effectively identify and divide syllables, they need to be well versed in syllable types and syllable division patterns.

**Syllable Types –** Seven of the most common syllable types in multisyllabic words are closed, open, magic e, vowel teams, bossy r, diphthongs, and consonant + le. As students advance in their reading instruction, they will also encounter the schwa syllable type and suffixes.

**Syllable Division –** There are four syllable division patterns: vowel-consonant/consonant-vowel (VC/CV, such as rab/bit), vowel/consonant-vowel (V/CV, such as ti/ger), vowel-consonant/vowel (VC/V, such as lem/on), and vowel/vowel (V/V, such as li/on). Teaching students to effectively decode words based on syllable division also helps students encode words (Schukraft, 2020).

**References**

Jiban, C. (2022, Feb 15). What the Science of Reading tells us about how to teach decoding—including phonics. https://bit.ly/3vhvHdu

Schukraft, S. (2020, July 20) The importance of teaching syllable division & decoding strategies. https://bit.ly/3RZDMgZ

## Syllable Posters

The three posters are meant to be displayed and referenced in the classroom.

The "What Are Syllables" poster can be used to introduce the seven basic syllable types.

The "Spot and Dot" poster can be used to help learners count the number of syllables in a word.

The "Multisyllabic Words" poster can be used to help learners identify the different syllable types in multisyllable words.

This page is intentionally blank.

# What Are Syllables?

Syllables are word parts. You can figure out how many syllables are in a word based on how many vowel sounds you hear in the word. There are seven syllable types, and understanding each one helps us read words.

**Pig Rule**

**Gnu Rule**

**Mule Rule**

**Toad Rule**

**Bird Rule**

**Owl Rule**

**Turtle Rule**

This page is intentionally blank.

# Spot and Dot

## Counting Syllables

Use Spot and Dot to find the number of syllables in words.

1) Look at the word.
2) Spot the vowels.
3) Dot the vowels.
4) How many vowel sounds do you hear in the word? That is the number of syllables.

| cat | tiger | ostrich | mice | flamingo |
| --- | --- | --- | --- | --- |

This page is intentionally blank.

# Multisyllabic Words

The words below have multiple syllables with different syllable types.

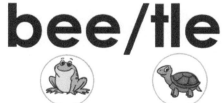

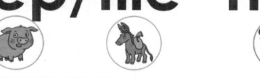

| | | |
|---|---|---|
| joy/ful | ti/ger | rai/sin |
| rep/tile | mu/sic | bee/tle |

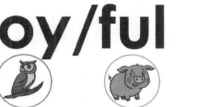

This page is intentionally blank.

**MODULE 4: The Road to Decoding**

# Lesson 8: Decodable Text

*Module 4, Lesson 8 of the Science of Reading Academy focuses on decodable texts and their crucial role in early literacy instruction. Decodable texts serve as a bridge for students to apply their phonics skills in meaningful reading contexts. They are designed to align with the phoneme-grapheme correspondences taught in structured literacy programs, providing focused practice while ensuring the text remains comprehensible, instructive, and engaging. Educators are encouraged to select decodable texts that match their scope and sequence, allowing students to build fluency and confidence in decoding while supporting broader literacy skills such as comprehension, vocabulary, and writing. Below is the transcript for the Module 4, Lesson 8 video.*

**(00:07)** Hello, and welcome back to the Science of Reading Academy. We are in Module 4, which has focused on all things decoding. To wrap up our Module 4 series, we are going to talk today about decodable text.

**(00:24)** Here in education, we really love our buzzwords, and decodable texts seem to be the buzzword of the time. This really does make sense to me, though, because decodable texts are almost like that missing piece of the puzzle when it comes to turning our early learners into decoders. So we've done all of this amazing work with them. We've done the phoneme-grapheme mapping. We've talked about all of the important phonemes that they need to know, and we've helped them connect those to the spellings, and we've given them lots of explicit systematic practice, but without that decodable text that allows them to apply those phonics skills to a meaningful text, there's just that missing piece, right? So you can think of decodable text as the training wheels to beginning reading. They help students try out their new phonic skills in a safe, meaningful way.

**(01:30)** Now, there are so many decodable texts out there to date because it is such a popular buzzword. So it's really important to know that just because a text is labeled decodable doesn't mean it's automatically going to be decodable for every student that picks up that book.

**(01:51)** A decodable text will align with previously taught phonic skills and provide focus practice on a specific phoneme-grapheme correspondence. So in order to know if a text will be decodable for your students, you're going to have to look at the decodable text company or publisher and figure out what their scope and sequence is and then compare that to your scope and sequence and figure out if they are a good match or not. It does not have to be a perfect science because we'll talk in a little bit that a text doesn't have to be 100% decodable by all of your students. In fact, it's better if there's some words in there that are perhaps not decodable, but it is really important to know that just because you go to the store and pick up a tub of books that say decodable doesn't automatically make them decodable.

**(02:52)** So when we're thinking about evaluative criteria for choosing what decodable text to use with our students, we want to make sure that these books are comprehensible, instructive, and engaging. So comprehensible is referencing that this story makes sense, so it's not using very obscure vocabulary. It's not having very stilted language. The story makes sense. Students can follow the storyline, the conversation sounds right, all of those components. That is very hard when it is at the beginning of a decodable text series. So you are going to have to think about that as well, but it really does need to make sense to you so that it can make sense to your students.

**(03:47)** The next criteria is that decodable texts are instructive. So most of the words can be decoded based on sound spellings previously taught. So books really don't need to be 100% decodable. There are going to be irregular words. There are going to be story words, there's going to be names, all of that, and that is in order to preserve that first goal of the story being comprehensible. So if you have students that can only read CVC words, in our normal everyday conversation, we are not just limited to CVC words and six high-frequency words, right? So authors have to incorporate some story words in order for the stories to still be comprehensible as well as instructive. So there's really not a consensus agreement on the percentage of words that need to be decodable, but around 75% decodable is a really good goal.

**(04:59)** Finally, the last criteria is that the books are engaging. So the story should be interesting and worth reading, rereading, and writing about. We don't want students to go, oh, that's a decodable book, and this is a real book. We want them to want to read the books, right? Just like with any other book. So think about that as well. Think about the pictures and the story, the characters are they representative, all of those things can go into your evaluating criteria as well.

**(05:38)** This story is an example from Laprea Education that aligns with their Structured Literacy with E.A.S.E. program. And so when we look at this, we can see that this story is comprehensible. So there is a character, there is a storyline, there's dialogue. All of those things are going to add to that. We know it's instructive because it is aligned to that phonics program's scope and sequence. And it's engaging. We can look at the pictures. They're very colorful. They are objects and animals that are familiar to children, so they're going to want to read about them, like cats and mice. All of those things are going to add to the story being engaging.

**(06:29)** So take some time now to try it out. Choose a decodable text from your library, or if you don't have access to a decodable text, look one up online. You can check out the preview at the end of today's lesson. You'll also have a downloadable bonus content that is going to include four different decodable texts, so you can utilize that as well. Whichever decodable text you choose, take a moment to evaluate that and see if it is comprehensible, so it has a storyline that makes sense; if it's instructive, and now remember, that's really going to depend on what has been previously taught to your students, so maybe just think through your grade-level scope and sequence; and is it engaging, so are students going to want to read that book? After you've done that, you can go ahead and jump back on the video. We're going to talk about what we can do to really leverage our decodable texts to get as much use of them as we can.

**(07:41)** Okay, so leveraging decodable texts. This quote and image come from Wiley Blevins' book, *Differentiating Phonics Instruction for Maximum Practice*, which I've referenced before on these videos, and I would highly recommend that you read it. He has a lot of wonderful things to say, not just about decodables but other aspects of word recognition as well. But since decodable texts are so beneficial to developing a student's word recognition skills, teachers are really starting to dedicate more and more instructional time to their use, and that's a really good thing. But with that, we want to make sure that we are still addressing all areas of the reading rope, and decodable texts really can help us do this.

**(08:30)** So this pie chart here talks about how decodables can be used for more than just phonics practice. So yes, phonics application is going to be a component of your instruction with decodable texts as well as building fluency. In fact, you can see that these are bold because that's going to be the majority, about 50%, of what you do with those texts, but we still want to incorporate other elements as well, such as syntax and text cohesion, writing and spelling, comprehension and early reading behaviors, so things such as print concepts and tracking. All of those components are still important to teach to students, and we can use decodable texts to teach those as well as vocabulary and oral language. So not only can decodable texts be used for these, we should be using decodable texts for these components. So make sure that you're being very intentional with how you utilize decodable texts so that we're not just focusing on the decoding.

**(09:43)** This also comes from Blevins, and it's a decodable text instructional routine. When you look at these components, you're going to notice that this routine is very similar to what we would do with a leveled text. Before we start reading, we're going to prepare students to have success by making sure that they have the academic vocabulary and they have the high-frequency words that they're going to read in that text.

**(10:12)** You also are going to want to make sure that students are familiar with the phonics skill that is going to be focused on in the text. So it's possible that you've done that in a whole-group Tier 1 setting, but it's also possible that your students might be reviewing a skill that was taught in Tier 1 instruction in previous years, and so it's more of a Tier 2 teaching that you're doing, and you're going to need to provide that explicit instruction in your small group before they start reading the book. So be mindful of those things before reading.

**(10:46)** During reading the book, you're going to provide that corrective feedback. Check in on students. How are they doing with decoding and applying their phonics knowledge to a text, and how are they doing at understanding and comprehending what they're reading?

**(11:05)** After reading, you're going to check on their comprehension. How did they do at understanding and following the story? Help them make connections between other books as well as what you're learning in a whole group. Reinforce that vocabulary and provide students an opportunity to extend their learning by doing a written response. So all of those things are good components of a decodable text instructional routine.

**(11:37)** This is a quote from Laura Stewart, and she says, "Decodable text promotes the habit of attending to the letters in the word as the primary means of recognizing the word." The texts that we choose and put in front of our students really matter. If we are choosing books that force our students to rely on context to figure out what words are, we're not developing the reading circuit and their brain, but if we are giving students books that are allowing them the opportunity to sound out and to make connections between graphemes and phonemes multiple times in one text, we are strengthening that reading circuit and helping them orthographically map that pattern. That's what we want. So that self-teaching hypothesis that we've talked about earlier can be true for that student, that the more they read that pattern, the better they're going to get and the more they're going to be able to transfer their isolated skills practice to any text that they read. So it's really important that we are intentional with the texts that we give to our students.

**(12:57)** Today's learning extension is a series of podcasts from *Melissa and Lori Love Literacy*, and it is all about the research on decodable texts, so a great listen if you're wanting to know more about how to evaluate the decodable texts that you choose, as well as some of the research that supports this practice.

**(13:21)** We're at the end of Module 4, so we have some wonderful bonus material for you available to download. From Lesson 4, we have our phonological and phonemic awareness assessment. From Lesson 5, we have our word mapping mats. Lesson 6, we have some high-frequency word activities. Lesson 7, we have syllable posters, and then Lesson 8, we have four different decodable texts for you to download, as well as an editable lesson plan template that is going to walk you through developing a well-rounded word recognition lesson plan. So wonderful, excellent bonus material for you to check out.

**(14:07)** Thank you so much for joining us for our last lesson of Module 4. Please remember to comment in our SOR Academy Facebook group. We just love hearing from you. And then make sure you join us for Module 5, focused on language comprehension.

## Decodable Texts and What to Look For

## Evaluative Criteria

Comprehensible

Instructive

Engaging

## Try It Out!: Choose a decodable text and evaluate if it is comprehensive, instructive, and engaging.

Additional Notes

## Leveraging Decodable Texts

## Additional Notes

## Decodable Text Instructional Routine

Before Reading

During Reading

After Reading

# Bonus Content

**Use the questions below to prompt discussion amongst your colleagues.**

1. **Purpose and Importance:** Why are decodable texts considered crucial in early reading instruction? Discuss how they support the development of phonics skills and decoding strategies.
2. **Criteria for Selection:** According to the video, what criteria should educators consider when selecting decodable texts for their students? How does aligning these texts with an instructional scope and sequence enhance their effectiveness?
3. **Balancing Decodability and Engagement:** How can educators strike a balance between ensuring a text is comprehensible and engaging while still being largely decodable? Discuss the implications of including nondecodable words in these texts.
4. **Instructional Strategies:** Explore the instructional routine recommended for using decodable texts effectively. What are the key components of this routine, and how do they support both decoding skills and broader literacy goals?
5. **Research and Practice:** Based on the discussion of the self-teaching hypothesis and orthographic mapping, how do decodable texts facilitate independent reading skills and transfer of phonics knowledge? Discuss the research supporting the use of decodable texts in literacy instruction.

**To extend your understanding of this topic, work through the activities below with a small group of peers.**

**Text Evaluation Workshop**
In small groups, evaluate a selection of decodable texts based on the criteria discussed (comprehensibility, instructiveness, engagement). Compare findings and discuss implications for classroom use.

**Decodable Text Scavenger Hunt**
Search online or in educational catalogs for decodable texts aligned with various phonics programs or scope and sequence documents. Share findings and discuss how these texts could be integrated into different instructional contexts.

**Phonics Skill Integration Exercise**
Create lesson plans or activities that integrate specific phonics skills into decodable text readings. Share these plans with peers and discuss their potential effectiveness in supporting student learning.

**Reading and Response Session**
Select a decodable text and simulate a reading session where one participant reads aloud while others observe. Discuss strategies for providing corrective feedback and promoting comprehension during and after the reading.

**Podcast Discussion on Research**
Listen to the recommended podcasts about research on decodable texts. Summarize key findings and implications for classroom practice. Discuss any new insights gained and brainstorm ways to implement evidence-based practices in teaching decodable texts.

**Additional Resources**
Scan to access four decodable texts, each representing a different phonics focus skill. Each book would appear at a different part of a sequential scope and sequence; therefore, the skills would build and spiral.

MODULE 5

# Supporting Language Development

In Module 5, we'll explore the "top half" of Scarborough's Reading Rope as we discuss all things language comprehension. First, we'll discuss the importance of building background knowledge, highlighting how our prior experiences and knowledge shape our understanding of what we read. We will unpack how the structure and meaning of language influence our comprehension. Finally, we'll focus on developing fluency, examining how fluency can be a vital bridging process to reading comprehension. These discussions will provide educators with valuable insights into fostering effective language comprehension skills in their students.

As you watch the videos in this module, use the pages that follow to write notes about what you are learning as well as reflect on the new information presented to you.

## Watch

The following videos are part of this learning module. Go to ScienceOfReadingAcademy.com to access each of the videos.

Lesson 1: Building Background Knowledge
Lesson 2: Developing Vocabulary
Lesson 3: Syntax and Semantics
Lesson 4: Verbal Reasoning
Lesson 5: Developing Fluency

## Before you begin

To activate your schema about the module topics, use your current knowledge and experience to reflect on the questions below.

1. How do you think having background knowledge about a topic can help with understanding a text?

2. Why do you think having a strong vocabulary is important for reading well?

3. How do you think understanding sentence structure and word meanings helps in reading and writing?

**A note about the bonus content in this module:**

Each lesson in this module focuses on one aspect of supporting language development. To help illustrate these aspects, we have provided published lessons from the Structured Literacy with E.A.S.E. program as well as an editable language comprehension lesson plan template. Read below for more detail.

**Additional Resources—Published Lesson Plans**
Scan to access four complete lesson plans from the Structured Literacy with E.A.S.E. program. These lessons go along with the decodable texts you received in the previous module. The purpose of sharing these samples is to show how language comprehension can be supported in a comprehensive structured literacy lesson. The details provided in the bonus content for each lesson in this module draw your attention to a specific part of the sample lessons that coincide with the lesson topic.

**Additional Resources—Editable Lesson Plan Template**
Additionally, you can scan to access an editable template that walks you through developing a language comprehension lesson. It is important to note that this lesson template complements the word recognition lesson. Both templates should be used to create a well-rounded lesson that addresses all strands of Scarborough's Reading Rope. You will be prompted to force a copy of the template into your own drive. The template has directions in each box to guide you through lesson planning. Delete the directions to type in your actual lesson plans.

# Lesson 1: Building Background Knowledge

*Module 5, Lesson 1 of the Science of Reading Academy emphasizes the critical role of background knowledge in reading comprehension. Background knowledge refers to the information and understanding a person already possesses before encountering new material. Dr. Conner discusses how studies illustrate that background knowledge significantly enhances comprehension. Students who had prior knowledge about a topic related to the reading material outperformed those who did not, regardless of their reading ability. This underscores the importance of educators fostering diverse and rich content knowledge across subjects to help students better understand and engage with what they read. Below is the transcript for the Module 5, Lesson 1 video.*

**(00:06)** Hello, and welcome back to the Science of Reading Academy. My name is Dr. Lindsey Conner, and I am so excited to dive into a brand-new module today. Module 5 will focus on how we can support students' language development.

**(00:22)** Word recognition gets a lot of attention and buzz when it comes to the Science of Reading, but the research is absolutely clear. Reading is more than just word recognition. We must be intentional about developing all strands of the reading rope, including those associated with language development. Today we will specifically be discussing background knowledge and its critical role in reading.

**(00:50)** I always like to go back to Scarborough's Reading Rope to really help center our learning. During Module 4, we talked about word recognition, and those are the bottom three strands of the rope, the phonological awareness, decoding, and sight recognition. During Module 5, we will really be discussing that top half of the rope, so background knowledge, vocabulary, language structure, verbal reasoning, and literacy knowledge.

**(01:24)** When working with early readers, you'll most likely have separate parts of your day that focus on word recognition and language comprehension, but as students become more proficient with their reading skills, these two components will become increasingly interwoven to allow for seamless decoding and comprehending at the same time.

**(01:49)** This quote by Jennifer Jump and Kathleen Kopp reflects that principle. They state, "In considering the language comprehension of the reading models, students must have both the understanding of the structures of the language and the knowledge and vocabulary needed to connect them together." And we know that as educators, that reading skills don't occur in vacuums, right? We must empower students with the skills for interweaving all of these components together.

**(02:24)** So to help us do that, we can help facilitate background knowledge with our students. *Background knowledge* refers to the information and understanding that a person already has before encountering new information or learning something new. So the definition listed says, "Knowledge of facts and concepts about a topic, problem, or situation students have when engaging with instructional content." So this is certainly not limited to reading, but this preexisting knowledge will help individuals make sense of any reading that they do. So background knowledge can come from various sources, including personal experiences as well as educational experiences.

**(03:19)** So one study that really helps us understand the importance of the background knowledge, particularly in reading comprehension, is often referenced as the Baseball Study. This study was conducted by researchers Donna Wright and Lauren Leslie in 1988. It provides insightful findings on how what we already know can significantly influence our ability to understand new information. In this study, the researchers worked with middle school students, dividing them into groups based on their reading skills—so if they were good readers or poor readers, as well as their knowledge of baseball, whether they had high knowledge or low knowledge. The students were asked to read a passage about a baseball game, and afterwards they were tested on how well they understood and remembered the details.

**(04:20)** The results were eye-opening. Students who were good readers with high knowledge of baseball performed well. That probably doesn't surprise you, but what was surprising was that good readers who had low knowledge of baseball struggled more than poor readers who knew a lot about the game. This clearly demonstrated that having background knowledge about a topic can significantly enhance comprehension, sometimes even more so than general reading ability.

**(04:57)** So what does this mean for us in education? This study really highlights the crucial role of building background knowledge in students. It's not just about teaching reading skills. It's also about providing rich, diverse content knowledge across subjects. By doing so, we can help students make a better sense of what they read and learn more effectively. Really, the Baseball Study teaches us that background knowledge is a powerful tool. It shows that what students bring to the table in terms of prior knowledge can greatly impact their reading comprehension.

**(05:36)** So let's try it out. I'm going to display a pretty technical passage on the next slide. I want you to pause the video and read the passage. Your task is then to summarize the main idea of the passage in one sentence. Okay, here we go.

**(06:00)** Okay. So after pausing and reading that passage, think: How did your prior knowledge impact your comprehension, whether that was positively or negatively? My guess was if you didn't know much about that topic, which I certainly did not, then it was difficult for you to follow what was even being talked about in that selection. If you were given a test where you were asked to summarize the main idea of this passage, you probably would perform poorly, but you really don't need an intervention on summarizing the main idea, right? If I gave you a passage on classroom management, you could summarize that in no time flat. What you need is more background knowledge on anaerobic fermentation, and this theme is often true for our students. We're providing them interventions on skills and strategies when it really was just a lack of background knowledge about that particular subject. So we need to be cognizant of how background knowledge impacts our students when they are reading.

**(07:14)** Here's an example of one way that you can build background knowledge with your students. So this is from the Structured Literacy with E.A.S.E program, and they call these Background Builders. So this Background Builder is an informational paragraph about pollution, and that background information is going to help students better comprehend the plot and the decodable text about a stuck duck. There are other ways that you can build background knowledge with your students, including videos, songs, and even photographs. You just need to be intentional about figuring out how to pull in those pieces to help aid your students' understanding.

**(07:57)** Our learning extension for today is an article from Reading Rockets about building background knowledge. So this has some great tips and tricks for you to check out.

**(08:08)** Thank you so much for joining us. For the first lesson of Module 5, please remember to join our SOR Academy Facebook group and comment on our Module 5, Lesson 1 thread. We can't wait to hear from you.

## Scarborough's Reading Rope: The Top Half

## Additional Notes

## Background Knowledge

## Baseball Study: What does it teach us as teachers?

## Additional Notes

## Pause and Reflect: How did your prior background knowledge positively or negatively impact your comprehension of the passage?

# Bonus Content

**Use the questions below to prompt discussion amongst your colleagues.**

1. **Understanding Background Knowledge:** How does Dr. Conner define background knowledge in the context of reading comprehension? Why is it crucial for students' overall reading development?
2. **Research Insights:** Discuss the findings of the "baseball study" and their implications for teaching. What does this study reveal about the relationship between background knowledge and reading comprehension?
3. **Integration of Skills:** According to the module, how can educators integrate word recognition skills with language comprehension skills as students progress in reading proficiency? What strategies can facilitate this integration?
4. **Educational Implications:** Reflect on the quote by Jennifer Jump and Kathleen Kopp about language comprehension in reading models. How can educators apply this principle in their instructional practices to enhance students' reading abilities?
5. **Practical Applications:** Based on the examples provided, such as Background Builders and other techniques, discuss practical ways educators can build and activate background knowledge in diverse classroom settings. How can these strategies be adapted across different subjects and grade levels?

**To extend your understanding of this topic, work through the activities below with a small group of peers.**

**Text Analysis and Background Knowledge**
Select a passage or article that is unfamiliar to the group. Read the passage individually and discuss how each person's background knowledge influenced their comprehension. Compare and contrast the interpretations based on varying levels of prior knowledge.

**Background Knowledge Mapping**
Create a visual map or chart that illustrates how background knowledge connects to different aspects of reading comprehension, including vocabulary acquisition, inference making, and text understanding. Share and discuss these maps to identify common themes and strategies.

**Case Study Analysis**
Review case studies or classroom scenarios where students' background knowledge significantly impacted their reading comprehension outcomes. Discuss strategies that could have been employed to better support these students and enhance their comprehension abilities.

**Content Integration Workshop**
In small groups, develop lesson plans that integrate background knowledge activities into specific content areas (e.g., science, history). Share these plans and discuss how they align with both literacy and subject-specific learning objectives.

**Resource Exploration**
Explore resources and materials, such as videos, songs, photographs, and informational texts, that can be used to build background knowledge in various subjects. Evaluate these resources based on their potential effectiveness in enhancing students' understanding and engagement.

**Additional Resources**
Building Background Knowledge DAY 2 in the lesson plan: Use the questions in the "Before Reading" Questions heading to activate and build schema before reading. Allow students time to think-pair-share before sharing responses with the group. Possible answers are included in parentheses following each question in the lesson plan. (Note, Day 1 also includes a front-loading activity, Background Builders, where the teacher can go over any important topics/concepts with certain learners prior to asking them to read the decodable text. Also, Semantics Activities (Day 2) are used to build background knowledge; more detail about semantics activities in Lesson 3.

# Lesson 2: Developing Vocabulary

*Module 5, Lesson 2 of the Science of Reading Academy underscores the critical role of vocabulary development in enhancing reading proficiency. Vocabulary is a foundational strand within language comprehension that directly impacts overall reading ability. Dr. Conner emphasizes the importance of both breadth and depth of vocabulary knowledge, highlighting how a wide range of known words and a deep understanding of their meanings correlate significantly with reading comprehension and fluency. She introduces the concept of lexical quality, which encompasses various components like orthography, morphology, syntax, semantics, and phonology, all crucial for robust vocabulary skills. Furthermore, she discusses Isabel Beck's three-tiered framework for categorizing vocabulary, emphasizing the strategic focus on Tier 2 words — high-utility academic terms critical for understanding complex texts across subjects. Below is the transcript for the Module 5, Lesson 2 video.*

**(00:07)** Hello, and welcome back to the Science of Reading Academy. We're in Module 5, exploring language development and its role in developing proficient readers.

**(00:17)** During our last lesson, we examined the significance of background knowledge in reading comprehension. Today we will focus on strategies for developing vocabulary. These two concepts are closely related. Background knowledge provides the context that enriches understanding, while vocabulary supplies the words necessary to articulate and comprehend that knowledge. It's important to be intentional in developing both areas as they really work together to strengthen a student's reading proficiency and overall literacy skills. So I'm really excited to dive deep into the importance of developing vocabulary with you all today.

**(01:04)** To really help center our learning, we can return to the reading rope model, which was developed by Dr. Hollis Scarborough. This model illustrates how multiple strands of language skills intertwine to create skilled reading. You'll see vocabulary here is the second strand in the language comprehension subset. So vocabulary is really important. You'll remember from Module 2 that if one of these strands is weak or missing, this whole strand right here, so this whole language comprehension strand, is compromised, which will eventually impact all of reading. A robust vocabulary will really allow students to make sense of the words they decode, which will enrich their overall comprehension and engagement with the text. Without a strong vocabulary, students may struggle to grasp the meaning of what they read, making it much harder to achieve fluid and meaningful reading.

**(02:11)** This quote states that "Both the vocabulary breadth and depth were significantly correlated with reading comprehension and reading rate." We know that this means that students with a wide range of known words—that breadth—and a deep rich understanding of these words—or the depth—are more likely to comprehend text effectively and read at a faster pace. So *breadth* is referencing the number of words a person knows, while *depth* is referencing how well a person knows the words. When students encounter new words, a broad vocabulary helps them make educated guesses about meanings, and a deep understanding enables them to grasp subtle nuances and connections within the text.

**(03:06)** Now, one area we really need to think about to help us ensure vocabulary depth is lexical quality. *Lexical quality* refers to how well a word is represented in a person's mental lexicon, which is basically like your brain's dictionary that's storing all of the words that you know. And a high-quality lexical representation is going to include the following components. First, you're going to have orthography. That's the spelling of the word, which involves recognizing and remembering the letter patterns and sequences that form the word. Strong orthographic knowledge helps students quickly identify and read words accurately.

**(03:54)** There's also morphology. *Morphology* is going to focus on the structure of words such as their roots, their prefixes, and their suffixes. This will allow students to not only decode complex words but also understand their meanings and see how words relate to each other.

**(04:15)** *Syntax* here in the yellow refers to the grammatical rules that govern how words are combined into sentences. A solid grasp of syntax helps students understand the relationship between words in a sentence and how different sentence structures can alter meaning.

**(04:34)** *Semantics* involves the meaning of a word, including its definitions, connotations, and the context in which it can be used. Semantic knowledge ensures that students not only recognize a word but also understand its meaning and use it appropriately in different contexts.

**(04:54)** And finally, phonology. *Phonology* is the study of the sounds of a language, which include the phonemes that make up words. So this is going to be your phonemic awareness portion, right? Knowledge of phonology aids in pronunciation, decoding unfamiliar words, and distinguishing between similar sounding words.

**(05:18)** So when we put all of these components together, we're creating a really comprehensive and high-quality mental representation of a word. When students have this strong lexical quality, they can easily retrieve and use words in their reading and writing, which leads to better comprehension and more fluent reading.

**(05:39)** So if you can think back to when we talked about orthographic mapping, we know that we have to connect all four processors together. The meaning processor, the context processor, the phonological processor, all the processors must work together. And lexical quality is very much related to that and the fact that we want high-quality representations of words in order to be able to retrieve them more easily.

**(06:10)** When it comes to vocabulary instruction, understanding the three tiers of vocabulary can really help us prioritize which words to teach. This framework here was developed by Isabelle Beck and colleagues, and it categorizes words into three levels based on their frequency and complexity. Now, one thing that's really important to note is this tiered system is different than the tiers of support system where you might think of Tier 1 as being things that all students receive or Tier 2 as being small-group instruction. This is not that. This is totally different. Just same category words here. So when you're thinking of Tier 1 vocabulary words, these are everyday words that most students will already know and use regularly. They include simple words like *dog, house, run, up, happy*. Since most students know these words, they do not typically need direct instruction, so Tier 1 vocabulary will just often come through conversation and listening and reading. They're words that students are going to pick up on most of the time automatically.

**(07:26)** Now, Tier 2, those are high-utility words. They're really going to focus on academic vocabulary. Those words are going to occur across a variety of subjects and contexts, but they're not going to be commonly used in everyday conversation. So examples might include *analyze, predict, evaluate, contrast*—almost test-taking words come to mind when I think of Tier 2. Tier 2 words should be a primary focus for vocabulary instruction because they're versatile and they improve students' ability to comprehend academic text and engage in classroom discussions.

**(08:10)** Now, Tier 3 words at the very top here, these words are specific to particular subjects or fields of study such as *photosynthesis* and biology or *alliteration* and literature. Tier 3 words should be taught as they arise within the context of subject-specific lessons. Instructions should include direct teaching and opportunities for students to engage with these words in meaningful ways that are related to the content that they are learning. Really though, the majority of our direct vocabulary instruction is going to focus on Tier 2 vocabulary words.

**(08:53)** So challenge yourself, pause the video, and take a minute here to classify each of these words that come from an elementary science text. So you're going to say, if each word—*side, depend, pollinate, mimic, sun,* and *quadratic*—are Tier 1, Tier 2, or Tier 3 words. So remember, Tier 1 words are everyday words. Tier 2 words are high-utility academic words, and Tier 3 are content-specific words. So pause, jot down your thoughts, and then come back for the answers.

**(09:34)** Okay, let's see how you did here. So Tier 1 words, those everyday common words, would be *sun* and *side*. Your Tier 2 words would be *mimic* and *depend*. So if you think about that, you can use those words in a variety of contexts. They do not have to be specific to a subject. Tier 3 is *quadratic* and *pollinate*, and those are going to be more subject specific: *quadratic*, more math specific, and *pollinate*, more science specific. And so those aren't going to have as much of a transfer across a student's academic day.

**(10:18)** Here's an example from the Structured Literacy with E.A.S.E. program, where they've pulled out two Tier 2 vocabulary words from a decodable text that students read. So students will learn and explore the word *selfless* as well as the word *gig*. So they're talking about synonyms, antonyms, and definitions so that students are getting multiple tiers of that lexical quality. And these words are in that Tier 2 high-yield vocabulary band.

**(10:54)** Alright, so we're almost done with our video. It's a great time to pause and reflect and think: How is vocabulary knowledge directly connected to comprehension, and how do you as an educator decide which new words to teach students? So pause, jot down your thoughts, and then join us back for our learning extensions.

**(11:21)** Okay, thank you so much for joining us today for this lesson focused on vocabulary. There are two learning extensions for you. The first is a podcast about the second, which is a book. So both are from Tanya S. Wright, who is a wonderful expert on vocabulary development. So in the podcast, you can hear her speaking about her book, and then her book itself is a wonderful resource.

**(11:53)** Thank you so much for joining us today, and please remember to join and visit the SOR Academy Facebook group to comment on the Module 5, Lesson 2 thread. We can't wait to see you for Lesson 3.

## Scarborough's Reading Rope: The Second Strand
What happens if one strand is weak?

Additional Notes

## Vocabulary Breadth vs. Vocabulary Depth

Breadth

Depth

## Lexical Quality

Orthography

Morphology

Syntax

Semantics

Phonology

## Three Tiers of Vocabulary

Tier 1: Everyday, common words

Tier 2: Academic vocabulary

Tier 3: Content-specific words

Additional Notes

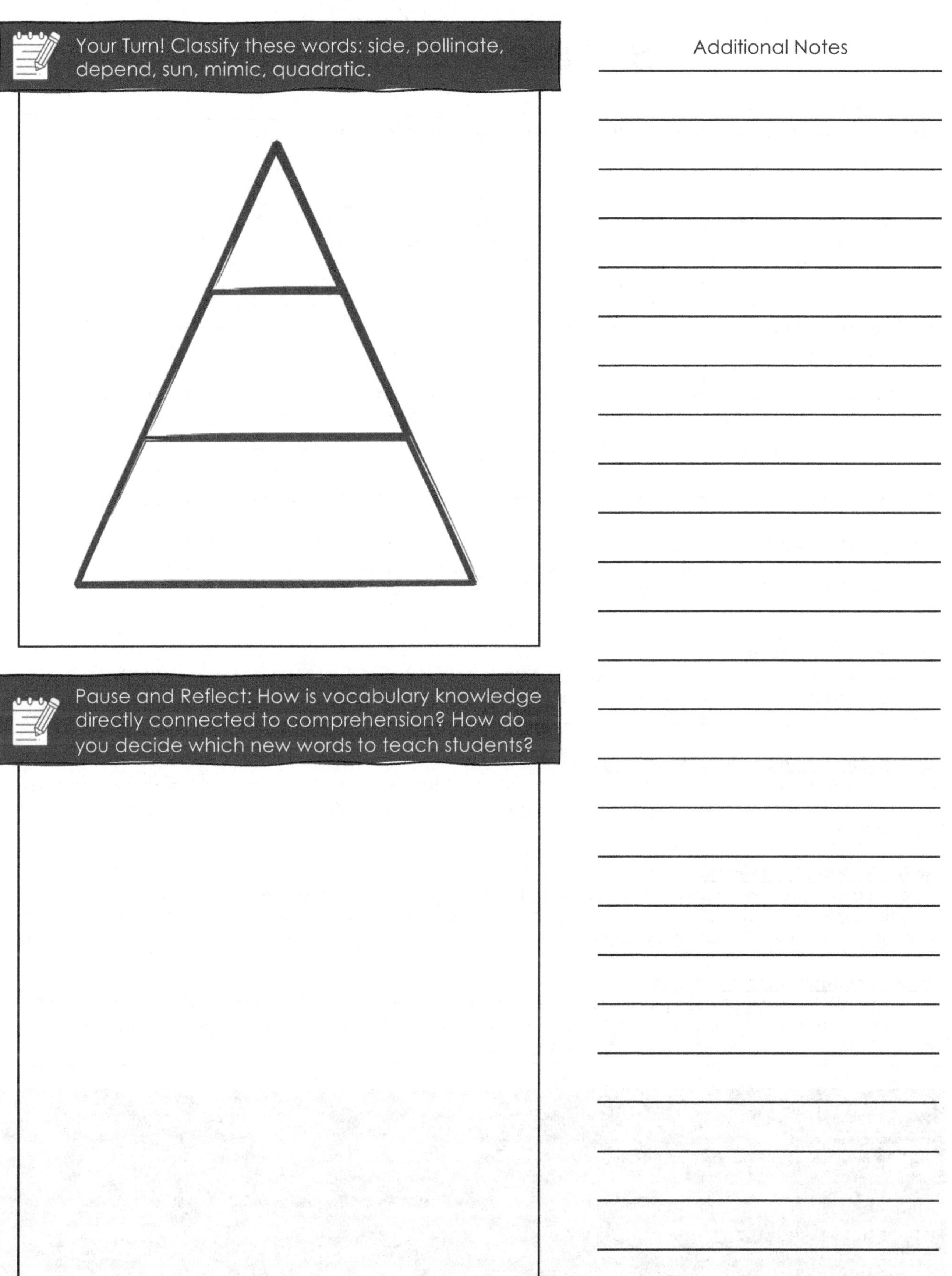
Your Turn! Classify these words: side, pollinate, depend, sun, mimic, quadratic.
Pause and Reflect: How is vocabulary knowledge directly connected to comprehension? How do you decide which new words to teach students?

Additional Notes

# Bonus Content

**Use the questions below to prompt discussion amongst your colleagues.**

1. **Role of Vocabulary in Reading:** According to Dr. Conner, how does vocabulary contribute to overall reading proficiency? Discuss its role in both decoding and comprehension processes.
2. **Vocabulary Depth and Breadth:** Explain the concepts of vocabulary breadth and depth as discussed in the video. How do these aspects influence students' ability to comprehend texts effectively?
3. **Components of Lexical Quality:** Dr. Conner mentions several components of lexical quality (orthography, morphology, syntax, semantics, phonology). Discuss how each component contributes to building a strong mental lexicon. Why is this important for students' literacy development?
4. **Three Tiers of Vocabulary:** Describe the three-tiered framework for categorizing vocabulary (Tier 1, Tier 2, Tier 3). Why is it crucial for educators to prioritize Tier 2 vocabulary in instructional planning? Provide examples to illustrate each tier.
5. **Strategies for Vocabulary Instruction:** Based on the video, what are some effective strategies educators can use to teach vocabulary? How can these strategies be adapted across different grade levels and subjects to enhance students' comprehension skills?

**To extend your understanding of this topic, work through the activities below with a small group of peers.**

**Vocabulary Analysis Workshop**
In small groups, analyze vocabulary lists from different subject textbooks or reading materials. Classify each word into Tier 1, Tier 2, or Tier 3 categories. Discuss strategies for effectively teaching Tier 2 words in various academic contexts.

**Lexical Quality Stations**
Create learning stations focused on different components of lexical quality (orthography, morphology, syntax, semantics, phonology). Participants rotate through stations to explore how each component contributes to vocabulary development and comprehension.

**Vocabulary Depth and Breadth Case Studies**
Review case studies or student profiles where vocabulary depth or breadth significantly impacted reading comprehension. Discuss instructional strategies that could have supported these students' vocabulary development.

**Semantic Mapping Exercise**
Choose a complex text or passage and conduct a semantic mapping exercise as a group. Identify key vocabulary words and discuss their meanings, connections, and contextual usage. Reflect on how semantic mapping can enhance comprehension skills.

**Tiered Vocabulary Lesson Planning**
Collaboratively develop lesson plans that focus on teaching Tier 2 vocabulary words. Consider incorporating activities such as word webs, synonym/antonym exploration, and context-based usage scenarios. Share and critique these lesson plans to refine instructional practices.

**Additional Resources**
Vocabulary DAY 3 in the lesson plan: Use the lesson plan wording to discuss vocabulary from the text. Begin by asking students to blend the sounds in any *decodable* words on the list. Then, discuss the vocabulary terms with students. Help students locate the definition, then locate and/or brainstorm synonyms and antonyms (when applicable) for each word. To support dictionary skills, you can do this using a physical or online dictionary. Students can create illustrations and/or an original sentence for each word using a reading journal, notebook paper, or a dry-erase board. (Note, **Day 1** also includes a front-loading activity, Building Vocabulary, where ELLs use pictures from the text to name items/concepts in the picture. In addition, **Day 2** includes specific words from the text that should be reviewed with ELLs.)

**MODULE 5: Supporting Language Development**

# Lesson 3: Syntax and Semantics

*Module 5, Lesson 3 of the Science of Reading Academy delves into the fundamental concepts of syntax and semantics within language development. Syntax, focusing on sentence structure and grammar rules, and semantics, centered on nuanced meanings and word relationships, are pivotal in shaping proficient readers. Dr. Conner emphasizes their integration into language comprehension, highlighting their roles in enhancing reading, writing, and communication skills. Educators are encouraged to provide direct instruction in both syntax and semantics to foster comprehensive language understanding among students. Below is the transcript for the Module 5, Lesson 3 video.*

**(00:07)** Hello, and welcome back to the Science of Reading Academy. We're in Module 5, focused on exploring language development and its role in developing proficient readers. So far, we have covered the crucial roles of background knowledge and vocabulary in language comprehension, emphasizing how they really form that foundation of skilled reading. Today we will shift our focus to two essential components of language structure: syntax and semantics. Understanding these elements is key to developing proficient readers who can navigate complex text with ease. And I know at least for me as an educator, this is an area where I still have a lot of learning to do. So I'm excited to dive in with you all today.

**(01:00)** So we'll again go back to Scarborough's Reading Rope. We are really focused on this language comprehension component, and we've talked about background knowledge and vocabulary. Today, syntax and semantics are really subcomponents of the language rope component language structure. So they'll both fall into this strand right here.

**(01:26)** You can kind of think about it this way: Syntax, or sentence structure, combined with semantics, which is nuanced meanings, is together going to form the foundation of language structure. Now, if you're anything like me, it's really tricky to keep syntax and semantics separate in my mind, so I always remember semantics, with the M, is all about meaning, and that has helped me keep them straight so far. So when you are combining these two, syntax and semantics, you are helping students develop a comprehensive understanding of language structure, which is going to not only help their reading but also help their writing and even their communication skills.

**(02:20)** So when we teach syntax, we're talking about all of the rules that govern how words are arranged into phrases and clauses and sentences. So these are lessons on grammar, right? Word order, sentence structure, all of those pieces are those grammar standards that we teach. Whereas semantics is dealing more with the meaning, and so it's going to be lessons on comprehending and interpreting the meanings of words in different contexts. So things like figurative language and really grasping nuances of our language, such as connotations and other things like alliteration, metaphors, those types of things.

**(03:08)** So this quote states that "Since both syntax and semantics play a role in language, to learn to comprehend more complex text effectively, students should have direct instruction in both the structure of a language and how it constructs meaning." These two areas are sometimes overlooked in direct instruction, but it really is important to purposefully plan for both. So let's look at some possible lesson ideas and discuss if they're focusing on syntax or semantics.

**(03:50)** Here's our first activity, a lesson on subject–predicate agreement. So syntax or semantics? If you guessed syntax, you are correct. Syntax involves the rules and structures that govern how words are arranged to form sentences, and subject–predicate agreement is a key aspect of these rules.

**(04:18)** Alright, syntax or semantics: creating a word web to investigate the relationships among words. If you guessed semantics, you are correct. Remember, semantics, with the M, is dealing with the meaning of words and the relationships between them. A word web helps students explore and understand these relationships, which will deepen their knowledge of word meanings and how they connect to each other within different contexts.

**(04:53)** Okay, what about this one? Syntax or semantics: completing a sort with a word's synonyms and antonyms. Alright, if you said semantics, you are correct. Thinking about a word's synonyms and antonyms is going to focus your brain on a word's meaning. So that is semantics.

**(05:17)** Last one here. Syntax or semantics: providing practice on combining sentences. This one was kind of tricky. This is primarily a syntax activity, right? Students are using the rules and structures regarding how words and phrases are arranged to form more complex sentences, but they might also be tapping into the meaning of words a little bit, so you might incorporate some semantics as well, but primarily this would be a syntax activity.

**(05:52)** Alright. So put it in your own words. Pause the video to provide your own definition of syntax and semantics, which, by the way, this activity of having students put new vocabulary words into their own words can be a really helpful activity to build up that vocabulary and focus on semantics. So pause and then come back for some activity ideas.

**(06:23)** Alright, so syntax in action; so syntax is focusing on that word structure. This is an activity called Sentence Anagrams, and the activity of Sentence Anagrams is going to involve rearranging the words of a given sentence to form a new sentence that still makes grammatical sense. It's a really fun and engaging way for students to practice and reinforce their understanding of syntax and sentence structure.

**(06:52)** So you're going to want to start with a complete sentence that has a clear meaning and is grammatically correct. So, for example, you might start with, "The quick brown fox jumps over the lazy dog." Students are then going to rearrange the words of the sentence to create new permutations while maintaining grammatical accuracy. Using our example, an anagram might be, "The lazy dog jumps over the quick brown fox." The challenge is really to ensure that their rearranged sentence still conveys a coherent meaning that is similar to the original sentence. This is going to encourage students to consider how different word orders can impact the clarity and emphasis of a sentence. So you could do it on a Google slide and just display it up on your board for students, but you could also do it in a pocket chart on index cards and start with the sentence written correctly and then have students rearrange it from there. So it's a really fun, almost like a brain teaser, and students enjoy doing it.

**(08:02)** Another activity is Prepositions. So you can display a picture of a chess game board or really any game that is going to have pieces that students move. And then you're going to place students in either partners or small groups and have them practice "moving" the chess pieces across the board using prepositions. So if you are teaching those younger grades and you're really working on positional words, this can be a great activity for you to really enforce that semantics. So, for an example, "He moved the chess piece over the king and beside the queen." This would be tricky if students don't know those chess piece names, so that's where you might pull in another board game that students might have more connection to.

**(09:00)** Alright, pause and reflect. Think about your classroom and the group of students that you see every day. What strategies will you use to teach syntax and semantics? After you've jotted down your thoughts, then come back and listen for today's learning extensions.

**(09:20)** If you want to learn more about the intricacies of linguistics, the podcast series *Linguistics with Lara* is a great listen. For you language gurus, this is going to give you all of the information you could ever want to know about our language. And this blog post by Shanahan really discusses the importance of sentence level comprehension, and this particular article has great practical implications for your work in the classroom, so this would be a more actionable next step for your learning extension if you're interested in that.

**(10:02)** Alright, thank you so much for joining us today for Module 5, Lesson 3. We can't wait to see you next time for Lesson 4. Have a great day.

## Syntax + Semantics = Language Structure

Syntax

Semantics

Language Structure

## Syntax or Semantics?

1. A lesson on subject-predicate agreement

2. Creating a word web to investigate relationships among words

3. Completing a sort with a word's synonyms and antonyms

4. Providing practice on combining sentences

## Put It in Your Own Words: Provide a definition of syntax and semantics in your own words.

Additional Notes

## Syntax in Action: Sentence Anagrams

## Semantics in Action: Prepositions

## Pause and Reflect: What strategies will you use to teach syntax and semantics?

Additional Notes

# Bonus Content

**Use the questions below to prompt discussion amongst your colleagues.**

1. **Syntax vs. Semantics:** How would you explain the difference between syntax and semantics to your students? Why are both important for understanding language?
2. **Teaching Approaches:** What instructional strategies would you use to teach syntax and semantics effectively in your classroom? How would you differentiate these strategies based on students' language proficiency levels?
3. **Integration into Curriculum:** How can you integrate lessons on syntax and semantics across different subjects or disciplines? Provide examples of how these language elements are crucial beyond English language arts.
4. **Practical Application:** Discuss a specific activity or lesson plan that you think effectively teaches either syntax or semantics. How does this activity align with the learning needs of your students?
5. **Assessment and Feedback:** What methods would you use to assess students' understanding of syntax and semantics? How would you provide constructive feedback to help students improve their grasp of these concepts?

**To extend your understanding of this topic, work through the activities below with a small group of peers.**

**Sentence Anagrams**
Provide students with sentences that they rearrange to form new grammatically correct sentences. Discuss how different arrangements affect meaning and emphasis.

**Semantic Word Web**
Create a word web exploring synonyms, antonyms, and associations of key vocabulary words. Discuss how these relationships deepen understanding of word meanings.

**Grammar Games**
Develop a game where students practice using prepositions or other syntactic elements in context, such as describing movements on a game board or map.

**Literature Analysis**
Analyze a piece of literature to identify examples of syntax and semantics. Discuss how the author's use of language contributes to the text's overall meaning and impact.

**Real-World Applications**
Assign students a task to find examples of syntax and semantics in real-world contexts, such as advertisements, news articles, or instructional manuals. Discuss the effectiveness of language choices in these contexts.

**Additional Resources**
Syntax and Semantics DAY 1 (syntax) and DAY 2 (semantics) in the lesson plan: Lessons in this sample program cycle through three syntax activities (taught during Day 1 Encoding) and seven different semantics activities (taught during Day 2 Background Knowledge). Syntax activities include sentence anagrams (organizing mixed up words into a coherent sentence using the logic of English), sentence elaboration (reading a sentence and pulling out the who, where, what, when, why, and how within them), and sentence combining (combining two or more shorter sentences into one coherent sentence). Semantics activities include synonyms, comparatives and superlatives, homophones, categorization and classification, semantic map, prepositions, and pronouns.

# Lesson 4: Verbal Reasoning

*Module 5, Lesson 4 of the Science of Reading Academy explores the crucial concept of verbal reasoning and its significant role in fostering proficient readers. Verbal reasoning encompasses the ability to analyze and infer from language-based information, crucial for comprehending text beyond its literal meaning. Dr. Conner emphasizes the integration of verbal reasoning with foundational skills like background knowledge, vocabulary, and language structure, stressing its pervasive impact across academic learning. Through explicit instruction in skills like making inferences and drawing conclusions, educators are equipped to scaffold students' development of these critical cognitive abilities, enhancing their reading comprehension and academic success. Below is the transcript for the Module 5, Lesson 4 video.*

**(00:07)** Hello, and welcome back to the Science of Reading Academy. We are in Module 5 and talking about all things language development and how it contributes to creating proficient readers. In today's lesson, we will explore the concept of verbal reasoning and its critical role in reading comprehension and language development. Verbal reasoning involves the ability to understand and analyze language-based information, so this is going to include things like making inferences and drawing conclusions. It's going to continue to build on several of those language skills that we've been talking about, background knowledge, vocabulary, and language structures. So let's get started.

**(00:53)** I am sure you are not surprised to see Scarborough's Reading Rope up on the screen. We always like to go back to it to anchor our learning. So we've been talking about this language comprehension rope here and the importance of background knowledge, vocabulary, language structure, and today we're really talking about verbal reasoning, so what that is and how it impacts our students.

**(01:22)** "Academic learning requires students to have considerable capacity for verbal reasoning and to be able to verbalize their verbal reasoning." So that quote includes the word *verbal* quite a bit, but really it just means that students must not only understand and analyze language-based information, but they also have to be able to express their thoughts clearly and effectively. This is going to impact reading comprehension as well as just about every other area of academic learning—everything from writing to discussions. This verbal reasoning component is essential.

**(02:07)** Now, we can define *verbal reasoning* as the ability to infer and draw conclusions to understand the text beyond the literal meaning. If you're anything like my state of Missouri, when you look at your reading standards, especially your reading comprehension standards, these words *infer, draw conclusions* are going to be all over it. Pretty much anything that we're asking our students to do with reading comprehension is going to require some sort of inferencing and some sort of drawing conclusions.

**(02:48)** So the question of course, is how do we teach verbal reasoning? And really it's not going to be, hey, here's a lesson on verbal reasoning. It's going to be on those subskills, those drawing conclusions lessons and that inference lesson. And honestly, for many of your students, they're going to need an explicit lesson on how to make an inference, and it's not going to just be a one and done lesson. It's going to be something that has to just become part of your vocabulary and part of your practice as an educator. So when we're explicitly teaching inferences, students need that modeling of how to take information from the text, so how to take text clues and combine it with the background knowledge in order to make that inference. And this process, when we're teaching this, that is supporting students' verbal reasoning skills.

**(03:45)** Here is an example from the Structured Literacy with E.A.S.E program that prompts students to make inferences regarding a decodable text. And something that this program does a great job of is providing that scaffold for students where it explicitly states, "Use your background knowledge and clues from the text to answer the questions." So students are prompted right away, hey, I'm going to need to use my background knowledge, and I'm also going to need to use text clues in order to be successful on this task. And that's just a really simple shift that you can make when you're writing your formative assessments, writing your assignments, however you're giving students practice with the skill, it's providing them that scaffold of what they're going to need in order to be successful with these types of questions.

**(04:37)** Alright, today's lesson was really brief. It's one of those things that is so simple but takes so much time and effort for our students to master. So take a moment, pause, and jot down your thoughts. How is making inferences an essential skill for comprehension? And after you've written down your thoughts, jump back on the video for a wonderful learning extension.

**(05:04)** Okay. Today's learning extension is a podcast by Dr. Rob Jackson, who is really focused on educational leaders, and he has a series that's going through each strand of the reading rope and how you can develop it. And there's not a lot of research out there, and I shouldn't say a lot of research, but there's not a lot of buzz out there about verbal reasoning, but he does a great job at combining lots of different sources into one succinct podcast, so a great listen if you would like to learn more.

**(05:41)** Alright, thank you so much for joining us today for Module 5, Lesson 4. Don't forget to visit the Facebook group and come back for Lesson 5. We have one more lesson in this module. We'll see you then.

## Verbal Reasoning

## Verbal Reasoning in Action! Teach Inference Making

Text Clues

Background Knowledge

Inference

## Put It in Your Own Words: How is making inferences an essential skill for reading comprehension?

Additional Notes

# Bonus Content

**Use the questions below to prompt discussion amongst your colleagues.**

1. **Definition and Importance:** How would you define verbal reasoning to your students? Why is it crucial for their overall academic success, beyond just reading comprehension?
2. **Teaching Strategies:** What instructional methods do you find most effective for teaching students how to make inferences and draw conclusions? How do you scaffold these skills for different levels of learners?
3. **Integration across Subjects:** In what ways can verbal reasoning skills be integrated into subjects beyond language arts? Provide examples of how these skills are applicable in science, social studies, or mathematics.
4. **Assessment and Feedback:** How do you assess students' proficiency in verbal reasoning? What types of feedback do you provide to help students improve in this area?
5. **Cultural and Linguistic Considerations:** How might cultural backgrounds or language proficiency affect students' development of verbal reasoning skills? What strategies can teachers use to support diverse learners in this aspect?

**To extend your understanding of this topic, work through the activities below with a small group of peers.**

**Inference Practice**
Provide students with short texts and ask them to identify text clues and use background knowledge to make inferences. Discuss how different interpretations can lead to varied conclusions.

**Discussion Circles**
Organize small groups to discuss challenging texts where students must justify their inferences and conclusions based on evidence from the text. Rotate roles such as facilitator, notetaker, and summarizer.

**Verbal Reasoning Games**
Create games like "What's Missing?" where students listen to a description or a story and then identify missing details or draw conclusions based on the information provided.

**Case Studies**
Present case studies or scenarios where students must apply verbal reasoning skills to understand motives, predict outcomes, or evaluate decisions made by characters or historical figures.

**Comparative Analysis**
Provide students with two versions of a text where details or interpretations vary slightly. Have them analyze how these differences impact the overall understanding and require different forms of verbal reasoning.

**Additional Resources**
Verbal Reasoning DAY 3 in the lesson plan: After students have finished reading the decodable text, use the "After Reading" Questions to guide discussion. These questions require students to use inference skills as well as teach students about nonliteral language. Allow students time to think-pair-share before sharing responses with the group. Possible responses are included in the lesson plan.

In many instances, the Metacognitive Strategies activities (Day 3) and Comprehension Skills and Strategies activities (Day 3) can also help build verbal reasoning skills.

**MODULE 5: Supporting Language Development**

# Lesson 5: Developing Fluency

*Module 5, Lesson 5 of the Science of Reading Academy delves into the critical skill of developing fluency in reading, which acts as a pivotal bridge between word recognition and comprehension. Using the framework of the active view of reading, the video highlights fluency as a key bridging process that integrates word recognition and language comprehension. Fluency encompasses three main components: accuracy, rate, and prosody. By focusing on these components, educators can help students move beyond basic decoding to fluid, expressive reading that enhances comprehension. This comprehensive approach underscores the importance of fluency in nurturing proficient readers who engage deeply with text beyond surface-level decoding. Below is the transcript for the Module 5, Lesson 5 video.*

**(00:07)** Welcome back to the Science of Reading Academy. We'll be wrapping up Module 5 today, which is focused on strategies for supporting language development. In today's lesson, we will focus on developing fluency, which is really a crucial bridging skill that helps students combine their word recognition skills with their language comprehension skills as they are on that path to becoming skilled readers.

**(00:35)** In the past several lessons, we've been referencing the reading rope to help us anchor our learning. Today, I want to bring your attention back to the active view of reading by Duke and Cartwright. One thing that's a little different about their model is that they specifically highlight the bridging processes, which, when we think about the reading rope, that's where the word recognition strand and the language comprehension strand are being interwoven together. One of those bridging processes is fluency, and so we're really going to hone in on that today to help us intertwine these two concepts.

**(01:18)** I find this flowchart really helpful, and it's developed by Wiley Blevins, and it just helps me know where fluency fits in the big picture of reading. One thing that's really helpful for me when I am using this chart is when I'm sitting down with teachers and we're looking at a student that is struggling in the area of reading, and we're really trying to pinpoint what the cause is for that student to be struggling, and this chart can really help us figure out where the breakdown is. This is not meant to be a black and white, you must master phonemic awareness before you master decoding; it doesn't work that way. It's not really a strict rule; it's just a general guide to help us really pinpoint those issues.

**(02:10)** So when we think about reading, it's going to start with phonemic awareness, so that's really foundational for decoding. So students are hearing sounds, they're putting them together, and they are learning that words are made up of individual sounds and individual sounds can be put together to make words. Once that understanding is underway, students can then begin decoding, so adding letters to that process and figuring out what print says. As students get more and more practice with decoding words, sounding them out, their brains are going to begin orthographically mapping those words, and the more words that they have orthographically mapped, the more they're going to be able to have automatic word recognition. This automatic word recognition is going to facilitate fluency, right, because students are now having that automaticity. They can read without having to expend too much cognitive effort on decoding. When students are having to sound out words sound by sound, remember all of those sounds, and then put it together, that's taking all of their cognitive effort when we really want them to be able to do that automatically because their brains orthographically mapped it so that they can focus on fluency. Once students are able to devote more mental resources to fluency and understanding what they read, that's going to enhance their reading comprehension.

**(03:49)** So why I bring this up is because it's really important: Before we start focusing interventions on fluency, we need to ensure that foundational skills like phonemic awareness and decoding are well established, and this approach is going to ensure that students have a solid base upon which to build their fluency and comprehension skills. If we skip the top part here, then when we're focusing on fluency, we're really just asking students to get faster and faster at memorizing, and that is not going to aid their reading comprehension. So just one thing to keep in mind as we talk about fluency.

**(04:30)** Now, when we do talk about fluency, it's not just about reading quickly, right? It encompasses several key components that together will create a fluent reader. So let's break these down. First, we have accuracy. *Accuracy* refers to the ability to read words correctly. This means recognizing words automatically and understanding their meanings. Accurate reading ensures that students are decoding words correctly, which is essential for comprehension. If a student misreads words frequently, it can lead to misunderstandings and hinder their ability to grasp the overall meaning of the text.

**(05:10)** Second is *rate*, so that is the speed at which a student reads. While it's important not to read too quickly, a certain level of speed is necessary to maintain the flow of reading. Reading too slowly can disrupt comprehension because it makes it harder to remember what was read earlier in the sentence or the paragraph. The goal is really to find a balance piece that allows for both speed and understanding.

**(05:38)** Finally, prosody. *Prosody* is the ability to read with expression. This involves using appropriate intonation, stress, and rhythm to convey meaning. Prosody helps bring the text to life and aids in comprehension by reflecting the natural flow of spoken language. It indicates that the reader understands the nuances and emotions and the text, which can greatly enhance the reading experience. That might remind you of verbal reasoning, right? So we've got to incorporate that in order for students to be able to be fluent readers.

**(06:18)** So when we talk about fluency, we're really looking at the integration of these three areas: accuracy, rate, and prosody. A fluent reader is going to do all three, and this combination allows the reader to focus on understanding the text rather than just on the mechanics of reading itself, so this is really a bridge between decoding and comprehension. As students become more fluent, they can shift their cognitive resources away from decoding words to understanding and interpreting the text, so this is why building fluency is so critical in developing proficient readers.

**(07:01)** "For nonfluent readers, on the other hand, the work of decoding can monopolize their attention. This means their cognitive resources are less available for making connections between sentences, relating what they are reading to what they already know, and making the inferential leaps a text requires." So this quote really emphasizes the need to foster fluency within our striving readers, right? They're so focused on decoding that they don't have any extra attention to that fluency, so we can combine their decoding instruction with that fluency instruction so they're getting both.

**(07:45)** There are ways you can scaffold the development of fluency with your readers. The first is echo reading, so that's going to be where a fluent reader, such as a teacher, reads a section of the text, and the student or students echo. There's partner reading where students are going to take turns reading portions of the text, and you can purposefully partner your students up so that they are hearing from a more fluent reader as practice. There's choral reading, so the class is going to read a portion of the text in unison with the skilled reader, the teacher, and independent reading, so students are going to read and reread a text independently. You really can use all layers with a single text, which is going to allow students to have multiple exposures, which will help develop their fluency. You can do these fluency scaffolds with a decodable text, with a trade book, with a poem. There's lots of options here and lots of scaffolds that you can pull out.

**(08:47)** So take a moment to summarize and synthesize: How do you currently support fluency practice with your instruction? And based on our learning today, what shifts might you make going forward? Pause, jot down your thoughts, and then jump back on so we can talk about our learning extension.

**(09:10)** Alright, today our learning extension comes from Dr. Timothy Rasinski, and he is a leading expert on fluency. So there's a podcast with him all about effective fluency instruction. Highly recommend that you listen to it. And then there is this *Megabook of Fluency*, which if you want strategies and activities that you can take and incorporate in your classroom, at least K–8 but probably K–12, this book would be a great resource for you. He has a ton of fantastic ideas that are all about fluency, so recommend that you check that out as well.

**(09:56)** Alright. Thank you so much for joining us. This was our last lesson of Module 5, so don't forget to comment on the Facebook group and then definitely come back and join us for Module 6. See you then.

## Active View of Reading

Active Self-Regulation

Word Recognition

Bridging Processes

Language Composition

Reading

## Blevins' Flow Chart

Phonemic Awareness

Decoding

Automatic Word Recognition

Fluency

Reading Comprehension

Additional Notes

## Fluency

Accuracy

Rate

Prosody

## Fluency Scaffolds

Echo Reading

Partner Reading

Choral Reading

Individual Reading

## Put It in Your Own Words: How do you currently support fluency practice with your instruction? What shifts might you make going forward?

## Additional Notes

# Bonus Content

**Use the questions below to prompt discussion amongst your colleagues.**

1. **Foundational Skills:** How do phonemic awareness and decoding contribute to the development of fluency? Why is it essential for students to master these foundational skills before focusing on fluency?
2. **Components of Fluency:** What are the key components of fluency (accuracy, rate, prosody), and how do they interact to enhance reading comprehension? Which of these components do you find most challenging to teach effectively?
3. **Instructional Strategies:** What instructional methods have you found effective in improving students' reading fluency? How do you differentiate these strategies for students at different proficiency levels?
4. **Integration Across Subjects:** In what ways can fluency practice be integrated into other subject areas beyond language arts? How might this integration enhance overall literacy skills?
5. **Assessment and Feedback:** How do you assess students' fluency in your classroom? What types of feedback do you provide to help students improve their fluency skills?

**To extend your understanding of this topic, work through the activities below with a small group of peers.**

**Fluency Progress Monitoring**
Collaboratively design a fluency progress monitoring tool that includes components for accuracy, rate, and prosody. Discuss how this tool can be used to track student growth over time.

**Fluency Scaffolding Techniques**
Role-play different fluency scaffolding techniques such as echo reading, partner reading, choral reading, and independent reading. Reflect on when and how each technique might be most effective.

**Text Analysis**
Analyze a sample text to identify passages where fluency practice could benefit students. Discuss how modifying text complexity or genre might impact fluency development.

**Fluency Intervention Strategies**
Brainstorm and share effective strategies for intervening when students struggle with fluency. Consider both short-term interventions (e.g., repeated reading) and long-term strategies (e.g., integrating fluency into daily routines).

**Fluency in Context**
Explore case studies or scenarios where fluency impacts reading comprehension differently across various student populations (e.g., English language learners, students with dyslexia). Discuss tailored approaches to support fluency development for these groups.

**Additional Resources**
Fluency DAY 1 and DAY 2 in the lesson plan: In these lessons, you'll notice a scaffolded approach to fluency. Day 1 lessons ask students to read sounds, words, phrases, and sentences from the text, whereas Day 2 asks students to read the entire text. Teachers can use observational data from the Day 1 reading to help determine which form of reading students should engage in with the text on Day 2 (from most support to least: echo reading, partner reading, choral reading, and independent reading).

MODULE 6

# Executing an SOR Approach

In Module 6, our focus is on practical implementation. Each lesson will focus on five key essentials educators need to translate the research into practice. We'll explore the key essentials for word recognition, language comprehension, sound walls, supporting ELL students, and literacy assessments. Through these discussions, educators will gain valuable insights and practical tools for implementing a Science of Reading approach in their classrooms.

As you watch the videos in this module, use the pages that follow to write notes about what you are learning as well as reflect on the new information presented to you.

## Watch

The following videos are part of this learning module. Go to ScienceOfReadingAcademy.com to access each of the videos.

Lesson 1: 5 Essentials for Word Recognition
Lesson 2: 5 Essentials for Language Comprehension
Lesson 3: 5 Essentials for Using a Sound Wall
Lesson 4: 5 Essentials for Supporting ELL Students
Lesson 5: 5 Essentials for Literacy Assessment

## Before you begin

To activate your schema about the module topics, use your current knowledge and experience to reflect on the questions below.

1. What strategies do you think are important for helping students recognize words quickly and accurately?

2. How do you think building background knowledge and teaching vocabulary can help students understand what they read?

3. What methods do you believe are effective for supporting students who are learning English as a second language?

**MODULE 6: Implementation Tips and Tricks**

# Lesson 1: 5 Essentials for Word Recognition

*Module 6, Lesson 1 of the Science of Reading Academy outlines the five essentials for teaching word recognition, essential for building foundational reading skills. First, explicit, systematic instruction of phoneme-grapheme correspondences lays the groundwork for decoding words effectively. Second, incorporating spiral review ensures continuous reinforcement of learned skills, preventing knowledge decay. Third, teaching high-frequency words through orthographic mapping enhances comprehension by linking sounds to written symbols rather than relying on rote memorization. Fourth, providing multiple opportunities for both decoding and encoding reinforces phonics skills and promotes their application across different contexts. Lastly, supporting students with carefully chosen decodable texts allows them to practice their phonics knowledge in a controlled setting, building confidence in independent reading. Below is the transcript for the Module 6, Lesson 1 video.*

**(00:07)** Hello, and welcome back to the Science of Reading Academy. Today we are launching our sixth and final module, which is going to be all about implementation tips and tricks. Each lesson in Module 6 will be organized slightly differently. We're going to have five essential items that you need to remember about one of the topics we've covered. These lessons will be really quick and are designed to help you synthesize the learning of the previous five modules. Today's lesson will be five essentials for teaching word recognition. Let's jump right in.

**(00:47)** Alright. The first essential for teaching word recognition is to provide explicit, systematic instruction of phoneme-grapheme correspondences. Understanding the relationship between phonemes, or sounds, and graphemes, letters, is fundamental for learning to read. By teaching these correspondences explicitly and systematically, we give students the tools they need to decode words, which is that first step in becoming proficient readers.

**(01:20)** Here's an example from the Structured Literacy with E.A.S.E. program of what this might look like. There is direct teaching of the oral articulation of the digraph sound /th/, so it's talking about whether or not the sound is voiced or unvoiced, and it talks about what type of sound it is and gives some language to use with students, as well as giving them an anchor to the grapheme, or the visual representation. So this would be an example of how the instruction is explicit. The systematic portion is going to come through your scope and sequence and being mindful to have a scope and sequence that carries students across the elementary grades.

**(02:07)** Essential number two is to incorporate spiral review and practice of previously taught skills. Spiral review helps reinforce those skills that students have already learned by continuing to revisit them regularly. This repeated exposure ensures that students retain and strengthen their understanding over time, which is going to prevent that forgetting curve from taking hold. We know that mastery of a skill comes from continuous practice and application, and our students who have reading disabilities or dyslexia are going to need us to be intentional with our purposeful practice. So by incorporating spiral review, we're giving all students multiple opportunities to practice and refine their skills, moving from basic understanding to mastery. We can't just be explicit and systematic with our teaching; we also have to be intentional about spiraling the learning for our students.

**(03:13)** An example from this in the Structured Literacy with E.A.S.E. program is beginning each lesson with a skill review. So this program is beginning with a decoding graphemes warm-up where students are connecting sounds to graphemes. You'll also see this approach in the Orton-Gillingham method where they utilize the three-part drill that provides intentional spiraling of previously learned skills through the visual drill, auditory drill, and the blending drill.

**(03:47)** Your third essential is to teach high-frequency words through orthographic mapping, not memorization. So you'll remember that orthographic mapping involves connecting the sounds of language, or the phonemes, with the written symbols, or the graphemes, that represent them.

Instead of rote memorization, students learn to recognize and decode words based on their understanding of these sound–symbol relationships. This really deepens their comprehension and allows for greater flexibility in reading and spelling. It's going to prevent their memorization ability from running out of space because our capacity for memorization is limited, while our capacity for orthographic mapping appears unlimited. It's a much more efficient way to store words, whether they're regular or irregular, but definitely when we're working on high-frequency words, giving students lots of opportunity to foster that orthographic mapping.

(04:49) Here's an example from the Structured Literacy with E.A.S.E. program. Explicit teaching is provided about both the decodable parts and the irregular parts of these high-frequency words. On the word cards, students' attention is brought to the irregular parts by writing them in red, and you can see sound boxes in the corner as a reference as well for both teachers and students. These are subtle shifts in your word cards that make a really big difference. There's also explicit teaching about the word when they're introducing it, about the parts that can help anchor what students already know, so vowel teams that they've learned, three-letter blends; they're connecting meaning by using a sentence here. So all of those components are going to help foster that orthographic mapping process.

(05:45) Your fourth essential is to provide multiple opportunities for decoding and encoding the focus skill. So decoding is the reading, encoding is the spelling, and those are reciprocal processes that really reinforce each other. By providing repeated practice in both skills, students will strengthen their understanding and their application of phonics and word recognition. This is going to give them more practice opportunities, which is going to help them have a deeper understanding of that phonics skill, which is going to empower our students to apply these skills confidently across different literacy tasks. And we really need that transfer, right? Students need to be able to transfer their phonics skills from isolated practice to a decodable text to any text. That's our goal, and so giving them multiple opportunities in both modalities is really important.

(06:49) You can see this example here where students are first decoding words, so the portion of the lesson is focusing on decoding words, phrases, and sentences with this skill practice page before shifting to encoding the words with dictation. So the words are going to focus on this same skill, but they're going to practice different modalities, decoding and encoding, to facilitate that reciprocity.

(07:21) Your fifth and final tip for word recognition is to support students' word recognition skills with a carefully chosen decodable text. So remember, what makes a text decodable is if students have been taught the phoneme-grapheme correspondences within that book. Decodable texts are the training wheels of word recognition; just like training wheels on a bicycle provide support and stability while children learn to ride, decodable texts offer a scaffolded approach to reading. They enable students to apply their phonics knowledge in a really controlled and systematic manner. By encountering words that adhere to the phonetic rules they've learned, students gain confidence in decoding unfamiliar words independently.

(08:10) So here is an example from the Structured Literacy with E.A.S.E. program where students are given a decodable text in the lesson that matches the skills, the phonic skills, they've been taught through those decoding and encoding and phonemic awareness activities.

(08:29) Alright, this lesson has some very special bonus downloadable content. We have this wonderful word recognition lesson plan. So as you're trying to think through all of the things that you need to remember when teaching word recognition to students, this lesson plan template can be a great place for you to start. It is designed for you to be able to type in while also having a little reminder snippet, so it'll tell you what each section needs to incorporate, and you can just highlight and delete and type your thoughts in, or you can keep those thoughts on there as well.

**(09:09)** So thank you so much for joining. Give yourself a moment to pause, reflect, and put it in your own words. In your opinion, what is the most important tip others need to know for teaching word recognition? So jot that down so that you can share your learning with others.

**(09:28)** And thank you for joining us. Don't forget to comment on the Module 6, Lesson 1 thread in our Facebook group. We can't wait to see you for Lesson 2, all about language comprehension.

Provide explicit, systematic instruction of phoneme-grapheme correspondences.

Incorporate spiral review and practice of previously taught skills.

Teach high-frequency words through orthographic mapping.

Additional Notes

Provide multiple opportunities for decoding and encoding the focus skill.

Support students' word recognition skills with a carefully chosen decodable text.

Put It in Your Own Words: In your opinion, what is the most important tip others need to know for teaching word recognition?

Additional Notes

# Bonus Content

**Use the questions below to prompt discussion amongst your colleagues.**

1. **Explicit Instruction:** Why is explicit, systematic instruction of phoneme-grapheme correspondences crucial for teaching word recognition? How can this approach benefit both struggling readers and advanced learners?
2. **Spiral Review:** What role does spiral review play in reinforcing previously taught word recognition skills? How can teachers effectively integrate spiral review into daily lessons to maximize retention?
3. **Orthographic Mapping:** Explain the concept of orthographic mapping in teaching high-frequency words. How does this approach differ from traditional memorization techniques? What are the long-term benefits for students?
4. **Decoding and Encoding:** Why is it important to provide multiple opportunities for both decoding and encoding skills in phonics instruction? How does this dual practice enhance students' overall literacy skills?
5. **Decodable Texts:** Discuss the significance of using carefully chosen decodable texts in teaching word recognition. How do these texts support students' application of phonics knowledge and foster independent reading skills?

**To extend your understanding of this topic, work through the activities below with a small group of peers.**

**Phoneme-Grapheme Matching Game**
Create cards with phonemes and corresponding graphemes. Have teachers match them and discuss how they would explicitly teach these correspondences in their classrooms.

**Spiral Review Planning**
Design a weekly spiral review schedule for a specific phonics skill. Discuss the types of activities (e.g., visual drills, auditory drills) that would be effective based on Orton-Gillingham principles.

**Orthographic Mapping Analysis**
Analyze a set of high-frequency words and discuss strategies for teaching them through orthographic mapping rather than memorization. Create sample word cards with highlighted irregular parts.

**Decoding vs. Encoding Practice**
Provide excerpts from a text and ask teachers to identify sections suitable for decoding practice and others for encoding practice. Discuss how these activities reinforce each other.

**Decodable Text Evaluation**
Evaluate a decodable text for its suitability in reinforcing specific phoneme-grapheme correspondences. Discuss how such texts can be integrated into broader literacy instruction plans.

**Additional Resources**
See the Module 4, Lesson 1 bonus content page for access to an editable word recognition lesson plan template.

# Lesson 2: 5 Essentials for Language Comprehension

*Module 6, Lesson 2 of the Science of Reading Academy focuses on key strategies to enhance students' ability to understand text. The first essential stresses the importance of building background knowledge through activities like the Background Builder, which primes students to connect new information with what they already know. Tip two highlights selecting and teaching Tier 2 vocabulary to improve academic language proficiency. Sentence-level comprehension, including syntax and semantics, is emphasized in tip three through activities. Tip four encourages continuous instruction in making inferences, crucial for developing verbal reasoning skills. Finally, tip five promotes scaffolded fluency practice throughout reading instruction, ensuring students integrate reading fluency with comprehension skills effectively. Below is the transcript for the Module 6, Lesson 2 video.*

**(00:07)** Hello, and welcome back to the Science of Reading Academy. We're in our sixth and final module, all about implementation tips and tricks. You'll remember that each lesson in Module 6 is organized into five essential items you need to remember about one of the topics we've covered in our academy. These lessons are quick and are designed to help you synthesize the learning from our previous five modules. Today's lesson is five essentials for teaching language comprehension. Let's get started.

**(00:42)** Alright. Our first essential is to provide students with multiple opportunities to build background knowledge prior to engaging with text. If you can think back to our previous module where we talked about the Baseball Study, right, that really emphasized the importance of background knowledge for students, students that had more background knowledge about baseball who were poorer readers than some of their peers who had little background knowledge about baseball performed better on a comprehension test. So we really need to be intentional about building that background knowledge in order for students to be able to comprehend the text that we put in front of them.

**(01:29)** An example from the Structured Literacy with E.A.S.E. program is this Background Builder that they incorporate into all of their decodable texts. So this is a little reader about Cat Camp, and the Background Builder is about summer camp. So you might think, surely my students would know all about summer camp, but there are absolutely students in our schools who have no background knowledge on summer camp, and this quick warm-up activity is going to support their comprehension as well as some of these Before Reading Questions that are going to activate students' knowledge such as, Have you ever been to camp? What types of activities did you do at camp? Have you been lost before? How did you feel? So these types of questions and activities such as the Background Builder are going to prime your students' brains to pull from the background knowledge that they have or create the background knowledge that they didn't have before in order to find success with the comprehension task.

**(02:38)** Tip number two is to carefully select Tier 2 vocabulary words to teach. Now, you'll remember Tier 2 in this context is not small group. We're talking about high-utility academic words, so those Tier 1 vocabulary words are your everyday conversation words that just about everyone knows: *dog, cat, up, down*. Your Tier 3 vocabulary words are those academic words that are very specialized and specific to content. So Tier 2 is that sweet spot where it is high-yield academic words that are going to really benefit students.

**(03:24)** An example from the Structured Literacy with E.A.S.E. program are the words *scuff* and *swell*. So these come from the decodable text that students will read in the lesson, and these words are not words that most students are going to know, but students are going to be able to translate them and use them in a wide variety of contexts. So the activities and lesson that students will participate in with these words are going to help them across the academic context.

(04:01) Tip number three is to address sentence-level comprehension, including syntax and semantics. Sometimes we forget, and we focus on big picture comprehension, but sometimes we need to really back it up to the sentence level. Providing explicit instruction of syntax, which we remember is sentence structure, and semantics, the meaning of words, is one of those crucial skills that we must provide that explicit teaching of in order to help support students' verbal reasoning skills.

(04:39) Two activities to teach syntax and semantics within the Structured Literacy with E.A.S.E. program include Sentence Combining—which there is a high amount of research to support the effectiveness of sentence combining, so this is a great activity for students to do both orally and through written expression—and this one, Categorization and Classification, where students are brainstorming and sorting and then sharing their list with other groups and having other groups guess what their categories must be. So it's a fun, gamified way to practice that semantics activity, so we can really make these activities very fun and engaging for students while they're developing these really higher cognitive skills.

(05:32) Tip number four is to continuously teach inference making. This is also related to verbal reasoning, and it's really just one of those crucial skills we must teach and continue to teach with our students. Inferencing is really hard for some students to grasp because it's pulling on their background knowledge and clues from the text, so they're having to incorporate multiple sources of input in order to draw conclusions.

(06:02) An example from the Structured Literacy with E.A.S.E. program is a little mini-lesson where the teacher is providing the why for why making inferences is important, a little bit of instruction about what an inference is, and then a think aloud where the teacher is utilizing the text to think aloud for the students what that inference might be, as well as an opportunity for students to practice independently. So these multiple layers of scaffolding and continuing to provide students with an introduction to that skill are going to help them find success over time.

(06:43) Your fifth and final tip is to incorporate scaffolded fluency practice into your reading instruction, and you'll remember that fluency does not have to be just during a reading comprehension lesson. You can and should incorporate fluency into your word recognition lessons as well.

(07:04) An example from the Structured Literacy with E.A.S.E. program is where they have multiple layers of scaffolding that provide students the opportunity to read a decodable text while also practicing that fluency with support.

(07:23) Alright, we have another wonderful bonus downloadable content for you today, and this is our language comprehension lesson plan, and this is going to help you think through teaching all of those important skills that we've talked about, those essentials. And just like with the word recognition one, it's going to have a little explanation and reminder and then allow you to type in your own plans.

(07:55) Alright, take a moment to pause and put in your own words: In your opinion, what is the most important tip that others need to know for teaching language comprehension? Jot down your thoughts so that you can share with your team.

(08:11) Thank you so much for joining us again today for Module 6, Lesson 2. Our next lesson is going to talk about sound walls, so please make sure to come back and join us for that. We'll see you then.

Provide students with multiple opportunities to build background knowledge prior to engaging with texts.

Carefully select Tier 2 vocabulary words to teach.

Address sentence-level comprehension, including syntax and semantics.

Additional Notes

Continuously teach inference making.

Incorporate scaffolded fluency practice into reading comprehension.

Put It in Your Own Words: In your opinion, what is the most important tip others need to know for teaching language comprehension?

Additional Notes

# Bonus Content

**Use the questions below to prompt discussion amongst your colleagues.**

1. **Building Background Knowledge:** How can teachers effectively assess and build upon students' background knowledge before introducing new texts? What are some creative ways to engage students in building background knowledge, especially for topics they may not be familiar with?
2. **Selecting Tier 2 Vocabulary:** Why is it important to focus on Tier 2 vocabulary words rather than Tier 1 or Tier 3 in academic contexts? How can teachers ensure that vocabulary instruction supports comprehension across different subjects and texts?
3. **Sentence-Level Comprehension:** Why is understanding syntax and semantics crucial for overall comprehension? What strategies or activities can teachers implement to explicitly teach syntax and semantics effectively?
4. **Teaching Inference Making:** How can teachers scaffold instruction to help students develop their inference-making skills over time? What are some challenges students might face when making inferences, and how can teachers address these challenges?
5. **Fluency Practice in Reading Instruction:** How does scaffolded fluency practice contribute to students' overall reading comprehension? In what ways can fluency practice be integrated into different aspects of reading instruction beyond comprehension lessons?

**To extend your understanding of this topic, work through the activities below with a small group of peers.**

**Building Background Knowledge Activity**
Select a topic relevant to upcoming reading materials. Have small groups research and present key background information. Discuss how this information connects to the text.

**Vocabulary Word Study**
Choose Tier 2 vocabulary words from a text students will read. Have groups create word maps or visual representations that include definitions, synonyms, and examples of how the words are used.

**Syntax and Semantics Exploration**
Provide sentences with deliberate errors in syntax or ambiguous word meanings. Groups correct errors and discuss meanings. Create new sentences to demonstrate understanding.

**Inference Practice Stations**
Set up stations with different texts. Each station has questions that require inference making. Groups rotate through stations, discuss answers, and justify their reasoning based on text clues.

**Fluency Practice with Feedback**
Using decodable texts, have groups practice reading aloud with different levels of support (e.g., partner reading, teacher feedback). Discuss how fluency impacts comprehension and strategies for improvement.

**Additional Resources**
See the Module 5, Supporting Language Development introduction. The second page of the introduction includes a note about bonus content for the module, as well as access to an editable language comprehension lesson plan template.

**MODULE 6: Implementation Tips and Tricks**

# Lesson 3: 5 Essentials for Using a Sound Wall

*Module 6, Lesson 3 from the Science of Reading Academy focuses on essential strategies for implementing sound walls effectively in classrooms. Sound walls are emphasized as tools to help students connect spoken language with written symbols, promoting phonemic awareness and spelling skills. The video outlines five key tips: organizing vowel sounds in a "vowel valley" to visually represent their mouth positions, categorizing consonants based on articulation types, gradually introducing graphemes aligned with instructional sequences, providing explicit instruction on mouth positions for phonemes, and using the sound wall as a teaching aid rather than expecting independent use. Below is the transcript for the Module 6, Lesson 3 video.*

**(00:07)** Hello, and welcome back to the Science of Reading Academy. We're in Module 6 and talking all about implementation tips and tricks, so taking what we've learned in the previous lessons and modules and talking about really actionable steps for putting that learning into practice. Now, today's lesson is going to be five essentials for using a sound wall. And as many educators are beginning to make that shift toward a structured literacy approach in their classroom, they're starting to utilize sound walls, but sound walls are so different from word walls. There's oftentimes confusion about what that should look like and sound like, so we're going to learn together five essentials for using a sound wall. Let's get started.

**(00:57)** So when we think about using a sound wall, the first question that you might have is: What exactly is a sound wall? And that's a great question. A sound wall is essentially a tool that is used to help readers connect spoken and written language. It's organized by the sounds, or the phonemes, of words rather than just the alphabet. So sound walls really help students visualize those relationships between sounds and letters, which is going to help them with phonemic awareness as well as spelling.

**(01:34)** So we're used to starting with graphemes because that makes sense to us. We've learned all of our graphemes, but when you think about the brain and how the brain learns to read, it starts with sounds first, right? Even though it's visual input, we connect that right away to sounds and then bring in the graphemes and that written representation, so we want to facilitate that process for our learners by utilizing sound walls.

**(02:05)** The first essential tip is to place all vowel sounds together in a "vowel valley." When I think about the English language and when experts think about the English language, we know that vowels are what make our language so very tricky. When I think about working with my second grade students, the first obstacle that would really set some of my striving readers apart was just short vowel sounds and distinguishing between them. Vowels are tricky in our language, so being intentional with how we teach them is definitely important.

**(02:48)** This is an example of what a vowel valley would look like. So these are the cards from Structured Literacy with E.A.S.E.'s sound wall that is connected with their curriculum, and you can see in this sound wall that the vowels go down in this "V" shape. That's why it's called a valley. And what's really fun about this is if you make these sounds, you'll notice how your mouth also makes a valley. So it's going to get wider and wider and wider open until you're down here with the short /a/ sound, and then it will close progressively until you're with the /yū/ sound. So that's a fun activity to do and then also a great thing to do with your students. We also have our diphthong sounds here, so those make your mouth move. And then this is the schwa, the lazy sound in our language, and then our R-controlled vowels down here.

**(03:50)** The next tip is to organize consonants according to the manner of articulation. So similar to the vowel valley, the vowel valley is organized by mouth placement, and consonants are organized by articulation. There's several different classifications for how we articulate consonants, and those are the following.

(04:13) There are stop sounds. So with stop sounds, your lips are going to completely block or stop the airflow. So that's like the /b/ sound. So those sounds are often ones that we have to really be careful about not adding that schwa or that /u/ sound to. You'll hear teachers, I know I did it myself as an early educator, that will say /buh/, and we want to just say /b/; we want to clip those sounds.

(04:43) The next type are nasals. So nasals are pronounced through airflow that is blocked in the mouth but released through the nose. So if you have a cold, I have a little bit of an allergy cold right now, I can really notice when I'm pronouncing those nasal sounds that they're a little trickier. If you say the sound /n/, you can probably feel those vibrations in your nasal canal. So that is a nasal sound.

(05:16) The next type are fricatives. So fricatives involve friction, which makes sense, right? They sound similar. And fricative sounds are produced from friction in the mouth. So if you think about the /f/ sound, like with the letter "f," you're forcing air through a narrow channel, and that's what's helping to make that sound.

(05:38) Now, affricates are basically combo sounds. They're going to start as stop sounds, and then they're going to move to a fricative like the digraph /ch/, which is represented by the "ch"; I should have said by the /ch/ sound, which represented by the diagraph "ch."

(06:01) Then we have the glide sounds. So with those, you just make those sounds by where you put your tongue and your lip. So this is going to be the /y/ sound like with the letter "y" and the /w/ sound with the letter "w," and those are really hard to say in isolation, especially the "y" sound. I've worked with several teachers, and we've practiced how to pronounce that correctly because you really have to think about what your mouth is doing to say it without the schwa sound, so those are tricky.

(06:35) The last classification are liquids. And so with liquids, the tongue is partially going to close the mouth and redirect the airflow, like with the /l/ sound with the letter "l."

(06:48) When you are arranging the consonants for your sound wall, instead of putting them in alphabetical order, you're going to think through what and how those sounds are classified through articulation. So again, this is from the Structured Literacy with E.A.S.E.'s sound wall, and these are all their stop sounds. So one thing that makes this really easy for teachers is it's color coded, so all of their stop sounds are yellow. And another thing that's nice is you can arrange it by voiced and unvoiced sounds. So if you think about the /p/ and the /b/ sounds, if you look at the mouth pictures, they're almost identical, but one of them has their voice on or one of them has their voice off. And so sometimes students will mix those sounds up, not always with reading but definitely with spelling, and so this can be a helpful teaching point for you.

(07:45) The third tip is to only display graphemes that have been taught to students. If you put everything up all at once, it really just becomes beautiful wall art that doesn't mean a lot to your students, and it might even be overwhelming wall art. We talked about how there's 44 phonemes, but there are over 100 graphemes in our language, so if we put all of those up for students, they're not going to be as meaningful if we add to the display as we teach each grapheme. This is also where your scope and sequence can come into play because if you are a second grade teacher, you can reference what was taught in kindergarten and first grade and already have that displayed on your sound wall so that students can reacclimate to previous learning.

(08:37) An example of what this might look like perhaps in a kindergarten classroom is the /n/ phoneme has only perhaps been introduced for the grapheme, the letter "n." So the "kn" grapheme and the "gn" grapheme haven't been introduced yet, so the teacher has covered these with a post-it note, and as students learn those, then those graphemes will be revealed so that students know they now have another way to spell that sound.

(09:09) The fourth essential tip is to help students understand how their mouths look and feel when they are producing phonemes. So this is something that can be really easy for us to overlook when we're introducing sounds or teaching a phonics lesson because these are things that our mouth just does automatically without us thinking about it. But for many of our students, they need that explicit instruction. So when we demonstrate and discuss specific mouth positions and movements that are required for the different phonemes, this is really giving our students a tactile and a visual understanding of speech production. So this is where it gets really important, another place for us as educators to be intentional with how we say our sounds to make sure we're not adding a schwa when we pronounce a consonant.

(10:04) This is an example from the Structured Literacy with E.A.S.E. program. So you can kind of see their script here. They are introducing what the sound is classified as, so it's a fricative sound, and they tell you what that means. And this is great to share with your students so that they're thinking about what their mouth is doing and if their voice box is on. There's also guided practice for students to practice through gradual release, actually articulating that sound. And one of my favorite parts is this corrective feedback down here where it gives you exactly what to do if students are pronouncing a sound incorrectly, what you can say, and what you can have students do to fix that. So that is so helpful because sometimes we can see it happening, but we're not trained always in this area, and so having that information at your fingertips is super helpful.

(11:02) My fifth and final tip is to use the sound wall as a teaching tool. Do not expect students to use it without support. And what I mean by that is when I think about word walls, we used to be able to say to students when they didn't know how to spell the sight word, what's the first sound you hear? Go find it on the word wall; write it down in your writing. Sound walls don't really work that way. It is really challenging, both for adults but especially for students, to make a sound, to think what their mouth is doing or even look in a mirror to figure out what their mouth is doing, go match their mouth to another mouth on the wall, and then look at that wall poster to figure out all the different spellings that might be what they're thinking of for that sound. Now, sometimes students can do that for sure, but most of the time they're going to need prompting and support to achieve this, so it's not really an independent activity. And the research on this particular use of sound walls is still inconclusive, so instead, what we want to do is use sound walls as a teaching tool to help us review sounds and graphemes and to continue to make these connections for our students. So the teaching part of the sound wall is where the practice is really valuable.

(12:25) Alright, so take a moment, pause, jot down something that you want to try in your classroom with sound walls, and then come on back because I have a very exciting bonus download for you.

(12:41) Alright, our bonus content for this lesson is the Structured Literacy with E.A.S.E.'s vowel valley. So you'll receive all of the sound wall cards for the vowel valley so that you can have your very own in your classroom. This is a wonderful download that is available to you as a thank you for joining us for this lesson.

(13:06) Thank you so much for your time today. We hope that you will comment on the SOR Academy Facebook group and please come back and join us for Lesson 4 where we are going to be talking about five essentials for supporting our ELL students. See you then.

What is a sound wall?

Additional Notes

Provide all vowel sounds together in a "vowel valley."

### Organize consonants according to the manner of articulation.

Stop Sounds

Nasal Sounds

Fricative Sounds

Affricate Sounds

Glide Sounds

Liquid Sounds

### Only display graphemes that have been taught to the students.

Additional Notes

Help students understand how their mouths look and feel when they produce phonemes.

Use the sound wall as a teaching tool.

Take It to the Classroom: What is one element of a sound wall you want to try in your classroom?

Additional Notes

# Bonus Content

**Use the questions below to prompt discussion amongst your colleagues.**

1. **Understanding the Concept:** What is the primary purpose of a sound wall compared to a word wall? How does organizing by phonemes instead of alphabet letters benefit student learning?
2. **Organizational Strategies:** Why is it important to arrange vowel sounds in a "vowel valley" and consonants by manner of articulation? How does this organization support phonemic awareness and spelling?
3. **Implementation Challenges:** What challenges do you foresee in implementing a sound wall in your classroom? How might you address these challenges effectively?
4. **Teaching Strategies:** How can explicit instruction on mouth positions and movements for phonemes enhance students' phonemic awareness and speech production skills?
5. **Assessment and Adaptation:** How can you assess the effectiveness of your sound wall instruction? What adaptations might you need to make based on student responses and needs?

**To extend your understanding of this topic, work through the activities below with a small group of peers.**

**Sound Wall Design Challenge**
In small groups, design a mock sound wall using phoneme cards provided. Discuss and justify your arrangement based on phonemic principles. Present your design to the group for feedback.

**Interactive Sound Production**
Practice articulating various phonemes together. Use mirrors to observe mouth movements and provide feedback to peers on clarity and accuracy of pronunciation.

**Sound Wall Walkthrough**
Conduct a guided tour of a completed sound wall in a colleague's classroom. Discuss how graphemes are introduced sequentially and scaffolded based on student learning stages.

**Sound Wall Reflections**
Reflect individually on potential challenges and benefits of using a sound wall. Share insights with peers and brainstorm strategies to maximize its effectiveness in diverse classroom settings.

**Sound Wall Integration Plan**
Develop a step-by-step integration plan for implementing a sound wall in your classroom. Include strategies for introducing new phonemes, reviewing previous ones, and adapting based on student progress.

**Additional Resources**
See the following pages for vowel phoneme posters. These can be displayed in your classroom as a vowel valley—a visual representation of the mouth movements made when articulating vowel sounds. A quick Internet search will show examples of vowel valley displays.

This page is intentionally blank.

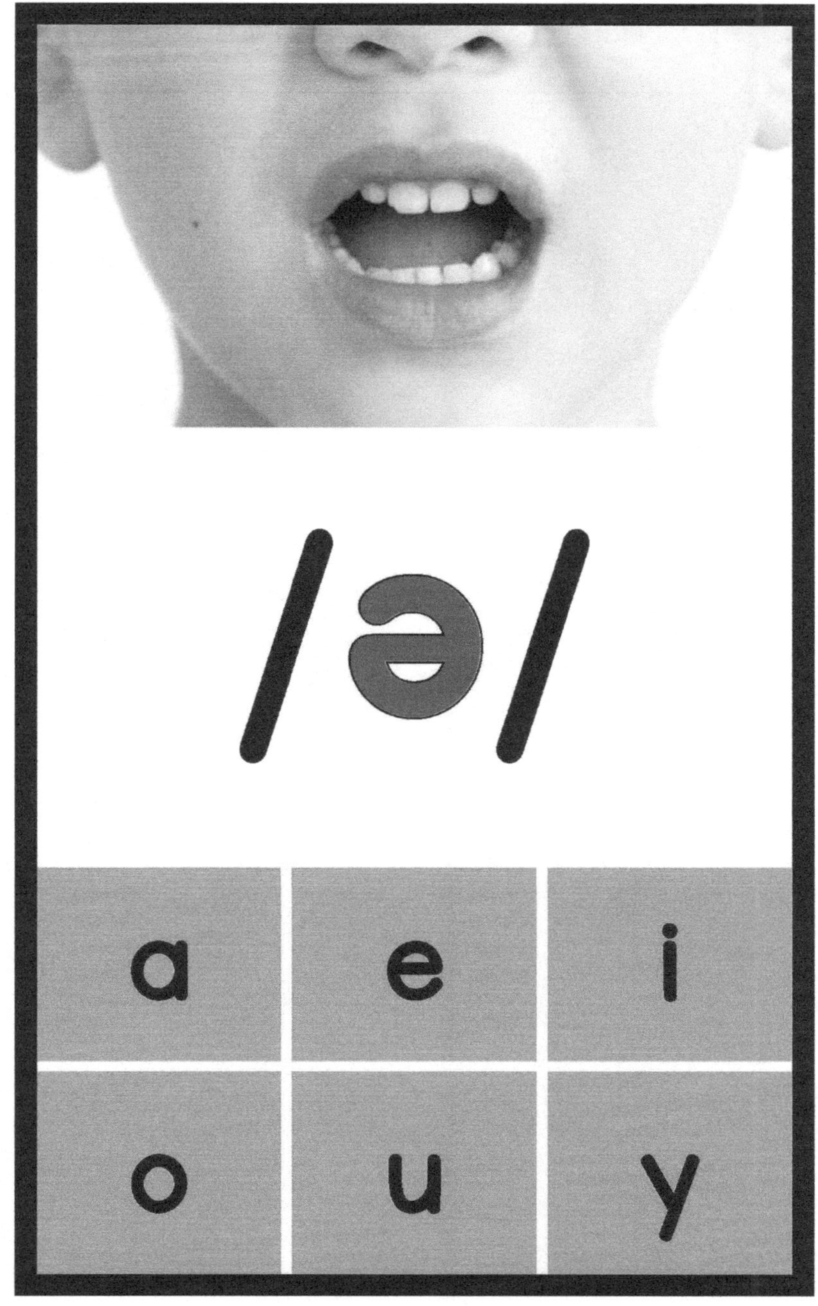
/ə/
a e i
o u y

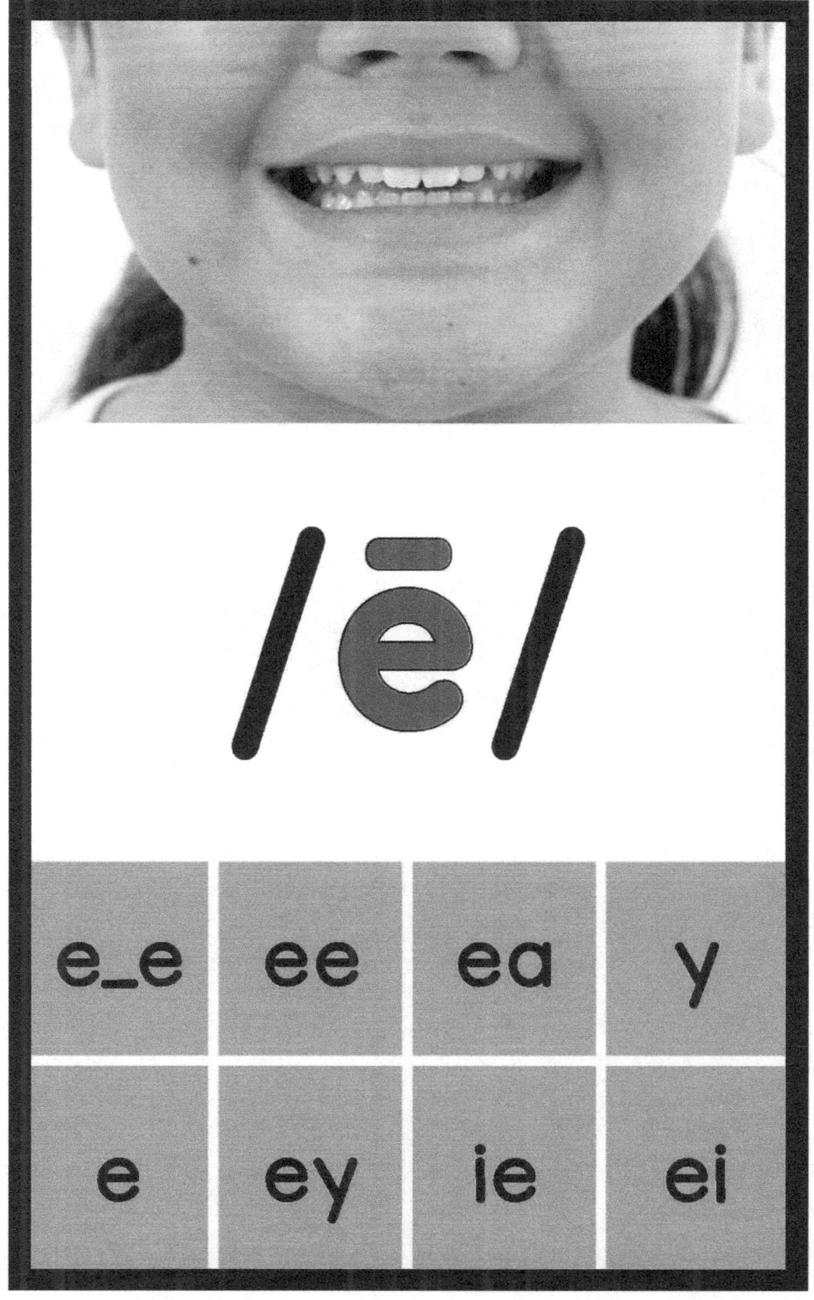
/ē/
e_e ee ea y
e ey ie ei

This page is intentionally blank.

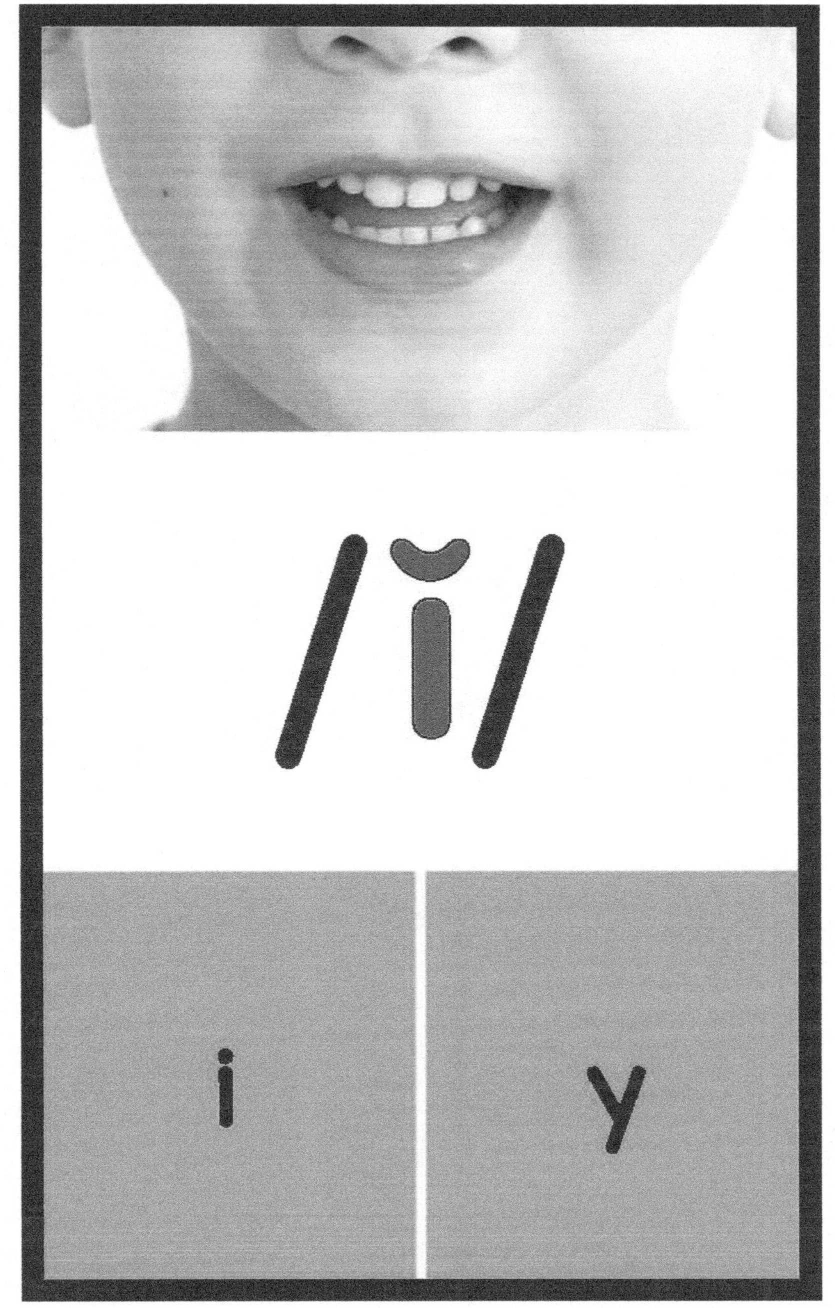

/ĭ/
i
y


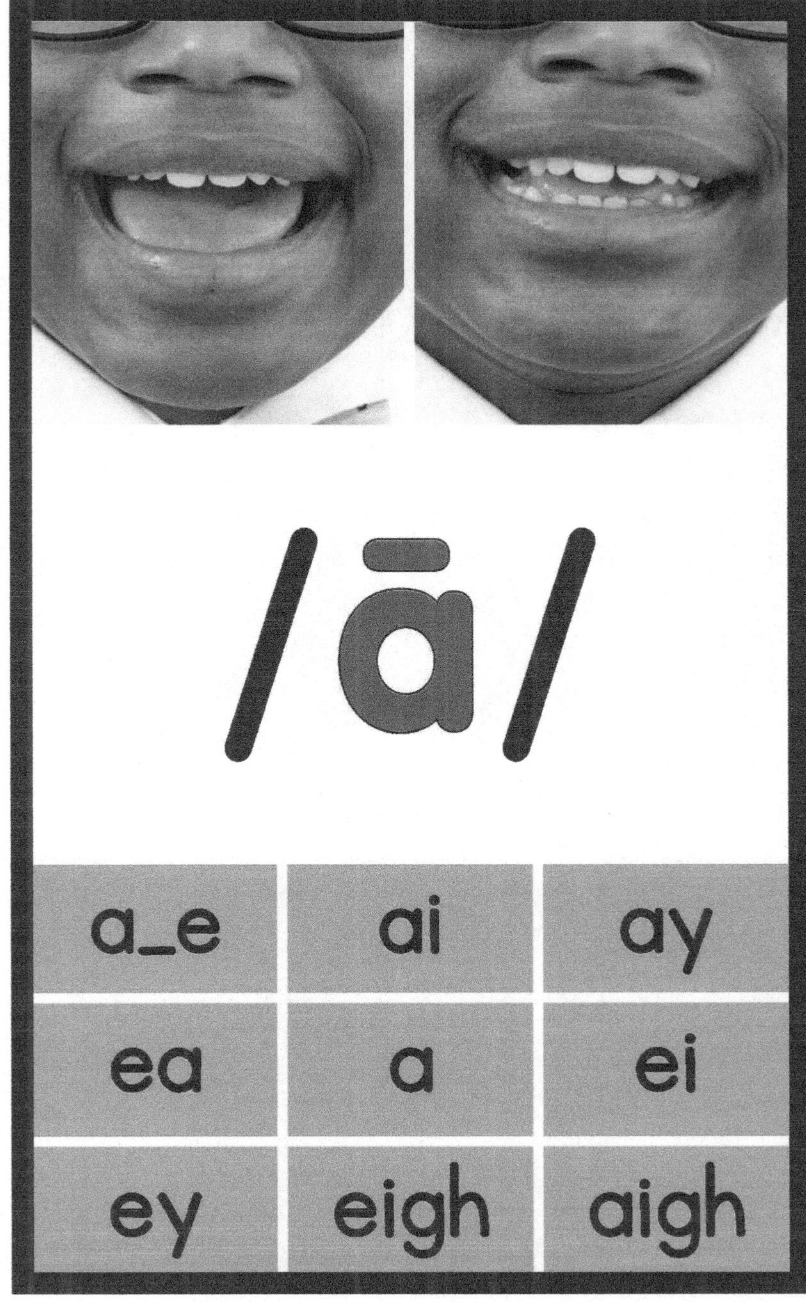

/ā/
a_e
ai
ay
ea
a
ei
ey
eigh
aigh

This page is intentionally blank.

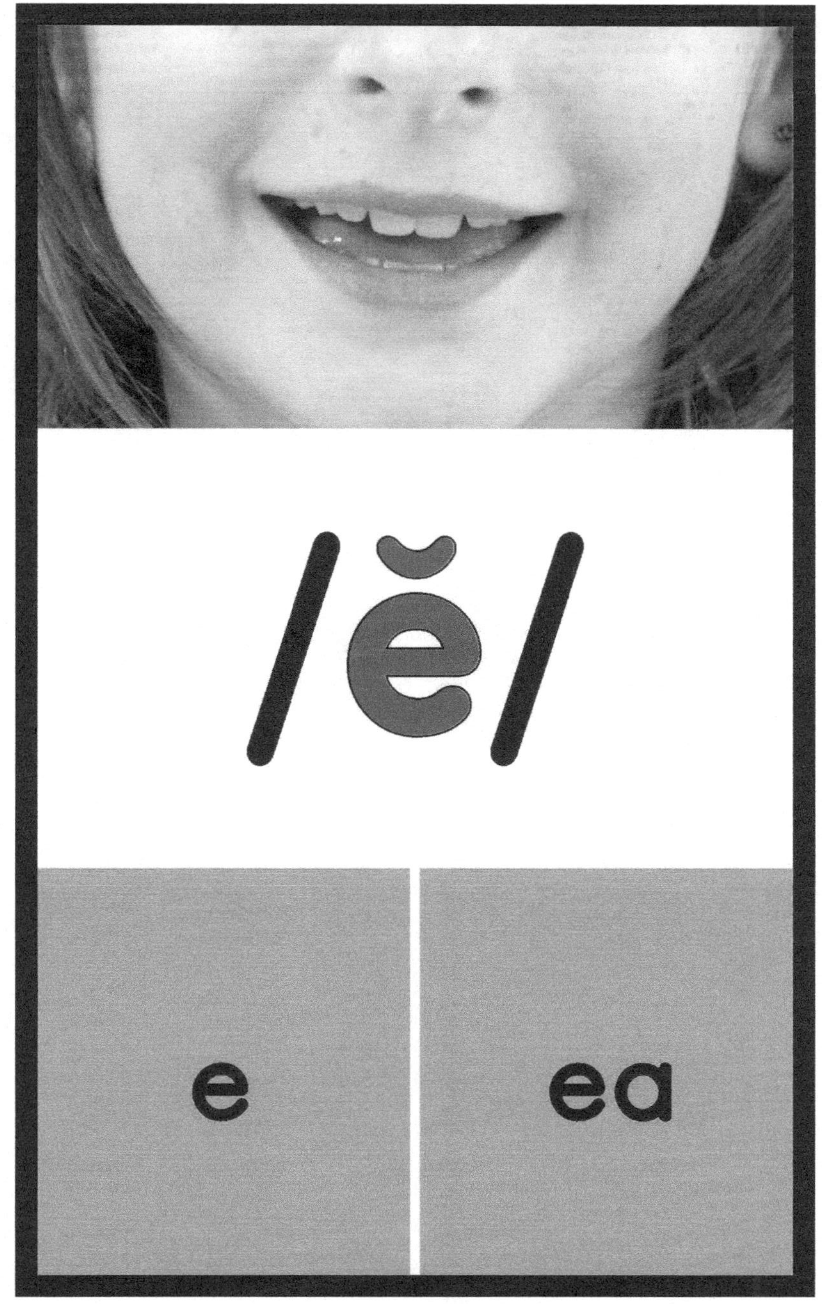
/ĕ/
e
ea

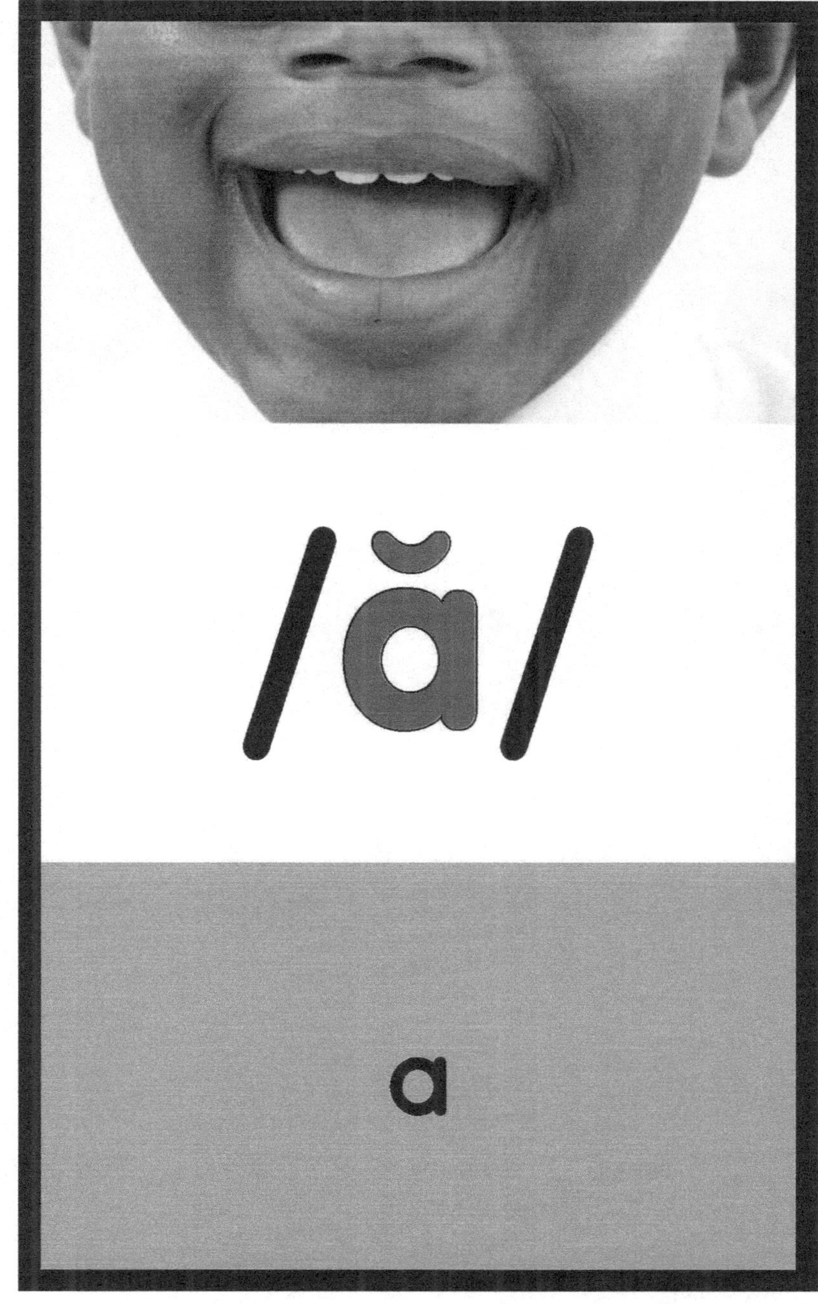
/ă/
a

This page is intentionally blank.

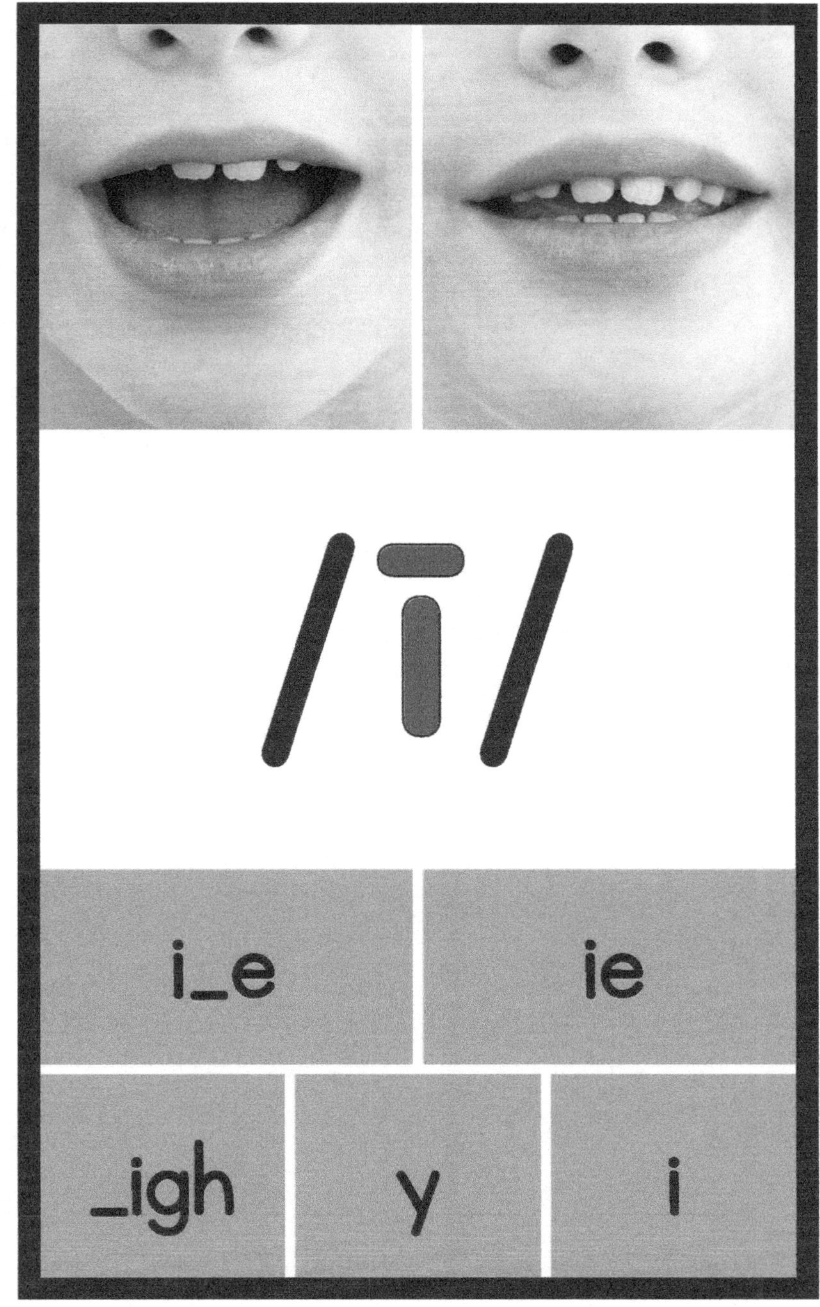

/ī/
i_e
ie
_igh
y
i


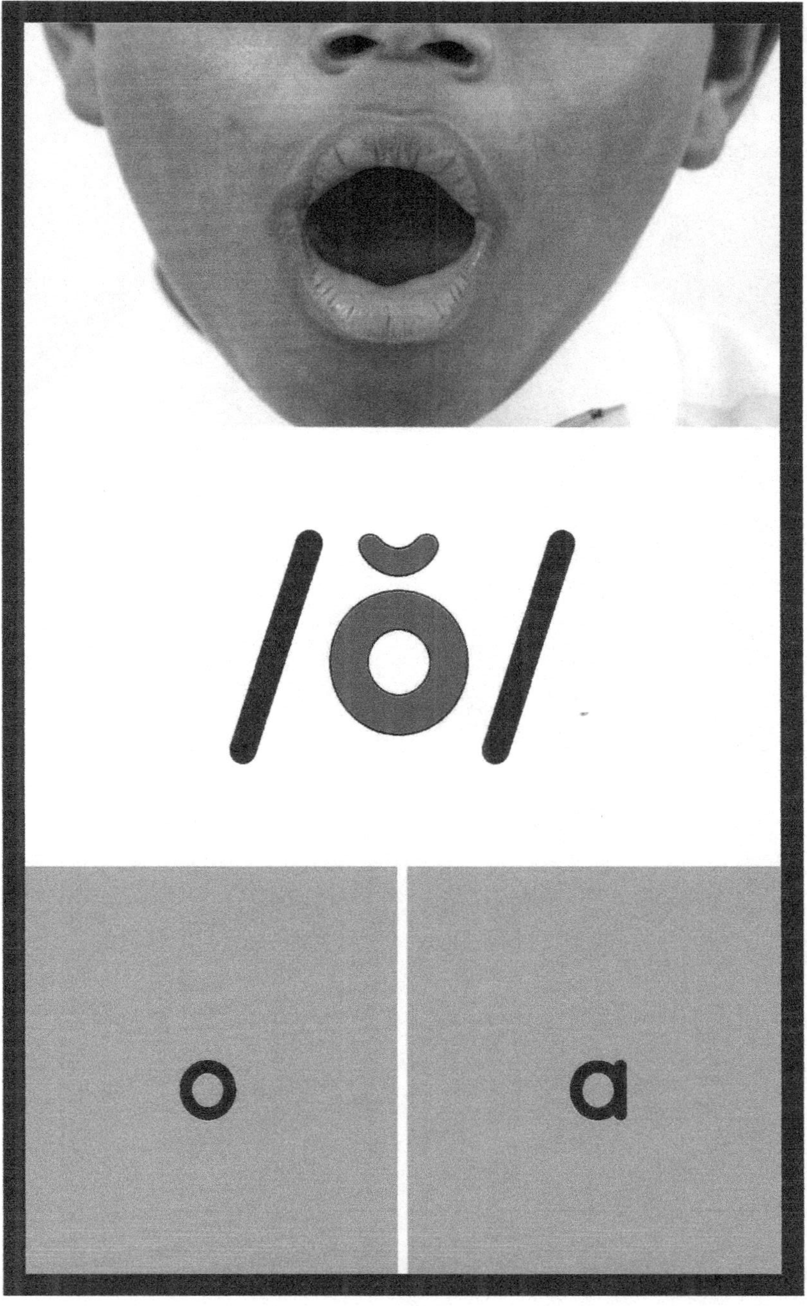

/ŏ/
o
a

This page is intentionally blank.

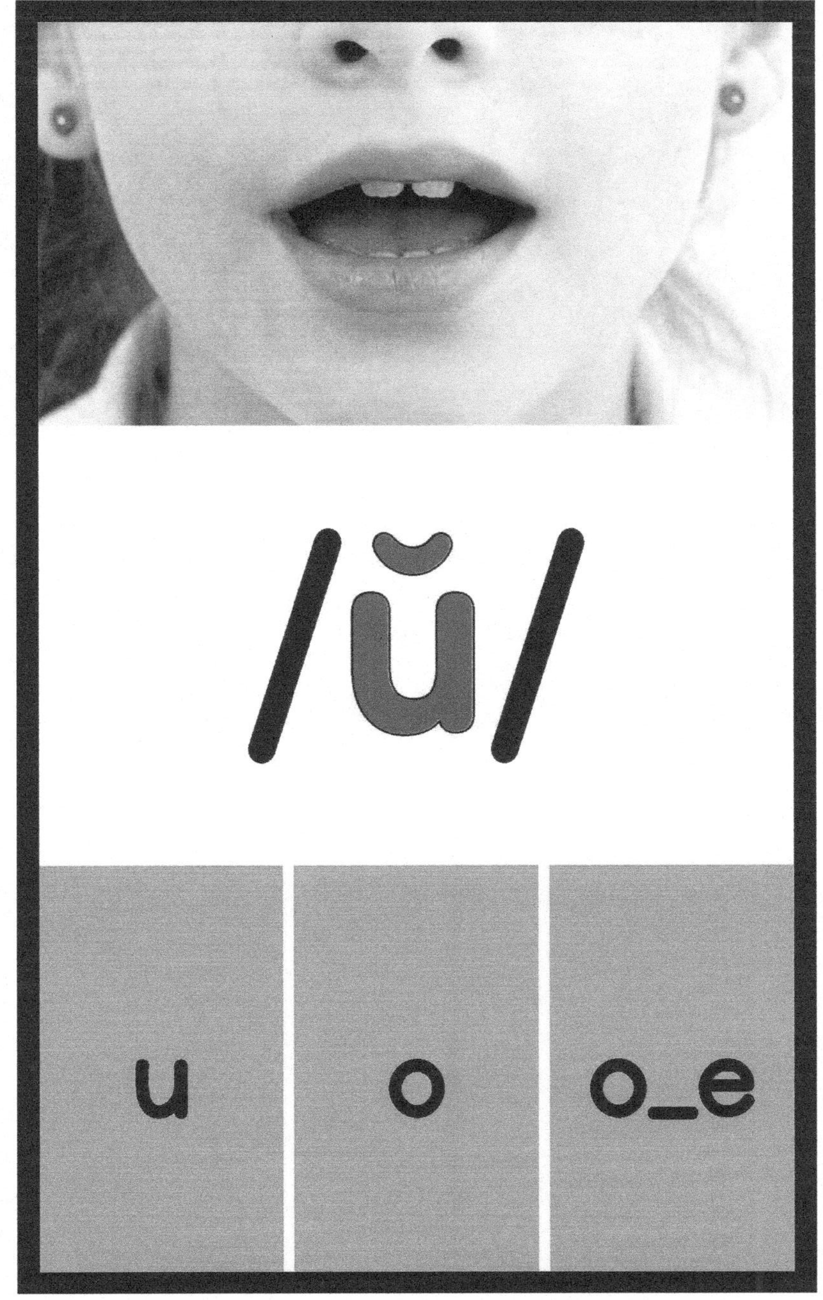
/ŭ/
u
o
o_e

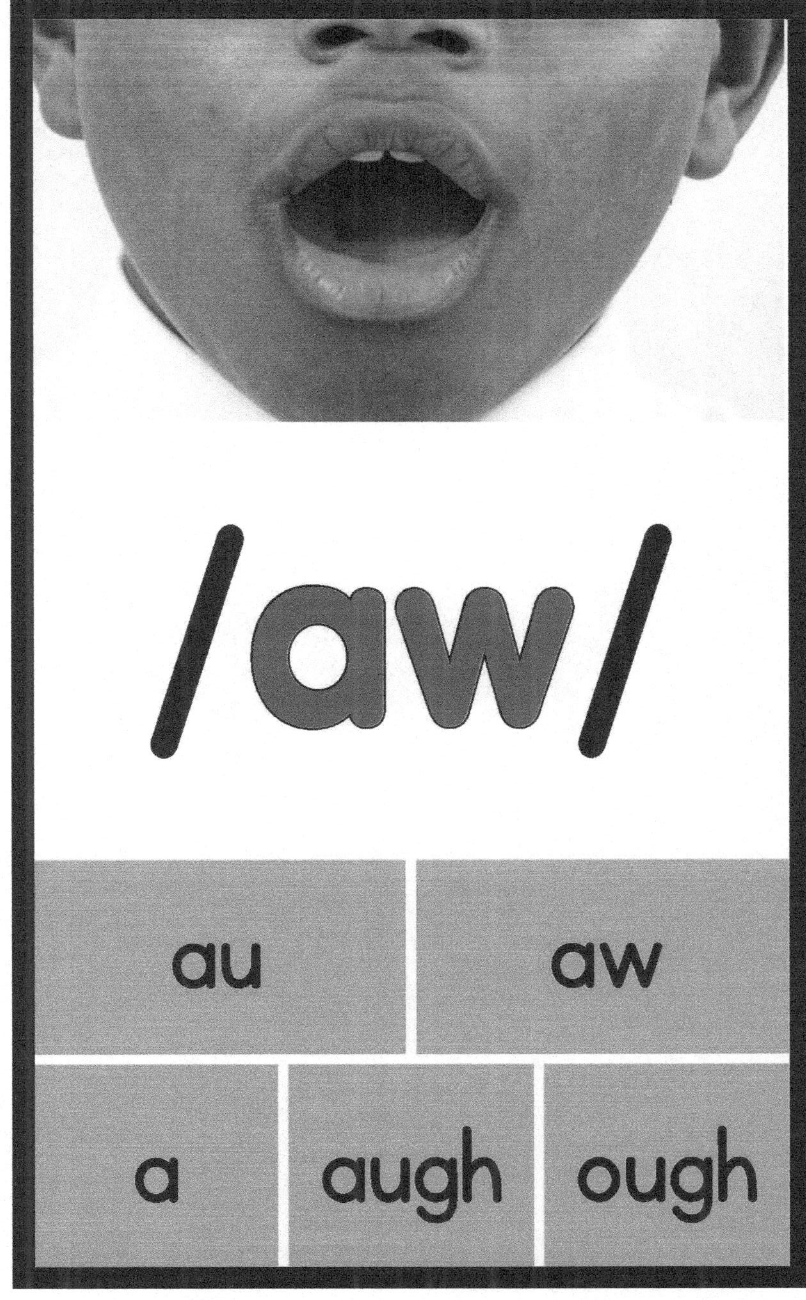
/aw/
au
aw
a
augh
ough

This page is intentionally blank.

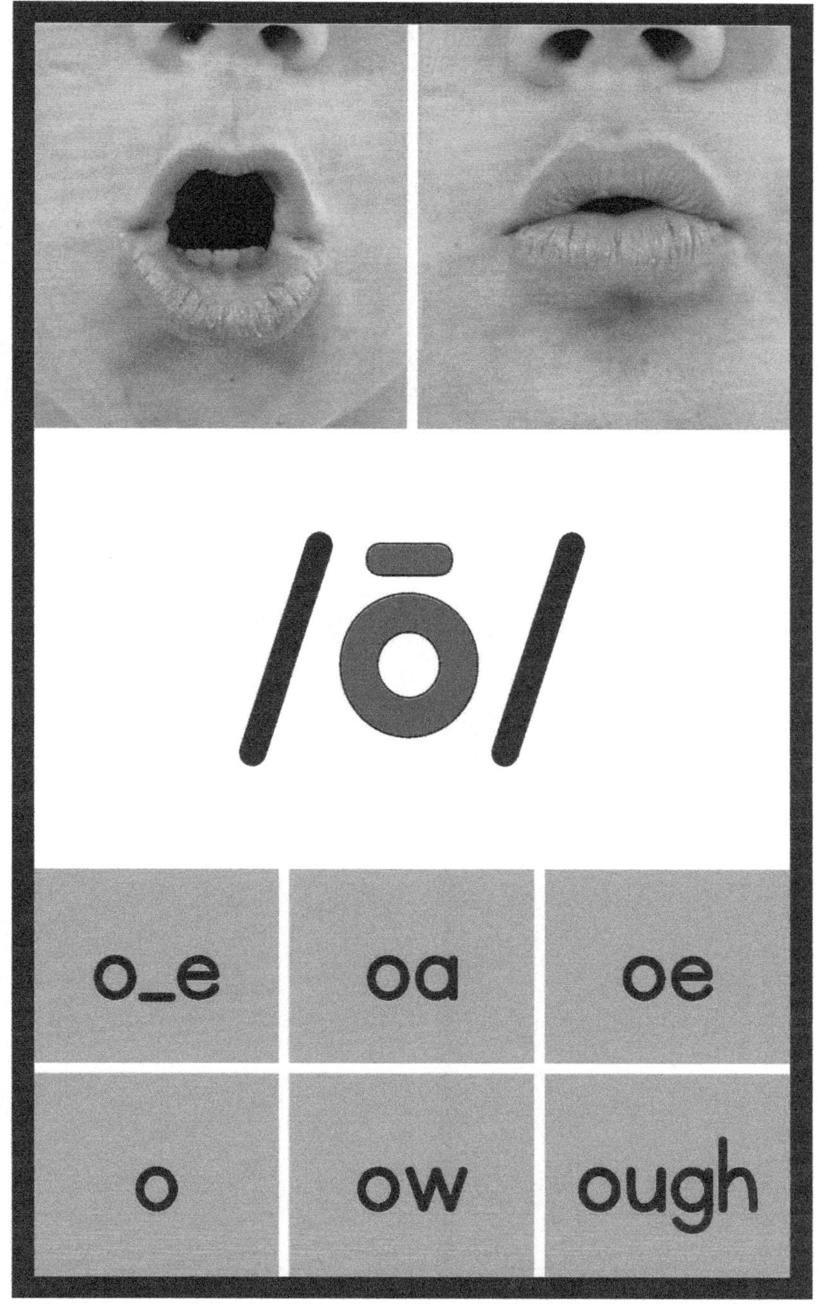

/ō/
o_e
oa
oe
o
ow
ough

/oo/
oo
u

This page is intentionally blank.

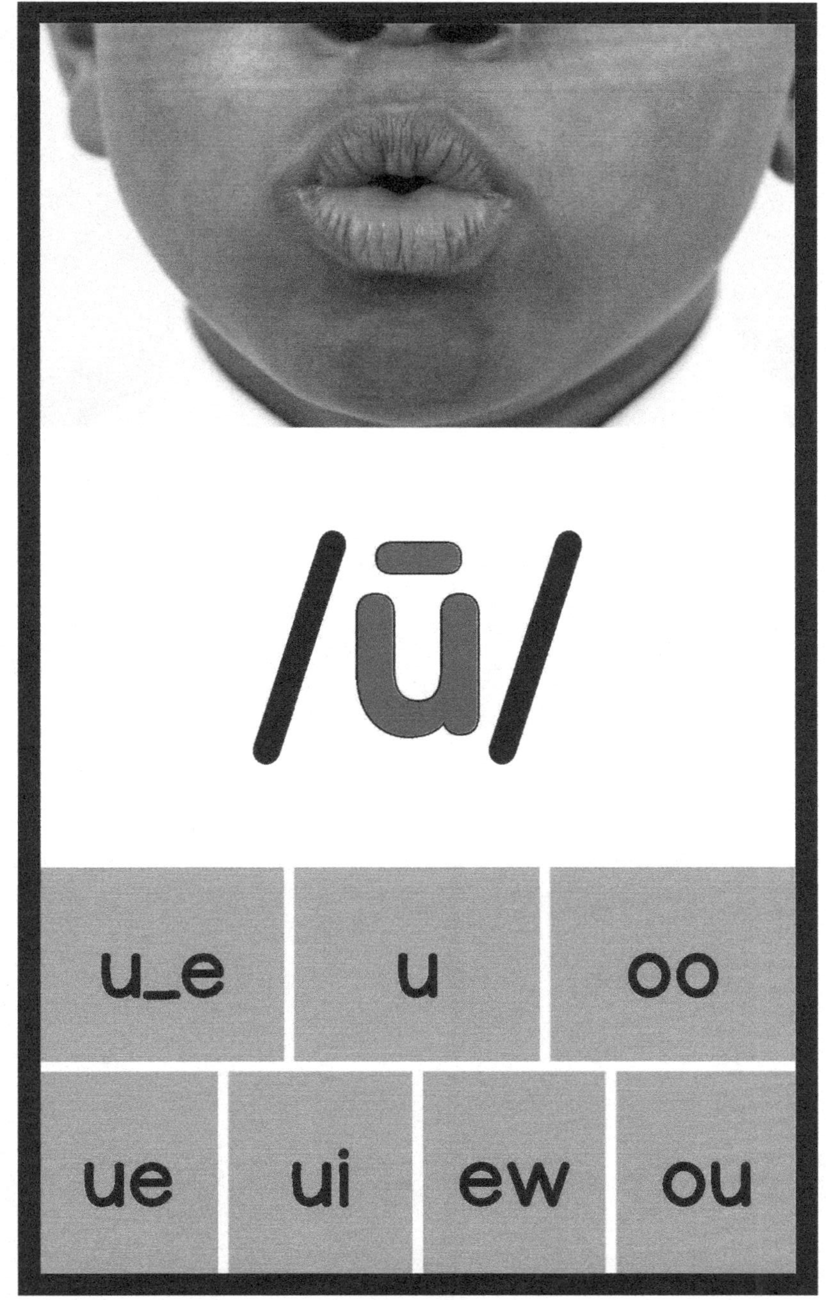
/ū/
u_e u oo
ue ui ew ou

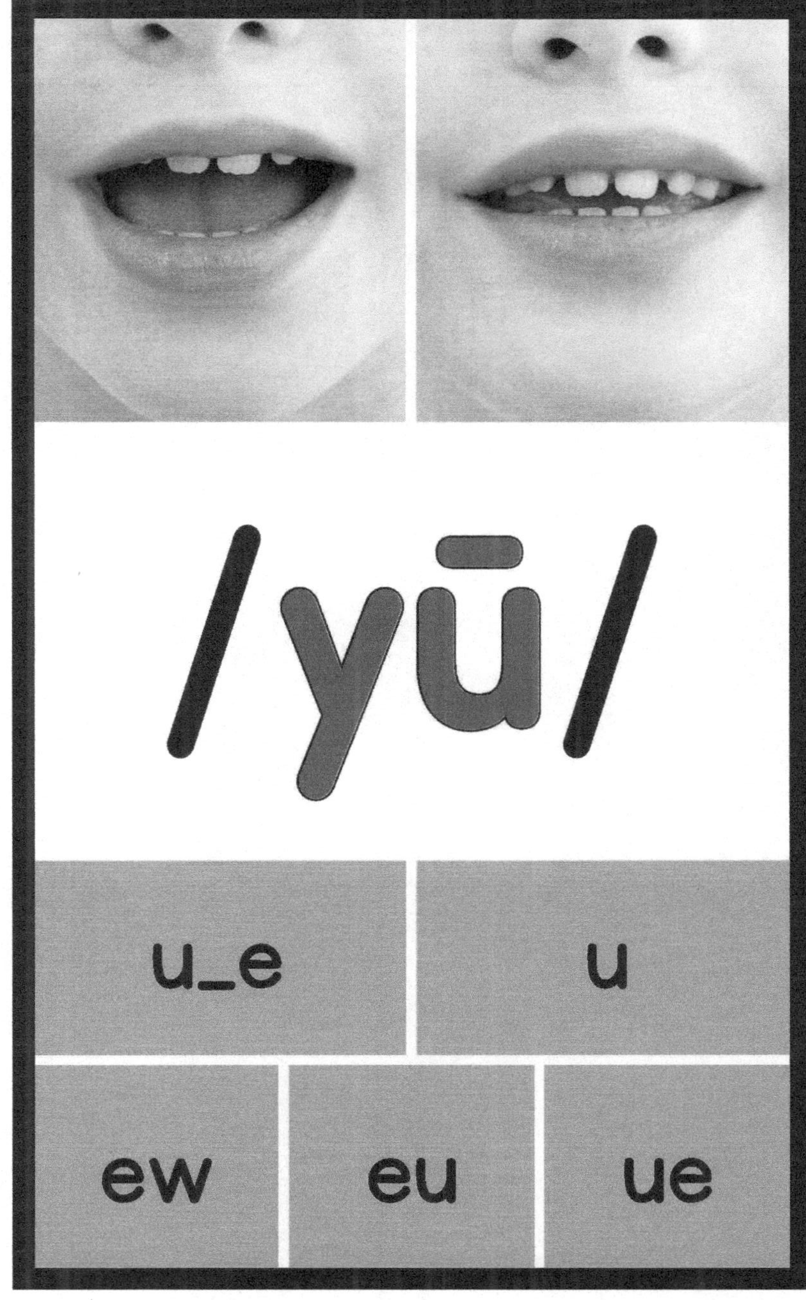
/yū/
u_e u
ew eu ue

This page is intentionally blank.

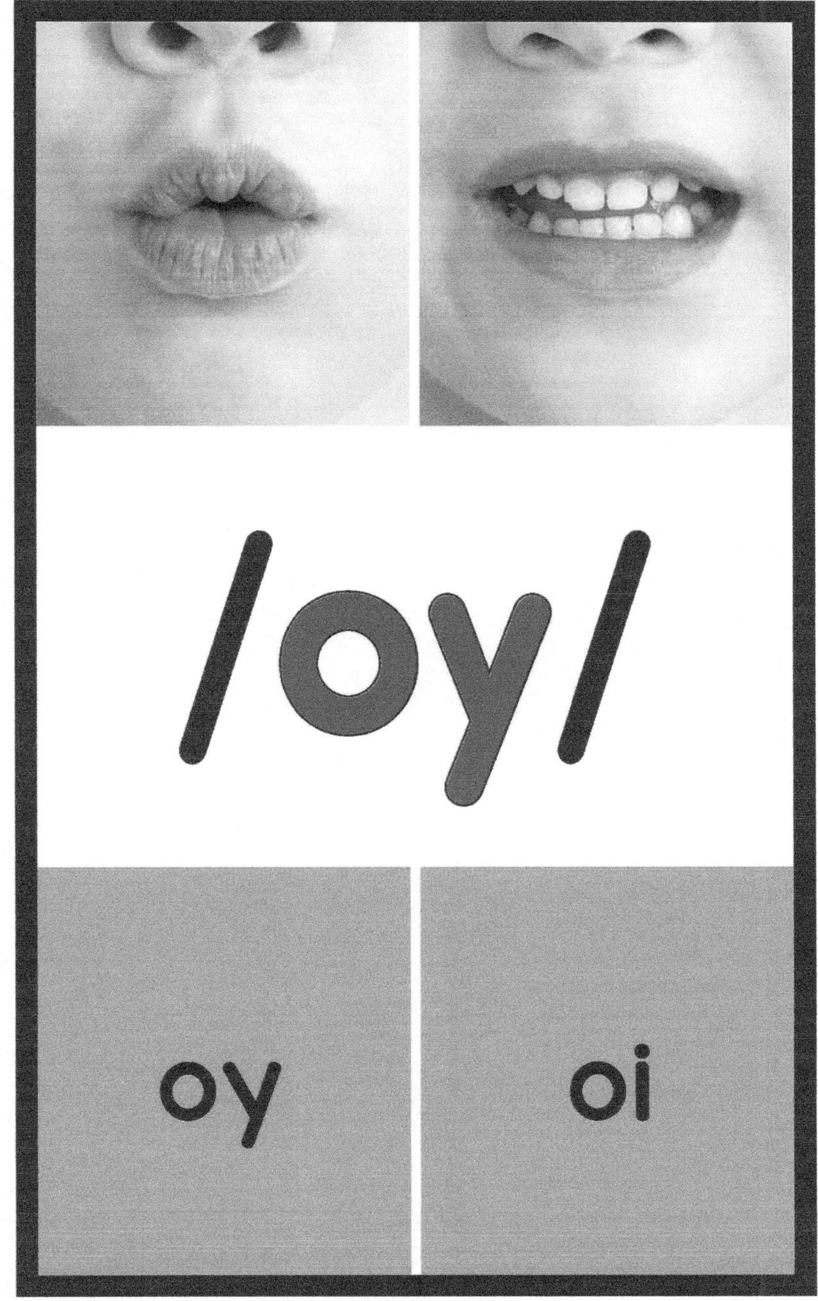
/oy/
oy
oi

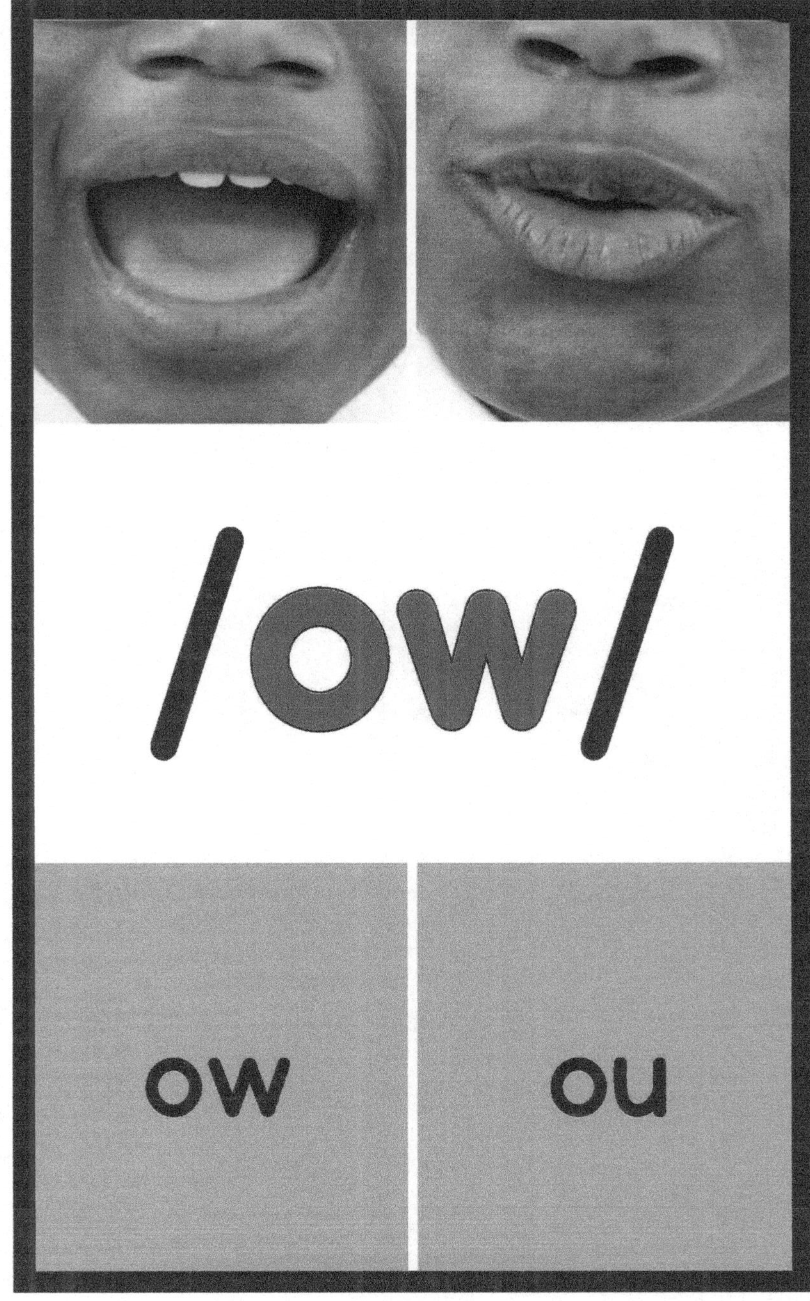
/ow/
ow
ou

This page is intentionally blank.

/ar/
ar

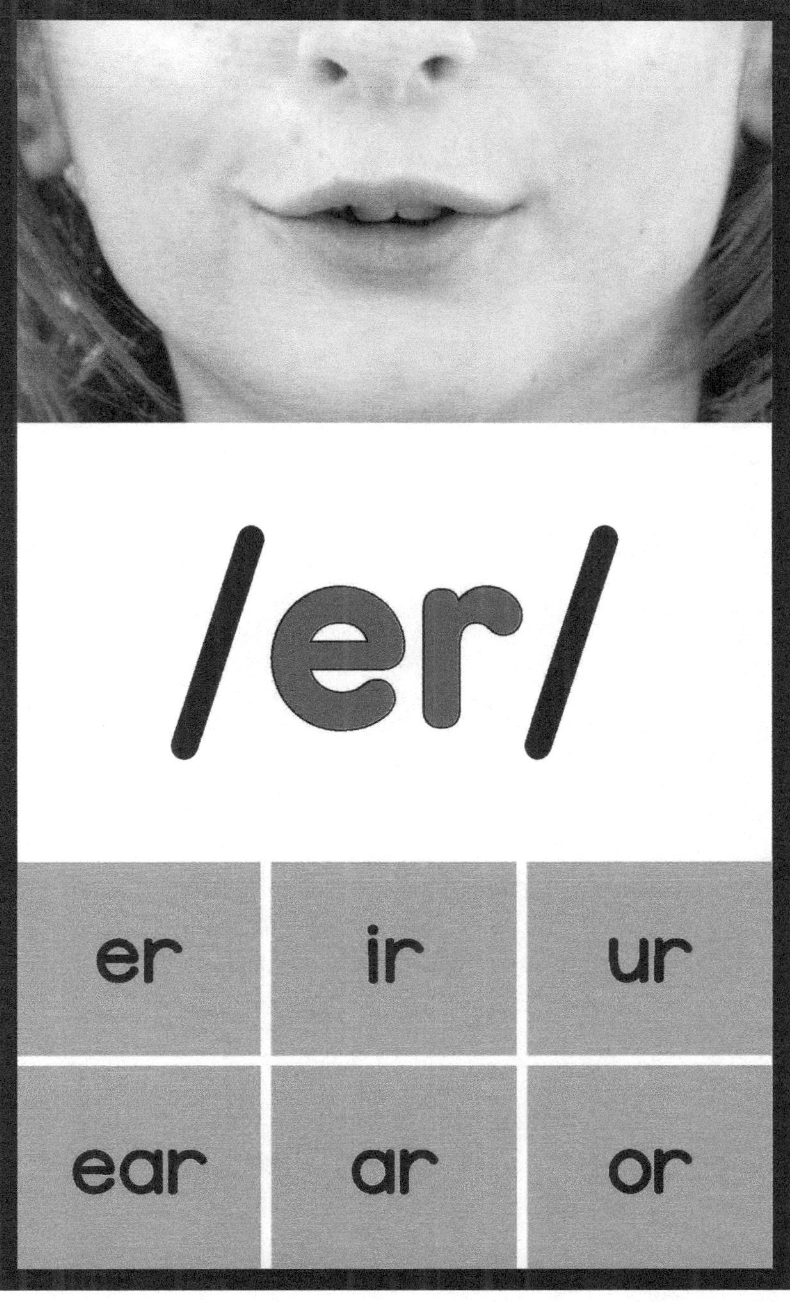
/er/
er
ir
ur
ear
ar
or

This page is intentionally blank.

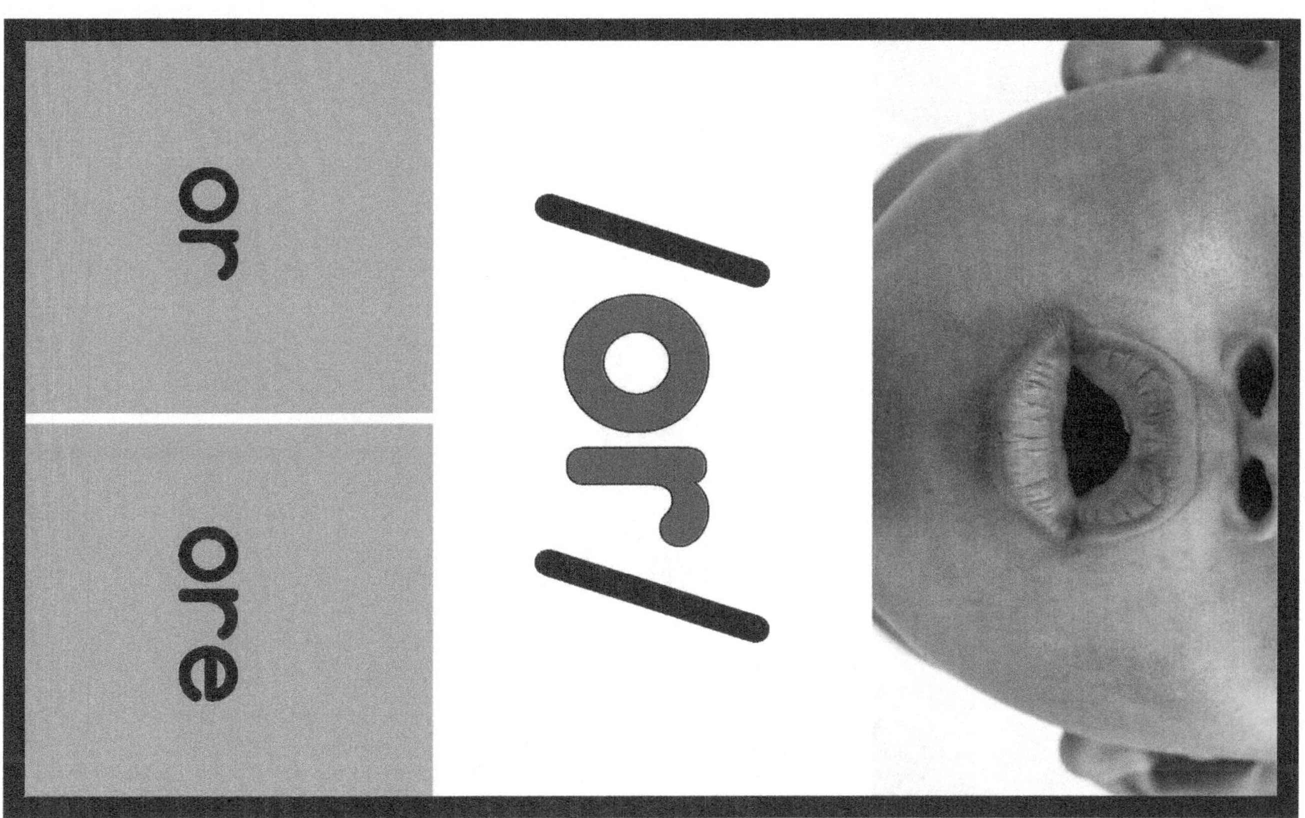
/or/
or
ore

This page is intentionally blank.

# Lesson 4: 5 Essentials for Supporting ELL Students

*Module 6, Lesson 4 from the Science of Reading Academy focuses on five essentials for supporting ELL students and introduces practical strategies to aid emerging multilingual learners in mastering English literacy. The essentials include leveraging students' native language to scaffold comprehension, building background knowledge across diverse topics, front-loading vocabulary from all tiers to ensure comprehension, integrating meaning into phonemic awareness activities to support orthographic mapping, and incorporating all language modalities—speaking, listening, reading, and writing—throughout lessons. These strategies aim to create a supportive learning environment where ELL students can effectively navigate new language and literacy challenges while leveraging their existing linguistic strengths. Below is the transcript for the Module 6, Lesson 4 video.*

**(00:07)** Hello, and welcome back to the Science of Reading Academy. We are in Module 6, focused on giving you practical tips and tricks for implementing the Science of Reading in your classroom. Today's lesson is all about five essentials for supporting your ELL students. Now, full disclosure, you might hear me reference them as EL students in the video because that's the term that I'm just used to using, but honestly, they both mean the same thing, right, ELL, EL students, emerging multilingual or emerging bilingual students. We're talking about students whose first language is not English, and we are helping these students both learn a new language while also learning to read that language. So we want to be intentional with supporting them to make sure that they find success in all academic areas. So let's get started with our five essential tips.

**(01:04)** The first essential is to leverage students' native language, which is sometimes referenced as *L1* when you're reading research, when you're introducing new content. So when students are encountering new concepts in their first language, or their home language, it's helping provide that bridge from familiar ground to new territory. This is going to help them grasp complex ideas much more quickly and accurately. Sometimes the things that we're doing in our classroom are hard enough for our native English speakers. So if you think about what your EL students are having to do cognitively, they have to translate everything that is coming in, and then they have to respond to that content. So not only do we want to make sure that we're being intentional to make sure that the content is comprehensible, so we call that *comprehensible input*, but we also want to make sure that we are being intentional with scaffolding our ELL students by allowing them the opportunity to think about things in their native language.

**(02:20)** So this is a snippet from the front matter in the Structured Literacy with E.A.S.E. program. So it gives some really good ideas for supporting your ELL students, such as using a translation app to name the items in students' native language before naming them in English. So just that simple little addition to your lesson can really support your ELL students.

**(02:46)** Another scaffold that they recommend is allowing students to discuss their answers to questions in their native language before asking them to discuss in English. And if you have multiple students in your class that speak the same native language, you can partner them up, but it's very possible that you only have one student that speaks a particular language in your classroom. They can just verbalize it to themselves or even have them record it saying their thoughts in their home language; that is both validating and helpful to those students.

**(03:21)** The second essential tip is to be intentional with building the background knowledge of your ELL students. So this is going to sound very similar to a tip from the five essentials for language comprehension lesson that was just two lessons ago, but honestly, that's a trend you're going to notice across this whole video is that good scaffolds and supports for your EL students are really just good teaching that will benefit all of your students. So this background building is going to help all of your students find common ground to comprehend text.

**(03:58)** Now, one thing that is really important to remember is that your ELLs will bring a wealth of knowledge and experience to your classroom, and their background knowledge will vary greatly from one student to another, just as with our native English speakers. So we should not make the assumption that just because a student's native language is not English that they automatically don't know things about a specific subject. We want to be intentional to figure out what they do know and then help build background for subjects that they may not be as familiar with, just as we would do with all of our students.

**(04:39)** Here is an example from the Structured Literacy with E.A.S.E. program where they have a Background Builder on mail delivery. So this is for the book *Spike Sends a Letter*, and you might think that many students would be familiar with the postal service here in America, but other countries have different methods of delivering mail, and there are some countries around the world that do not have mailbox as a common, everyday object. So connecting to what students already know about mail, so thinking about perhaps what they're used to or what happens in their house or at their home, and building from there is a great way to honor their prior knowledge while also building background knowledge that they are going to need in order to be successful with the story or the content that you're getting ready to teach.

**(05:33)** Essential tip number three is to front-load all tiers of vocabulary, not just Tier 2. So this is slightly different from the five essentials for language comprehension video where it was recommended to focus on Tier 2 vocabulary words. For your EL students, you may need to span all three tiers, but you'll definitely spend more time with Tier 1 words as students may not be familiar with the English version of that word. So remember, Tier 1 words are common, everyday words. So, for example, door might be a word that most of your students know, but some of your EL students may only know their native word for it. They don't need to learn the meaning, but they need to learn what to call it. So your Tier 1 instruction will look a little bit different than your Tier 2 instruction.

**(06:28)** This is an example of a Vocabulary Builder within the Structured Literacy with E.A.S.E. program. So you can see there are a wide variety of tiers of vocabulary words because this Vocabulary Builder was really designed with EL students in mind. So you can see Tier 1 vocabulary words such as *pig* or *friends* or *moon*. Those are things that we might not typically pause and have a vocabulary lesson on. Those don't need to be words where you're having a full-blown synonym, antonym, dictionary definition, all of those things. You just need students to know what that word is and associate it with something that is in the picture or in the story. Now, there are also some really awesome Tier 2 words on here, such as *sob* or *comfort*, and those are going to be words that you can have some of those deeper conversations with. So front-loading your vocabulary is just teaching it before students are encountering it, and this is a really helpful thing for your EL students.

**(07:38)** The fourth essential tip is to include the meaning of words as you complete phonemic awareness and phonics activities. So you're obviously not going to have time for a full vocabulary lesson after each phonemic awareness activity, or that would just take us all day long to get through any phonemic awareness learning at all. So this is more just an incidental practice and is just going to kind of become part of your everyday teaching. The reason we want to emphasize meaning is to help support the orthographic mapping process, so students need to connect sounds, visual representation, and meaning in order to fully orthographically map a word. Our EL students will need more intentional support in the area of meaning than other students might.

**(08:32)** So this is a Phonemic Awareness warm-up in the Structured Literacy with E.A.S.E. program, and not necessarily a warm-up, just a phonemic awareness activity. And so an example of how you might pull in meaning would be with this word right here, *kin*. You're asking students to segment the word *kin* into individual phonemes, /k/ /i/ /n/. You might also say *kin* is another word for family and then just move on. It doesn't need to be a full-blown vocabulary lesson, but just giving that little snippet can help students anchor that activity that they just did to meaning as well.

(09:12) The fifth and final tip for this lesson is to incorporate all four modalities of language and reading lessons, and those four modalities are speaking, listening, reading, and writing. I used to teach in a school that was predominantly filled with EL students, and this was something that we were encouraged to do across all areas of our day, was to make sure that no matter what we were teaching, we were being intentional with incorporating speaking, listening, reading, and writing, even if it was a math lesson, making sure that all four modalities were incorporated. We especially want to be intentional with the productive language areas, so the areas where students have to actually produce language like writing and speaking, because those are often much harder for students. But encouraging students to produce language from the start is worth the payoff in the end, so something to be intentional about when you're planning.

(10:17) Alright, you're going to take it to the classroom now. So pause and jot: What is one way that you will purposefully support your ELL students as you're working with them in the coming weeks and coming months?

(10:35) After you have jotted that down, don't forget to visit the SOR Academy Facebook group to comment on the Module 6, Lesson 4 thread. We really appreciate and enjoy hearing from you all. Please make sure you join us for the very last lesson of our Science of Reading Academy, which is going to be about essential tips for assessment. See you there.

Leverage students' native language (L1) when introducing new content.

Additional Notes

Be intentional with building the background knowledge of your ELL students.

Front-load all tiers of vocabulary (not just Tier 2).

Include the meaning of words as you complete phonemic awareness and phonics activities.

Incorporate all four modalities of language in reading lessons: speaking, listening, reading, and writing.

Take It to the Classroom: What is one way you will purposefully support your ELL students?

Additional Notes

# Bonus Content

**Use the questions below to prompt discussion amongst your colleagues.**

1. **Leveraging Native Language:** Why is it beneficial to leverage students' native language (L1) when introducing new content? How can this practice support both academic and linguistic development for ELL students?
2. **Building Background Knowledge:** How can you effectively assess and build upon the diverse background knowledge that ELL students bring to the classroom? What strategies can ensure equitable access to content for all students?
3. **Vocabulary Instruction:** Why is front-loading vocabulary important for ELL students? How might you differentiate instruction across Tier 1, Tier 2, and Tier 3 vocabulary words to support their language development?
4. **Meaning in Phonemic Activities:** How can integrating meaning into phonemic awareness and phonics activities benefit ELL students' orthographic mapping process? What are practical ways to incorporate meaning without overwhelming instructional time?
5. **Incorporating Modalities:** Discuss the importance of incorporating all four language modalities (speaking, listening, reading, writing) in lessons for ELL students. What challenges might teachers face in implementing this approach, and how can they overcome them?

**To extend your understanding of this topic, work through the activities below with a small group of peers.**

**Language Scaffolding Role-Play**
In small groups, role-play scenarios where one member acts as an ELL student encountering new academic content. Practice using scaffolding techniques such as translating key concepts into the student's native language or providing visual aids to enhance comprehension.

**Background Knowledge Exchange**
Each teacher brings an example of how they have integrated students' background knowledge into a lesson. Discuss these examples and brainstorm additional ways to effectively build upon students' diverse experiences.

**Vocabulary Front-Loading Strategy Swap**
Share different strategies for front-loading vocabulary among peers. Each teacher presents a strategy they find effective, such as using visuals or contextual sentences. Discuss which strategies might be most beneficial for different types of vocabulary (Tier 1, Tier 2, Tier 3).

**Phonemic Awareness and Meaning Connection**
Design a phonemic awareness activity that incorporates meaningful context for ELL students. Share and discuss these activities with peers, focusing on how to maintain balance between phonemic practice and meaningful vocabulary integration.

**Integrated Modality Lesson Planning**
Collaborate to plan a lesson that incorporates all four language modalities. Choose a topic relevant to both language and content objectives. Discuss how to scaffold speaking, listening, reading, and writing activities to support ELL students' language development throughout the lesson.

**Additional Resources**
See the Module 5 Supporting Language Development introduction. The second page of the introduction includes a note about bonus content for the module, as well as access to published lesson plans. Then, use the information on the following page to identify the areas of the lesson plan that support ELLs.

**Additional Resources**

Front-Loading with Background Builders Day 1 lesson plans, Background Builder half sheet. This passage is related to the text students will read on Day 2. Ask students to summarize what the passage was about. (For ELL students, invite them to first summarize in their native language before asking them to summarize it in English.) Discuss the major topic and any bold vocabulary words in the passage.

Front-Loading with Vocabulary Builders Day 1 Complete the Vocabulary Builder activity with students. Show students the images from the book on the Vocabulary Builder half sheet. Start by discussing what is happening in each picture. (For ELL students, invite them to first explain what they see in their native language before asking them to explain it in English.) Next, point out the different items and/or concepts in the image. (For ELL students, use a translation app to name the items in the students' native language before naming them in English.) Then, label the items. A short word bank is provided, but the labeling should not be limited to those words.

Front-Loading with Text Preview Day 1 Small-Group Support—Front-Loading. Invite students to either listen to a digital version of the Day 2 text or echo read the story with the teacher. This additional exposure will help their decoding on Day 2.

Utilizing the student's native language You'll notice in the examples above, it is recommended to allow ELL students to respond to questions in their native language before asking them to articulate their response in English. This allows them to process what they are comprehending in a language for which they already know the code. So rather than asking students to process their understanding *and* translate their thoughts into a new language at the same time, they are tackling one at a time: 1) processing their understanding in their native language then 2) translating those thoughts into English.

Additionally, when introducing new words, use a translation app so you can show the student what the word is in their native language. This will help them process the meaning of the new English word they are trying to learn.

# Lesson 5: 5 Essentials for Literacy Assessment

*In the final lesson of the Science of Reading Academy series, the focus is on the five essentials for literacy assessment. Emphasizing the critical role of assessment in tailored instruction, the video outlines key strategies. First, it advocates using diagnostic screeners to pinpoint student knowledge gaps across phonemic awareness, phonics, and more. Second, it stresses using this data to form needs-based groups and set precise instructional goals. Third, ongoing progress monitoring is highlighted to track student growth dynamically. Additionally, informal formative assessments are recommended for real-time insights into teaching effectiveness, complemented by summative assessments to gauge overall mastery. These essentials underscore the pivotal role of assessments in guiding effective teaching practices and ensuring student success in literacy development. Below is the transcript for the Module 6, Lesson 5 video.*

**(00:07)** Hello, and welcome back to the Science of Reading Academy. This is our final lesson of our series, and I just can't believe it. Thank you so much for taking the time out of your very busy schedules to come and learn with us. This lesson will be the fifth in our five essentials series, which are lessons that are designed to be quick and to help you synthesize the learning in the previous five modules. Today's lesson will cover the five essentials for literacy assessments.

**(00:39)** Now, assessment and data might not be the most exciting topics, but they really are crucial for making our teaching intentional and tailored to student needs. Assessment should be the heartbeat of our instruction. It drives everything we do and helps us stay attuned to the needs of our students. So let's get started on five essentials for literacy assessment.

**(01:07)** Alright, the first essential tip for literacy assessment is to utilize diagnostic screeners to determine what students already know. Now, there are a variety of diagnostic screeners out there, and really you just want one that is going to help you know what students know and what they still need to work on. This can and should include screeners on phonemic awareness, concepts of print, phonics, as well as other reading areas.

**(01:43)** Here are two examples from the Structured Literacy with E.A.S.E. program. So there's an alphabet letters and sounds assessment. So up at the top it says administer at the beginning, middle, and end of the year, so you're using it not only as a diagnostic screener, but you're also using it to continue to do progress monitoring. And this is a phonics assessment that is designed to help place students within the program. And so that is a very useful teaching tool to know what your students know as well as what they need to work on. And once you know what they need to work on, it tells you exactly where to take them in the program so that you can teach those skills.

**(02:24)** The second tip is to use the screener data to organize students into needs-based groups and to set goals. So we don't want to just collect all of this baseline data so that we can just check it off the list and say done with that; we spend a lot of time doing assessment and collecting data, and we want to use it to drive our instruction. So the data that we gather should inform our teaching, and it should most definitely inform our small-group goals.

**(02:54)** This is an example from the Structured Literacy with E.A.S.E. program, where teachers are prompted to form needs-based small groups based on if students need help with the previous skill, the focus skill, high-frequency words, or vocabulary support. So to know that, data is really going to be your best friend so that you can figure out what group students need to be in order to fill those needs. So this is a much different approach than just putting students in a group based on text level. You have to truly be a diagnostician to figure out what they need, fill in those gaps, and then move them out of that group because they might not continue to need that thing.

**(03:34)** And that relates to tip number three, which is to complete progress monitoring to observe and track student growth. Just because students were identified as needing support with short "a" doesn't mean they will still need that support three weeks later. So we need to check in with our students and keep collecting data to see how they are doing.

(03:58) So here are two examples from the Structured Literacy with E.A.S.E. program. One is progress monitoring within a lesson, so after teaching, you're going to do some dictation, some decoding—both of real words and nonsense words—and having students read a sentence. This is an example of progress monitoring after multiple lessons. So it's trying to figure out if students are retaining, synthesizing, and transferring that new knowledge. So these are going to give you two different pieces of data that together are going to tell you what you need to do with your student.

(04:38) Tip number four is to conduct informal formative assessments to inform how your teaching should adapt and evolve. So this is not always going to be something that you plan for and write down. This is more just an in-the-moment assessment that teachers take all the time to let us know how our lesson is going. This is getting the pulse of your classroom by doing a thumbs up or thumbs down activity, walking around and watching students respond through writing, or doing a quick showdown with whiteboards. All of those are examples of that informal formative assessment.

(05:18) One example might be during an oral articulation lesson. So if students are substituting the /e/ sound for the /i/ sound like we like to do here in the Midwest, you're going to hear that. That's going to be the input that you're receiving, and then you're going to provide with corrective feedback in the moment. That is you taking formative data and using it to change your teaching practice. And the nice thing about this is the corrective feedback is right here in the teacher guide for you.

(05:52) Tip number five is to include summative assessments to determine student mastery of taught concepts. So summative assessments will go at the end, and this is after learning has occurred, so after that Tier 1 instruction; it's going to give you information about what is going well or what is maybe not going so well.

(06:15) So this is an example of a Sequence 2 Postassessment. So a sequence is similar to a unit, so after students have completed several lessons of learning, this is a comprehensive exam to get a pulse on how they're doing at reading and retelling and some deeper comprehension questions, including vocabulary and inferencing and synthesizing. There's a dictation portion that's going to help you with the orthography knowledge that your students have. So this is a summative assessment that includes lots of skills, and it's going to give you a lot of great data points.

(06:57) Alright, so pause, jot down a thought: What is one takeaway about literacy assessments that you can bring back with you to the classroom, so something that either is affirming to you or maybe something that you want to shift? After you've jotted down your thought, make sure to jump back on the video so I can share one more bonus content with you.

(07:20) Alright, the bonus content for today is a Concepts of Print Assessment. So there's not a lot of concepts of print assessments out there, so this is a great resource for you. And it includes the text that you can print and share with your students that they will answer questions on. So this can be helpful to know with your very early and emerging readers what they need support with more on that language comprehension side in contrast to perhaps just a letter and sounds assessment. So this is going to help you fill in all those pieces that you need to have the full picture of your student.

(08:01) Alright, thank you so much for joining us for the Science of Reading Academy. It has been a true pleasure learning with you, and I hope that you have gained some helpful tips for you and your classroom and your students to take back. Please continue to visit our Facebook group and add your voice and add your learning because your thoughts are truly valuable. We appreciate your time and can't wait to hear from you again. Thanks.

Utilize diagnostic screeners to determine what students already know.

Use the screener data to organize students into needs-based groups and set goals.

Complete progress monitoring to observe and track student growth.

Additional Notes

Conduct informal formative assessments to inform how your teaching should adapt and evolve.

Include summative assessments to determine student mastery of taught concepts.

Take It to the Classroom: What is one take-away about literacy assessments you can bring back with you to the classroom?

Additional Notes

# Bonus Content

**Use the questions below to prompt discussion amongst your colleagues.**

1. **Using Diagnostic Screeners:** Why is it essential to use diagnostic screeners to assess what students already know? How can these assessments guide instructional planning for both individual students and groups?
2. **Organizing Students into Needs-Based Groups:** Discuss the benefits of organizing students into needs-based groups based on assessment data rather than text level alone. How can this approach support differentiated instruction in literacy?
3. **Progress Monitoring for Student Growth:** Why is ongoing progress monitoring crucial in literacy instruction? How can different types of progress monitoring, such as within lessons and across lessons, provide a comprehensive view of student growth?
4. **Informal Formative Assessments:** What role do informal formative assessments play in adjusting teaching strategies in real time? Share examples of effective informal assessment techniques and their impact on classroom instruction.
5. **Summative Assessments for Mastery:** How do summative assessments complement ongoing formative assessments in assessing student mastery of literacy concepts? Discuss the benefits and challenges of incorporating summative assessments into instructional planning.

**To extend your understanding of this topic, work through the activities below with a small group of peers.**

**Diagnostic Screener Exploration**
Explore different diagnostic screeners used in various programs or districts. Compare and contrast their effectiveness in assessing different literacy skills (phonemic awareness, phonics, etc.). Discuss which screener might be most beneficial for different student populations.

**Group Goal Setting Simulation**
Role-play a scenario where assessment data is used to form needs-based small groups. Each participant takes on the role of a teacher using assessment data to set specific goals for their groups. Discuss strategies for adjusting groupings based on ongoing assessment data.

**Progress Monitoring Analysis**
Analyze sample progress monitoring data from structured literacy programs. Discuss trends in student performance over time and implications for instructional adjustments. Share strategies for communicating progress monitoring results effectively with students and parents.

**Formative Assessment Techniques Showcase**
Each teacher presents a formative assessment technique they find effective (e.g., thumbs up/down, whiteboard showdown). Demonstrate how these techniques can provide immediate feedback and inform instructional decisions. Discuss adaptations of these techniques for different grade levels and subject areas.

**Designing a Comprehensive Assessment Plan**
Collaborate to design a comprehensive assessment plan for a specific literacy unit or skill. Include diagnostic, formative, and summative assessments. Discuss how each type of assessment contributes to understanding student learning and guides instructional planning.

**Additional Resources**
See the following pages for the Concepts of Print Assessment.

# Concepts of Print Assessment

## Assessment Details and Administration

Use the book Quin and Ben to assess concepts of print. Print the two pages front to back and fold in the middle. Students use/reference this book during the assessment. The test can be approached two different ways:

1) Ask/prompt students explicitly, using the phrases on the assessment sheet, to discover their understanding of each print concept.
2) Ask students to read the story as you carefully observe, marking all relevant items. When they finish, return to the skills that were not easily observed and ask students explicitly about the specific items.

Notes about test administration by concept:

- **Book Concepts** – Complete the items in this section before reading.
- **Letter Concepts** – Use the title page to complete the items in this section.
- **Reading Concepts** – Reference the first page for the items in this section. When assessing one-to-one match ("Point to the words as I read them."), use the back cover. The back cover is not decodable for students, but they should be able to follow along using one-to-one match.
- **Word Concepts** – Use page 1 of the story for the items in this section.
- **Directionality Concepts** – Use the first line of the first page for the items in this section.
- **Punctuation Marks** – Students read the story for the items in this section.

### Student Data Sheets

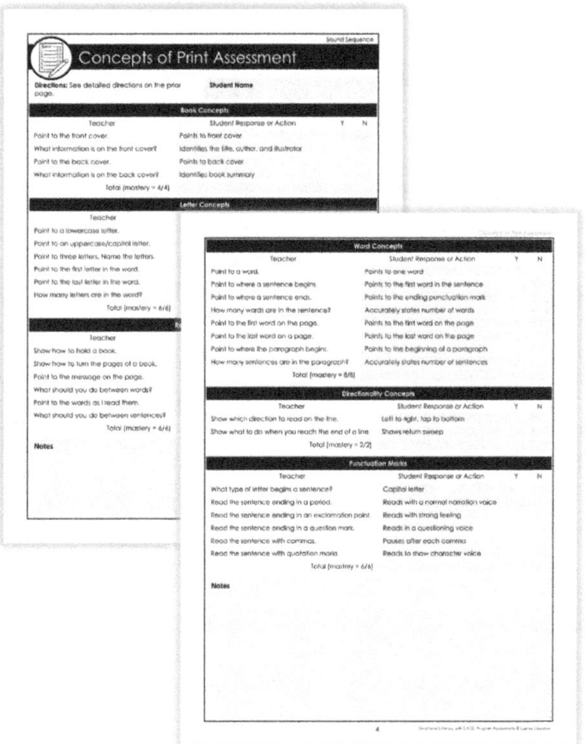

Sound Sequence

Concepts of Print Assessment

**Directions:** See detailed directions on the prior page. **Student Name**

| Teacher | Student Response or Action | Y | N |
|---|---|---|---|
| **Book Concepts** | | | |
| Point to the front cover. | Points to front cover | | |
| What information is on the front cover? | Identifies the title, author, and illustrator | | |
| Point to the back cover. | Points to back cover | | |
| What information is on the back cover? | Identifies book summary | | |
| Total (mastery = 4/4) | | | |

**Letter Concepts**

| Teacher |
|---|
| Point to a lowercase letter. |
| Point to an uppercase/capital letter. |
| Point to three letters. Name the letters. |
| Point to the first letter in the word. |
| Point to the last letter in the word. |
| How many letters are in the word? |
| Total (mastery = 6/6) |

| Teacher |
|---|
| Show how to hold a book. |
| Show how to turn the pages of a book. |
| Point to the message on the page. |
| What should you do between words? |
| Point to the words as I read them. |
| What should you do between sentences? |
| Total (mastery = 6/6) |

**Notes**

| Teacher | Student Response or Action | Y | N |
|---|---|---|---|
| **Word Concepts** | | | |
| Point to a word. | Points to one word | | |
| Point to where a sentence begins. | Points to the first word in the sentence | | |
| Point to where a sentence ends. | Points to the ending punctuation mark | | |
| How many words are in the sentence? | Accurately states number of words | | |
| Point to the first word on the page. | Points to the first word on the page | | |
| Point to the last word on a page. | Points to the last word on the page | | |
| Point to where the paragraph begins. | Points to the beginning of a paragraph | | |
| How many sentences are in the paragraph? | Accurately states number of sentences | | |
| Total (mastery = 8/8) | | | |

| Teacher | Student Response or Action | Y | N |
|---|---|---|---|
| **Directionality Concepts** | | | |
| Show which direction to read on the line. | Left to right, top to bottom | | |
| Show what to do when you reach the end of a line | Shows return sweep | | |
| Total (mastery = 2/2) | | | |

| Teacher | Student Response or Action | Y | N |
|---|---|---|---|
| **Punctuation Marks** | | | |
| What type of letter begins a sentence? | Capital letter | | |
| Read the sentence ending in a period. | Reads with a normal narration voice | | |
| Read the sentence ending in an exclamation point | Reads with strong feeling | | |
| Read the sentence ending in a question mark. | Reads in a questioning voice | | |
| Read the sentence with commas. | Pauses after each comma | | |
| Read the sentence with quotation marks | Reads to show character voice | | |
| Total (mastery = 6/6) | | | |

**Notes**

4

### Student Book Quin and Ben

Quin hops in a van to

Ben is Quin's pal. Ben hit his leg, hip, and gut. Can

Quin and Ben are pals. One day, Ben gets hurt when Quin is at work. Will Ben be able to get himself to the vet? Read to find out.

Quin and Ben

Written By: Charlotte Irons

Illustrated By: Eva Elfimova

This page is intentionally blank.

# Concepts of Print Assessment

**Directions:** See detailed directions on the prior page.

**Student Name**

| Book Concepts | | | |
|---|---|---|---|
| Teacher | Student Response or Action | Y | N |
| Point to the front cover. | Points to front cover | | |
| What information is on the front cover? | Identifies the title, author, and illustrator | | |
| Point to the back cover. | Points to back cover | | |
| What information is on the back cover? | Identifies book summary | | |
| Total (mastery = 4/4) | | | |

| Letter Concepts | | | |
|---|---|---|---|
| Teacher | Student Response or Action | Y | N |
| Point to a lowercase letter. | Points to a lowercase letter | | |
| Point to an uppercase/capital letter. | Points to an uppercase letter | | |
| Point to three letters. Name the letters. | Names three different letters | | |
| Point to the first letter in the word. | Points to the first letter in a word | | |
| Point to the last letter in the word. | Points to the last letter in a word | | |
| How many letters are in the word? | Accurately states number of letters in a word | | |
| Total (mastery = 6/6) | | | |

| Reading Concepts | | | |
|---|---|---|---|
| Teacher | Student Response or Action | Y | N |
| Show how to hold a book. | Holds the book correctly, facing them | | |
| Show how to turn the pages of a book. | Turns pages from right to left | | |
| Point to the message on the page. | Points to the print, not the illustration | | |
| What should you do between words? | Brief pause | | |
| Point to the words as I read them. | Shows one-to-one match when pointing | | |
| What should you do between sentences? | Long pause | | |
| Total (mastery = 6/6) | | | |

**Notes**

| Word Concepts | | | |
|---|---|---|---|
| Teacher | Student Response or Action | Y | N |
| Point to a word. | Points to one word | | |
| Point to where a sentence begins. | Points to the first word in the sentence | | |
| Point to where a sentence ends. | Points to the ending punctuation mark | | |
| How many words are in the sentence? | Accurately states number of words | | |
| Point to the first word on the page. | Points to the first word on the page | | |
| Point to the last word on a page. | Points to the last word on the page | | |
| Point to where the paragraph begins. | Points to the beginning of a paragraph | | |
| How many sentences are in the paragraph? | Accurately states number of sentences | | |
| Total (mastery = 8/8) | | | |

| Directionality Concepts | | | |
|---|---|---|---|
| Teacher | Student Response or Action | Y | N |
| Show which direction to read on the line. | Left to right, top to bottom | | |
| Show what to do when you reach the end of a line. | Shows return sweep | | |
| Total (mastery = 2/2) | | | |

| Punctuation Marks | | | |
|---|---|---|---|
| Teacher | Student Response or Action | Y | N |
| What type of letter begins a sentence? | Capital letter | | |
| Read the sentence ending in a period. | Reads with a normal narration voice | | |
| Read the sentence ending in an exclamation point. | Reads with strong feeling | | |
| Read the sentence ending in a question mark. | Reads in a questioning voice | | |
| Read the sentence with commas. | Pauses after each comma | | |
| Read the sentence with quotation marks. | Reads to show character voice | | |
| Total (mastery = 6/6) | | | |

**Notes**

Quin and Ben are pals. One day, Ben gets hurt when Quin is at work. Will Ben be able to get himself to the vet?

Read to find out.

# Quin and Ben

Written By:
**Charlotte Irons**

Illustrated By:
**Eva Elfimova**

Quin hops in a van to get to a job. Quin tags, bags, and mops at his job.

1

Ben is Quin's pal. Ben hit his leg, hip, and gut. Can Ben get on a bus to get to the vet? Yes!

2

Made in the USA
Monee, IL
06 January 2025

75993961R00129